ALL OUR WORKING LIVES

PETER PAGNAMENTA
AND
RICHARD OVERY

BRITISH BROADCASTING CORPORATION

PICTURE CREDITS

Picture research by June Leech

Page 9 John Topham Picture Library; 10 Popperfoto; 11, 14 BBC Hulton Picture Library; 16 EMI Music Archives; 18 Private collection; 19 ICI; 20 Express Newspapers; 21 BBC Hulton Picture Library; 24 *Oldham Evening Chronicle*; 26, 27 Oldham Libraries, Art Galleries and Museums; 28 Rochdale Libraries (Local Studies Collection); 29 Popperfoto; 32 Manchester Central Library; 34 (top) Robert Scott, (bottom) BBC Hulton Picture Library; 36 TUC Library; 37 Humphrey Spender; 38 John Topham Picture Library; 41 BBC Hulton Picture Library; 42–3 John Topham Picture Library; 47 Courtaulds P.L.C.; 48 John Topham Picture Library; 50 From Sir Geoffrey de Havilland's autobiography *Sky Fever* (Hamish Hamilton); 52 (top) *Flight*, (bottom) BBC Hulton Picture Library; 54 British Aerospace, Brough; 56 Working Class Movement Library, Manchester; 57 John Topham Picture Library; 58 (top) Keystone, (bottom) S. and G. Press Agency Ltd; 62, 63 John Topham Picture Library; 64 British Aerospace, Weybridge; 65 John Topham Picture Library; 70 Times Newspapers Ltd; 71 John Topham Picture Library; 72 British Aerospace, Filton; 74 British Aerospace, Warton; 76 Photo Graphic, Birkenhead, and Weidenfeld & Nicolson Archives; 78–9 John A. Owen; 81 British Steel Corporation; 82 Times Newspapers Ltd; 84 The Governor and Company of The Bank of England; 85 Keystone; 86 Times Newspapers Ltd; 87 *Steel is Power: The Case for Nationalisation* (Victor Gollancz, 1948), and Weidenfeld and Nicolson Archives; 88 Cartoon from *Steel News*, 1949 (copyright Associated Newspapers p.l.c.); 90 Aerofilms; 95 British Steel Corporation; 97 John Topham Picture Library; 100, 101 British Steel Corporation; 102 J Sainsbury plc; 104 (left) Leicestershire Museums, (right) Mary Evans Picture Library; 105 (top) BBC Hulton Picture Library, (bottom) National Union of Agricultural Workers; 106 BBC Hulton Picture Library; 107 (top) Bishopsgate Institute, (bottom) TUC Library; 108 Harrods Ltd; 110 J Sainsbury plc; 111 Private collection; 112 J. R. Bubear; 113 Private Collection; 117 BBC Hulton Picture Library; 120 (left) Popperfoto, (right) BBC Hulton Picture Library; 122 J Sainsbury plc; 123 Mothercare Ltd; 124 Photo Graphic, Birkenhead; 126 Mansell Collection; 127 Swan Hunter Shipbuilders Ltd; 130 Imperial War Museum; 132 Swan Hunter Shipbuilders Ltd; 133, 135 The Bede Gallery, Jarrow; 136, 137 Mansell Collection; 138 BBC Hulton Picture Library; 142 Erich Lessing – Magnum; 144 Austin & Pickersgill Ltd; 146, 147 *Glasgow Herald & Evening Times*; 150 Crosfield Chemicals, Warrington; 152 The Halton Chemical Project, Widnes; 153, 154 (top) ICI; 154 (bottom) John Topham Picture Library; 157 ICI; 159 Albright and Wilson Ltd; 160 ICI; 162 Camera Press; 164–5, 166 ICI; 168 Popperfoto; 171, 172 Cliff Williams, Clay Cross; 173 B. T. Batsford Ltd; 174, 175 Welsh Miners Museum, Cynonville, Port Talbot; 176 BBC Hulton Picture Library; 177 South Wales Miners' Library, University College, Swansea; 178 BBC Hulton Picture Library; 181 NCB; 182–3, 185 John Topham Picture Library; 186, 188 NCB; 192 Janine Wiedel; 194 Barnaby's Picture Library; 196 Imperial War Museum; 197 BBC Hulton Picture Library; 199 Norfolk Rural Life Museum; 200 National Union of Agricultural Workers; 201 Mansell Collection; 202–3 NFU; 204 John Topham Picture Library; 207 Keystone; 209 John Topham Picture Library; 211 BBC Hulton Picture Library; 214 *Farmers' Weekly*; 216 BL Heritage Ltd; 218 Popperfoto; 219 Ford's Photographic Department; 220, 221, 223, 224 BBC Hulton Picture Library; 226 Aerofilms; 229 John Topham Picture Library; 232 Press Association; 234 Austin Rover Group Ltd; 236 John Topham Picture Library; 238 Ford's Photographic Department; 241 BBC Hulton Picture Library; 242 Austin Rover Group Ltd; 244 ICL; 246 (top) Chris E. Makepeace, (bottom) Mullard Ltd; 247 EMI Music Archives; 248–9 Public Record Office (Crown Copyright); 250–1 BBC Hulton Picture Library; 259 ICL; 262 Press Association; 264 Scottish Development Agency; 265 Inmos (Photographer – John Perry); 266 BBC Copyright (Robert Hill).

All newspaper cuttings are from the British Library – Newspaper Library, Colindale.

Published by the British Broadcasting Corporation
35 Marylebone High Street, London W1M 4AA

ISBN 0 563 20117 7

First published 1984
© Peter Pagnamenta and Richard Overy 1984

Typeset by Phoenix Photosetting, Chatham
Printed in Great Britain by Mackays of Chatham Ltd

ALL OUR WORKING LIVES

CONTENTS

ACKNOWLEDGEMENTS

The BBC and the producers of *All Our Working Lives* would like to thank all the people who made the series possible by agreeing to talk about their time at work. They are far too numerous to list, but many will find themselves quoted in the programmes or the book, and we also thank those whom it was not possible to film, but who gave so much of their time during the preparation and research for each programme.

Equal acknowledgement is due to the many individuals and organisations who helped our film researcher, Christine Whittaker, find the film on which the series also depended: in particular to the National Film Archive, the Imperial War Museum, the Scottish Film Archive, the North West Film Archive, and the EMI-Pathe and British Movietone newsreel libraries. We were also assisted by companies, by nationalised industries, and by many trade unions.

For help with the technical, labour, and economic history of each sector, the producers turned to specialists in each field and to historians. Special thanks are due to our Series Adviser, Professor Leslie Hannah of the London School of Economics. The production team are also grateful for the generous advice they received from: Dr Peter Fearon and Dr Keith Hartley on the aircraft industry; Professor Roy Church and Dr Daniel T. Jones on the motor industry; Dr William Reader on the chemical industry; Professor Barry Supple and Dr Christopher Storm-Clark on the coal industry; Dr Douglas Farnie on cotton; Michael Mclear, Malcom Peltu, Dr Gary Werskey and Roger Woolnough on the electronics industry; Dr Graham Wilson, Dr Michael Topham and Mike Soper on farming; Michael Braham on retailing; Professor Anthony Slaven and Frederick Walker on shipbuilding; and Professor Peter Payne on iron and steel. Additional assistance came from Eddie and Ruth Frow, Professor John Burnett, Dr John Field, John Garnett, Dr Howard Gospel, Dr Terry Gourvish, Dr David Mayall and Geoff Tweedale.

For their own part, the authors of this book owe particular personal thanks to the producers and assistant producers who worked on each film and did the interviewing: Peter Ceresole, Angela Holdsworth, Ruth Jackson, Glynn Jones, Jonathan Lewis, Michael Waldman, Averil Ward, and to Holly Aylett, Maggie Brooks, Joanna Davis, Charles Furneaux, Peter Grimsdale, Roger Parry, Nikki Rendle and Colleen Toomey; to Leslie Hannah for his advice and guidance over the long haul; to Piers Brendon for his special help and encouragement; to Liz Green and Cassie Phillips for typing the manuscript; and to their patient families.

PREFACE

This book, like the BBC Television series which it accompanies, uses the candid memories of managers and workers across a range of British industries to give an account of Britain at work since the First World War. It is a story of achievement and reward, anxiety and adaptation, and because Britain's standard of living depends on the wealth generated by industry and those who work in it, it affects almost everyone.

The efforts of those who helped make the series over a two-year period are acknowledged separately. The most valuable result of the research is an archive of nearly three hundred filmed interviews with men and women who worked in a range of jobs from aircraft building to agriculture, steel-making to electronics, between the 1920s and the 1980s. We have made much use of these interviews both for quotation and indirectly.

First-hand recollections cannot possibly cover all the changes and developments of the period. The major industrial leaders of the 1920s and 1930s, when Britain came to accept that the Victorian prosperity was over, are long since dead. And many factors were quite outside the direct experience of those who worked in industry itself. Nevertheless their stories give us a unique opportunity to look at British working life from the inside. They reveal the different ways in which ten industries dealt with the new circumstances that arose as competition increased and technology changed, and they raise many broader questions. Where was job satisfaction or conflict greatest? When profits and wages were high, was this because the research and equipment were right, or because human relations were good, or because government intervened? Inevitably, one major question haunts the narrative. Why has Britain fallen so far behind her neighbours in western Europe, as well as America and Japan?

The sector-by-sector approach makes it easier to see what went right as well as what went wrong. It shows both strengths and weaknesses: great inventiveness combined with poor salesmanship, a great craft tradition combined with restrictive practices, countless opportunities taken or lost. There are no easy answers to Britain's problems, past or present. But here at least is an opportunity for men and women whose lives have been caught up in industry for over half a century to give their account of what it has been like.

The first and introductory chapter puts the major changes that have taken place in historical perspective. The concluding chapter looks back on Britain's industrial performance in a more general way, through the hindsight of those who have been caught up in it.

Peter Pagnamenta
Richard Overy

CHAPTER 1
WORKING LIVES

You had to build up and build up. They used to ask you, 'Can't you do a little more?' When I started work at first there were 20 to 30 starting the same morning as me. By Friday there was only 10, because they weeded you out. They just wanted people who could do the work.

Ethel Tillotson, on her move from a cotton mill to a new radio factory in 1938.

People's memories of their lives at work are personal and anecdotal. They are about good working conditions or bad, achievements and disappointments, higher or lower pay. Taken together these individual stories form a historical pattern which may be repeated across a whole industry, as all are swept forward or back by the same economic forces. Those who began their jobs around the time of the First World War bear witness, in these chapters, to the huge transformation in the nature of work that has taken place since then. They also shared in the changing fortunes of British industry. After the post-war boom and slump, and the depression of the thirties, came the pressure for all-out production in the Second World War. Then came the long period of full employment, when wages rose quickly. In the 1960s the boom faltered, and the fat years have been followed by the recession and lay-offs of the seventies and eighties.

The changes in markets, technology, and conditions have been greater than in any half-century since industrialisation began. They affected almost everyone, the farmer as well as the agricultural worker, the mill-owner as well as the spinner, engineers and designers as well as assembly workers. In most cases the changes were for the better.

The amount of time spent at the place of work each day has steadily decreased. Bert Barry, a riveter on the Wear, describes the long hours that were typical for millions of industrial workers at the end of the First War.

> You got woke up at about 5.30. A big hooter woke you up and you jumped out of bed and dashed down to the shipyard to get there for six o'clock. You worked till eight, and had half-an-hour for your breakfast, and then worked until twelve. Now for your dinner. At one you started work again, until five. You did that five days, and Saturday you worked five-and-a-half hours.

A week of fifty-five hours or more was standard until 1919, when many industries came down to forty-eight hours. But in less organised occupations the hours could be far longer. Len Sharman was twelve years old when he went to work for a farmer in Suffolk.

> We had a very rough time, and we had to work very hard. He used to call us at five o'clock in the morning, and we were on the go at seven o'clock at night, and my wage then was 10/- a week and my keep.

For domestic servants and shop assistants, hours could be almost unlimited. Rita Greendale describes her day in a Hull greengrocers in the 1920s.

> We normally started about seven in the morning. Get the stall out before half-past seven. And we used to have a snack on the counter at about twelve o'clock in the shop. It was one of the

Salford millworkers, 1930

9

few occasions when you were allowed in the shop, because we all worked on an outside stall. At five o'clock you had a sandwich or a banana or something, and then you just went on working. On a very early night we might close at nine or half-past. Mostly we were open till midnight.

People started work at a much earlier age. Before 1918 most began at twelve. Even when the school-leaving age was raised to fourteen, after the First World War, child labour was felt to be so essential to the highly successful Lancashire textile industry that special arrangements continued with the schools, for 'half-timers'. Before Ellen Coston started at the Jubilee Mill at Padiham in 1921 at the age of twelve, she had to be checked by the doctor, who pronounced her fit to start work.

I went half-time at twelve, and I went to school a half-a-day and in the mill half-a-day. We used to have a little green book and we used to have to take it with us to school and it was then marked that we had attended school, and we had to take it to the mill and they marked down that we had been there.

A 12-year-old cotton worker changing bobbins, 1920

The school-leaving age rose to fifteen after the Second World War, and did not reach sixteen until 1973.

At the other end of their working lives, as long as they were healthy and could hold on to their jobs, people continued working for much longer. When Ellen Coston started, some of the weavers she worked alongside were in their late seventies. When the first state pensions were introduced in 1909 they were means-tested, and only payable after the age of seventy. The idea of a period of retirement, that we now take for granted, was the exception for a privileged few.

The physical conditions of work have improved beyond measure. At the start of the century many workplaces were still crowded, dangerous, and insanitary. Though the Factory Acts laid down minimum conditions for health, and stipulated that walls should be whitewashed every fourteen months, the regulations were hard to enforce. Arthur Wardley describes the basic facilities at a large textile mill in the 1920s.

The toilets were outside in the yard. There'd be three WCs together, there'd be no roof on, open to the sky. Now just imagine, you are coming out of a hot spinning room, 80-odd degrees and an old pair of slippers on, middle of winter, three feet of snow on the ground, using the toilet, blowing a gale. You didn't stop long.

Eating arrangements at work were also primitive. Most industrial workers took in their own food. If they were lucky, they could find ways of warming it up on the boilers. In the steel-rolling mills the practice was to cut off a section of red-hot rail to heat food on. The two World Wars helped to bring in canteens, clinics and other welfare facilities. But there

The pithead of Marine Colliery at Cwm, Monmouthshire, after an underground explosion had killed 52 men in 1927

were always great variations between what a good employer would provide, and a bad. Paid holidays were introduced at the Brunner Mond alkali works at Northwich in 1884. It took nearly sixty years before this became the common practice.

Accidents were frequent. In 1912 the Board of Trade reported 3995 industrial fatalities. In the coal mines alone there were 1100. Seventy years later the equivalent figures were 579 overall and 42 in the mines. Injury was so widespread as to be part of the work process itself. It was regarded as inevitable that foundrymen would be splashed with molten metal. Textile workers risked injury every time they mended a broken thread. Riveters, unprotected by goggles, were hit in the eyes by flying chips of steel. Chemical workers were burnt by acid spills. Legislation was introduced to try to improve safety standards but many deaths went unrecorded because the victims died away from work, after debilitating lung or skin diseases. Coal dust in the mines, the red dust and gases of the steel-works, the fluff in the textile mills, all took their daily toll. Each industry had its own special hazards. Spinners contracted cancer of the groin from the oil that splashed on to them from the textile machinery. A shipyard worker describes how his father, a welder, died from breathing lead fumes.

> The insulated holds were entirely lined with sheet lead. Floor, ceiling, walls, and it was all hand-welded. In some cases the torch was blown by mouth, and you got the force of the flame by blowing down the tube which made the flame hot enough to melt the lead. Arising out of that we presume he got lung cancer. Now it's an industrial disease. Then it was just an unfortunate fact of life.

In many trades modern machines that would have reduced the risk of injury were slow to be introduced because labour was plentiful and equipment expensive. As health and safety legislation increased, employers often complained about their costs. Yet spectacular improvements were made over the period of a single working life. Clifford Hartley was a weaver in Earby.

> A modern mill is a marvellous place to work in today. Air conditioning, very little dust flying about, it's all got to be kept down to an absolute minimum. In the old days there were cobwebs hung down, and they swept down twice a year. Now it's swept down probably every week, or drawn out automatically by suction.

In terms of pay, the employee's share of the fruits of his own labour rose in comparison with the share that went to the managers or shareholders. In the 1920s a wage of 30/- to £3 a week was standard, in the 1980s the average industrial wage was nearer £140. Adjusted for inflation, wages rose threefold. The gap between the pay of the manager and the industrial worker was reduced. But differences between wages paid to groups of workers continued, so that a farm labourer is as poorly off in relation to everyone else today as he was in the 1920s.

Apart from pay levels there has been a shift in the whole method and basis on which people earn. Life for many managers was simple under the old 'contractor' systems, where one skilled man would hire his own gang, be paid a lump sum by the employer, and share out the pay at the end of the week. In the coal mines there were many variations of the 'butty' system, whereby the mine manager negotiated a rate for a particular piece of work with a collier, who then recruited and paid his own men. There were similar arrangements in most of the old industries. Bert Barry remembers how he was paid as a riveter.

> You had to go into the pub when you got your wages. One man in the squad got all the wages in bulk, and we had to go into the pub, and the managers always had a supply of change, and dozens of men would be in for change, buying beer.

Contractor systems were gradually replaced, but there were continuing distinctions between those who were paid on a time basis, whether by the week, the day, or the hour, and those paid by results. Piecework in Victorian times had been a relatively simple matter of price lists for each item produced or part of a job done. As industry became more complicated, so did payment systems, with new forms of incentive and bonus. Instead of being set arbitrarily by management, rates came to be negotiated with the unions. A Midlands car worker describes how the system changed.

> Before the war the foreman and the rate fixer used to come and look at you working and time you with a stopwatch. You'd got

to do the job. If you stopped, the watch stopped. So you didn't
have a lot of scope really, it was more or less the foreman and
the rate fixer who timed the job. After the war, when we had
the new wages procedure, all times were negotiated and
pounds, shillings and pence went out. It was man hours against
decimal hours. A job was worked out, it would take you so
many hours to do. At the end of the week each job was counted
up, how many hours the job had taken, how many hours you'd
got. You'd divide your man hours into that to come to your
piecework price.

The ways in which people were paid became fairer and more standardised, but the complicated legacy of the past was to have a permanent
effect on industrial relations, reinforcing the hierarchies of British
industrial life.

All the time the nature of the job to be done was altering. In heavy
industry work became less physically demanding as new machinery
was installed. In the shipyards, pneumatic and hydraulic power
hammers replaced hand riveting and caulking. Coal came to be cut and
moved not by human muscle alone, but with cutting machines and
conveyors. In the steelworks, furnaces came to be charged by machine,
rather than by hours of shovelling in the melting shops. In the chemical
plants cleaner and safer processes replaced back-breaking manual work.
But though physical conditions improved, the coming of mechanisation
reduced the demand for traditional skills, or required different ones. On
the farms agricultural equipment reduced drudgery but it also took
away the need for the skill of the hedger and the ploughman. Len
Sharman used to walk up to twelve miles a day behind the heavy
horses, and plough an acre a day with a single furrow.

In those days we used to plough what we call a ten-furrow
stretch. You'd draw a furrow up the field and you'd go around
five times and you'd start another one, so you had a furrow
every eight foot. Your drill wheels ran in the furrow and the
horses went on the soil. And, of course, that drained the land
as well. Well, of course, when tractors came in that was all
done away with. You start on one side, and you plough and
you get to the other side. Today there's no skill in ploughing.

In the textile industry automatic looms made the old skill of the
weavers redundant. In the engineering industry new types of machine
allowed the semi-skilled to produce work that would have previously
needed a journeyman fitter or a turner with five years apprenticeship
behind him. New tools were accompanied by new methods of organisation. At first 'Scientific management' and 'Time and motion' were
American imports, to be regarded with suspicion by trade unions and
employers alike. But eventually the well-planned lay-out of machines
and conveyor belts, and the precise timing and costing of jobs, came to

Changing skills: a horse plough-man inspects a tractor and plough at a Berkshire demon-stration in 1930

receive as much attention as wage rates or the price of raw materials. Jobs on production lines were broken down into smaller parts and shorter cycles. Cath Smith used to make curtains and upholstery in the trim section of the Standard car factory in Coventry. When she started, each girl made an entire piece of upholstery on her own sewing machine. When the conveyor belts were introduced in 1937 this changed.

> When the conveyors came in they were marked off, and the girls would sit along the conveyor. Probably there were about twenty-eight in the gang I worked on, fourteen facing that way, fourteen facing up this way. The first two girls would pick the work up and do probably the first three rows of fluting. The next two girls would do so many more rows of fluting. The next two girls would finish the fluting off. Then two youngsters took the work off the conveyor and marked it round the board. Put it back on the conveyor and and the next set of girls would be putting on what we call piping and ending. Those girls finished the job off.

The production line provided the most emotive example of an apparent decline in the 'quality' of work, especially in the car industry where it was first widely introduced, and where it was most alienating. Joe Dennis worked on the night shift in the noise and turmoil of a car plant in the 1950s, with the car bodies moving past ceaselessly.

> My wife always insisted that I had my breakfast before I went to bed. And I would get into such a state that I would sit down to a bacon and egg and the table would appear to be going away from me. I thought, 'Crikey, how long am I going to have to put up with this?'
> But the pay was good. It was a case of really getting stuck in and saying, 'To hell with it, get it while it's there'. And this is the way it went, but the elderly chaps couldn't stand the pace.

But not all new industry involved mass production, or assembly lines.

Much of the new technology was more demanding and interesting than what had gone before. Ken Webber worked in the 1950s at a new chemical plant in Runcorn, where carbide was produced from electric furnaces with a temperature of 4000 centigrade.

> The people who worked on the carbide plant were generally people who liked a challenge, and liked to be doing something that a lot of people wouldn't. The tappers looked on themselves as being really a pretty good team, and they were acknowledged in the town, 'He's a carbide tapper', you know, 'He's a tough guy'. They had a certain prestige.

Those who had an old skill could still admire a new process. Don Owen was a 'first hand melter' in a steelworks, controlling the bubbling metal in the open-hearth furnaces with a mixture of his eye and a sixth sense that took twenty-five years to acquire. In the 1980s, steel is made by the Basic Oxygen process, and the giant BOS converters are operated from an electronic control desk.

> The first hand melter was finished in the BOS plant. He still had a very responsible job, but as regards his eye making steel, or anything like that, it was all instrumentation. He never looked at a furnace. But it's a wonderful process. You can't compare it at all. They are making steel in the BOS plant which we could never make. A pity it never came out years ago.

In the old factories and workshops discipline was much harsher, and enforced by foremen with the right to hire and fire. If overtime had to be done, it was compulsory. If work was below standard, money was deducted from the wage packet. In the cotton mills three pence was taken off for a mistake in the cloth. Company rules were to be obeyed, and minor misdemeanours, such as making tea, or smoking, could lead to instant dismissal. When old industries with a particular tradition of insecurity began to decline, the fear increased. Jack Wylie was in the shipyards on Tyneside in the 1930s.

> Men were scared of being finished. Foremen had a lot of power and were able to hire and fire men without recourse to the management. A lot of men, unfortunately, thought if they could get in with the foreman, their job would be more secure. Men used to give the foremen presents – a packet of Woodbines with a ten shilling note tucked in. There was a foreman, who lived very near to where I lived, who regularly, every Sunday morning, had garden produce left on his doorstep.

Even in the growth areas, such as the car and electrical factories that were built between the wars, the same insecurity continued. So did the inequity between those on a month's notice, a week's notice, and those taken on by the hour. More cars were being sold each year, when Hayden Evans started at the Pressed Steel car-body plant in Oxford.

You had no guarantee any day of having a day's work. You might come in in the morning and they'd say, 'Oh, we haven't got any jobs, come back this afternoon', and then they'd say, 'Go over the café opposite and the foreman will come and fetch you when the job comes.' You would go over there and at four o'clock they'd come for you, and it's no exaggeration to say they'd want you to work till nine o'clock.

Unemployed men queuing outside the Gramophone Company at Hayes, Middlesex, which was taking on workers in 1932. Electrical and car firms were expanding, even during the depression

After the Second World War work became less casual, and new employment legislation in the 1960s gave the right to compensation and redundancy payments. But though shop floor discipline was less arbitrary, the chance of a sudden factory closure, or mass redundancies involving thousands at a time, was as great as ever.

One of the responses to this insecurity was the growth in trade union membership, though the defeat of the General Strike, and the depression, provided a setback to this between the wars. The unions remained strongest in the old industries, for the car firms, and many other new employers, tried to keep the unions out of their plants for as long as they could. Some used straightforward intimidation. Frank Dodd remembers the manager of a small chemical company in the 1930s.

> He refused to have a union in the place at all. And he threatened that he'd sack the first man that started one. And that first man was me, but he didn't sack me because I got the union too strong beforehand. But we still had a lot of difficulty. The men were really afraid to be seen talking to me because the foreman wanted to know what they'd been saying. Up to the time I started we got no time and a half for Sunday or any other holiday. He pointed out that he didn't get any more for his TNT that he made then, and therefore he didn't pay us.

By the end of the thirties, the new unions with a general membership, like the Transport and General Workers, were recruiting widely, but the spread was uneven. Farm workers and shop workers were still largely unorganised.

The position of the unions, and particularly the shop stewards, was consolidated during and after the Second World War. In 1935 there had been four million members, by 1950 there were nine million, and the unions had won recognition almost everywhere. Their strength brought new forms of collective bargaining and additional pressure for better conditions, but few improvements were conceded willingly.

At the same time the lives of supervisors and managers, owners and entrepreneurs were changing too. At the start of the century the small firm was still typical, often run by the family who owned it. Even in the larger companies, contact between workforce and management was close and regular, and owners who took a direct interest in their business could work as many hours as their men. But the distance between the two widened over the years despite calls for more participation and involvement. The job of 'manager' was itself subdivided so that production engineering, personnel management, finance and sales became separate functions. Yet in the 1920s many managers still operated by instinct, with the minimum of paperwork. The manager of a family shipbuilding firm remembers the informal way in which business could be conducted.

> I can remember my grandfather and my uncle coming back from London with an order on the back of a matchbox, and not even a contract was signed. An exchange of letters was quite good enough. There was good faith between two people. It was quite a long time after I started that contracts became a general procedure.

Even in the new industries that were growing up, powerful bosses could run their affairs in an individualistic and sometimes eccentric manner. Jack Fish worked for Blackburn Aircraft in the early 1930s.

Norman Blackburn said he wanted an aircraft to tour Europe, and he said to Alf Mills, 'Design me one, and I'll buy you an armchair'. That's how it started. Alf Mills designed this thing, which just started on a duplicate pad. I don't think he ever used a slide rule. It was a monocoque, all metal, and it was a good aeroplane.

This was a style of management that was on the way out. As businesses grew larger and absorbed smaller firms, ownership shifted from individual entrepreneurs to shareholders, or to the state. Policy came to be decided in government departments, or London head offices, or in the headquarters of multinationals, by anonymous bosses who might have little or no contact with the workforce they controlled. Many workers came to see themselves as small cogs in very large machines. The shop which Rita Greendale was working in during the 1950s was taken over by a nationwide group.

The first thing that happened was that instead of having a name you suddenly had a number. Mind you it was an enormous number. Suddenly, instead of being a nice friendly atmosphere, everybody was suspicious. Everything was under lock and key and you got notices around saying you could be searched at all times, and they sent plainclothes inspectors in.

The old managers: three brothers, S. R. Lysaght (managing director), W. R. Lysaght (chairman) and H. R. Lysaght, still ran the family steel company, John Lysaght Ltd, between the wars

The new corporate management: Directors of Imperial Chemical Industries, the huge chemical group formed in the 1920s to compete with the Germans and Americans, about to return from Brussels in 1928. Sir Alfred Mond is in the centre

These individual experiences of shop worker and farm labourer, car worker and shipbuilder, reflected the gradual shift from a Victorian economy to a new age. What had gone was the era of peace and industrial pre-eminence, free trade and cotton, of steam and rail, to be replaced by an age of armaments and protection, of corporations and multinationals, of aviation and electronics. One of the principal features of the new age was the very speed at which changes took place. Old industries collapsed, and new ones rose up more quickly in new places. Decisions to invest, or to pull out, or to switch products, were made more rapidly. Traditional ideas about the natural specialisation of a particular part of the country, and about who did what best, had to be forgotten. In the 1930s, former cotton workers found themselves making aircraft or radio parts in Lancashire. In the 1970s, the aircraft factories were themselves contracting, and one of the radio factories had turned to producing video discs. In the 1970s, miners in south Wales went to work making vacuum cleaners and refrigerators. Many of these changes involved shifts around the country, from the north and north-west, where the industrial revolution had begun in the eighteenth century, to the south-east and the Midlands. There were shifts even within the same industries. In the 1930s steelworkers from Glasgow came south to the new works at Corby in Northamptonshire, which offered excellent prospects with its cheap iron ore. Less than fifty years

19

David Low cartoon, 1946. In the years immediately after World War II, the Labour government campaigned to increase productivity and output per man

"I'LL ATTEND TO THE FOUNDATIONS LATER"

later steel-making at Corby ceased and the annual Highland Gathering in the town is the principal reminder of the great migration. In the 1960s and 1970s coal miners from Scotland and the north-east transferred to newer pits in Yorkshire.

The old basic industries contracted. In Scotland there are now 40,000 workers in electronics, more than in shipbuilding or steel. At the same time the balance between manufacturing industry and the rest of the economy was shifting so much that economists began to talk about 'de-industrialisation'. In 1950 the manufacturing and service sectors both employed the same numbers, 42 per cent of the workforce. Thirty years later manufacturing employed only 26 per cent, and 62 per cent were in service jobs, such as retailing, banking or insurance. There were more white collar jobs, fewer blue collar. More people have technical qualifications and training; they are more mobile. Few end their working lives doing the same job as when they started, or expect to do what their parents did.

Most saw these changes in a positive way, as working conditions improved and living standards rose. But others were less happy. The loss of a job, or the inability to use a skill, or an enforced move away from family and friends in an old-established community, contributed to a sense of deprivation and loss.

Similar shifts were happening in all industrialised countries, but in Britain they seemed to happen more painfully than elsewhere and with more debate and self-analysis. The great changes in technology, and in the style of management and labour relations, were accompanied by a sense of decline, partly because the traditions of the past had been so strong. The concern with industrial life also arose because so much insecurity and hardship continued alongside the growth. There was an expectation of employment for all, yet the fear of being out of a job

Coventry workers protest against the lay-offs of over 2000 when Standard re-equipped their tractor factory in 1956

determined many attitudes. The experience of millions on the dole in the 1930s, and of another generation in the 1970s and 1980s, could be put down partly to conditions of world trade that were beyond Britain's control, but it was also attributed to particular British failings at work. Perhaps the technology had not changed fast enough, or perhaps labour relations were too polarised, or managers were too sleepy. Except in the brief period of full employment and rising living standards for all, in the 1950s and 1960s, the British were the first to blame themselves.

The expectations that people had of industry were made more poignant by what was happening among Britain's major industrial competitors. Not only were they able to make cheaper goods, but their living standards rose faster and to higher levels. The United States had always been ahead, but it seemed a source of national affront to be over-taken by Germany, France, Scandinavia, and Japan. The most bruising comparisons were not those of total output, or share of world trade, but of Britain's competitive efficiency. The British worker could not produce nearly so much in an hour as his German or American equivalent. Productivity did not rise as fast as it did elsewhere.

The awareness that British industry was not working smoothly, or changing as fast, or producing the results that it should be, dates from before the turn of the century, and the start of the period of this book. A 'British disease' was diagnosed early, even if the cures for it have varied down the years. For some the remedies were largely political: they wanted to replace the capitalist system altogether, or to take certain sectors into public ownership. For others the solution had more to do with adjustments in economic policy: industry could become more efficient once tariffs were imposed, or the exchange rate altered, or if Britain joined the Common Market. For many others the cure had to be an internal one, self-administered by those who worked in industry. What really mattered was to rationalise production in larger units, or to change the attitudes of workers and managers towards each other and their work. Successive generations have grown used to hearing exhortations from government ministers and members of the royal family urging them to wake up, work harder, pull together, pull their fingers out, be more efficient.

The self-criticism was in full swing in Edwardian Britain, as the industrial supremacy the Victorians had taken for granted was seen to be slipping away. Already the United States and Germany were producing more steel and machinery than Britain, and were far ahead in the new industries of cars, chemicals, electrical engineering. At the Guildhall in 1901 the Prince of Wales said, 'The old country must wake up . . .', and expanded on this later:

> Abroad one finds an existing impression . . . that the superior technical and scientific knowledge of our foreign competitors is one reason why our hitherto pre-eminent position in manufacture and commerce is so considerably threatened.[1]*

The lack of technical training and scientific education were acknowledged to be genuine weaknesses. A simpler vein of criticism put the emphasis on the national character. Stereotypes were drawn, of the unenterprising and conservative manager who operated by rule of thumb, and the lazy and obstructive worker. Self-deprecating foreign comparisons were made as frequently then as now. The *Daily Mail* wrote admiringly of the German businessman:

> He is a glutton for work. He out-hustles even the Americans. He is up at half-past six every morning, at his simple breakfast of coffee and rolls . . . It is the German's love of work, love of business, that makes him, plus his thoroughness and scientific training, a menace to easier-going rivals.[2]

The Edwardians admired the welfare benefits and better conditions that the more paternalistic German employers provided for their workers, and they recognised how much the class system dominated labour relations in Britain as compared with other countries. A National Education Association pamphlet found that

* The footnote figures refer to the References on pages 283–4.

In America, the manufacturer works *with* his men, here he works *over* him. Here it is the everlasting feudalism of master and man: there the man is colleague of his master, and they run the machine together; no impassable chasm, industrial or social, divides them.

All these problems were under discussion when the First World War began, and shattered the foundations of the massive Victorian industrial machine for ever. The Great War put the British economy and British working methods under their severest test yet, exposing weaknesses and showing strengths. The wartime need for explosives, radios and vehicles transformed some of the industries that had been weakest before 1914, with a new infusion of research effort and government money. A giant aircraft industry was created from scratch. The car, electronic and chemical industries entered the 1920s still small by American standards, but firmly established. The old staples, cotton, coal, steel, shipbuilding, all played their part in the war, but emerged to face demands and markets quite different from those they had known before. Towards the end of the First World War all the issues that affected industrial performance were re-examined, with government encouragement, in preparation for the coming of peace. Management was urged to be more professional, to take better training, to invest more, and to sell more energetically. Labour was called on to be more co-operative and to abandon restrictive practices. These themes run through the chapters that follow, as different industries tried to cope with the changed conditions after 1918. But the factor that none of them could do anything about was the burden of history itself. The difficulties of the British industrial experience in the twentieth century were as much to do with the inheritance from the nineteenth century as anything else.

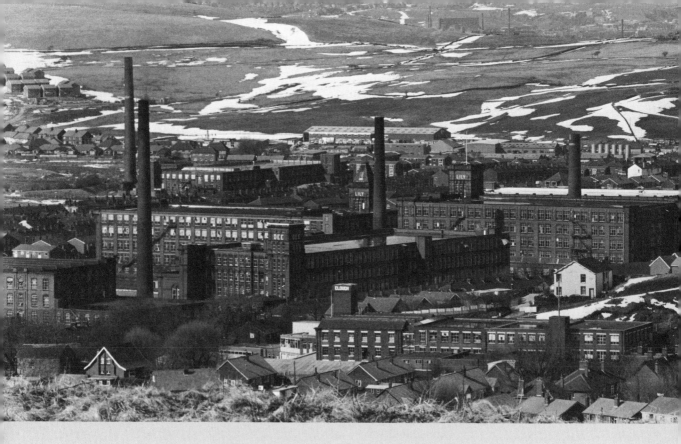

CHAPTER 2: COTTON
OVER A PRECIPICE

The best organised and most finely managed industry in Great Britain, if not in the world, is the Lancashire cotton industry. It is conducted with a thoroughness and a capacity that is at once the envy and despair of foreign rivals, and it furnishes in its continued progress an object lesson which other industries in the country may do well to take to heart.[3]

Charles Watney & James Little, 1912

If in the hot summer of 1914 you had said to a Lancashire man: 'My dear Sir, do you realise you are standing on the edge of a precipice?' his eyes would have popped out of his head. He would have asked you to see a doctor. The advance had gone on for generations: the increase was automatic. It was a natural law: it did itself.

So Lancashire believed. So England believed. And both of them were wrong.[4]

Godfrey Armitage, 1950

Eighty years ago, the smoking chimneys of the Lancashire mill towns marked one of the wonders of the industrial world. Concentrated into a few hundred square miles was a trade so well organised and efficient that it could produce cotton yarn and cloth at a quality and price that no one else could approach. It was a success rooted in the Victorian era of free trade, coal and steam engineering, and vigorous individual enterprise, and was sustained by a workforce of 600,000 men and women whose skill and experience was unparalleled. Unlike other British industries, which already felt the United States or Germany breathing down their necks, Lancashire had sensed no hint of competition from elsewhere before the First World War. They had two-thirds of the world trade, and cotton goods were by far the most valuable of Britain's exports, earning a quarter of all overseas earnings. A Burnley manager describes the part that exports played for the mills:

> They used to say that Lancashire wove the home trade before breakfast. They had an hour's start in the early morning before they had a break, and then they wove for the world for the rest of the day.

When the First World War ended there was a mood of overwhelming optimism in Lancashire. The men came back from France, and mills that had been turned over to munitions were reopened.

> I don't think anybody thought about change. We were all anxious to get moving again and get our mills in full production. We had all been producing ammunition or khaki cloth, and we had to get back to producing towels and sheets. There was no difficulty with producing. We could produce everything that was required.

> Government, hastily removing the wartime controls, shared this general belief. A Board of Trade Committee reported in 1918 that 'all the evidence we have received tends to prove that the strength of the British cotton trade in the competitive markets of the world is unimpaired', and for the first two years of peace every yard of cloth made could be sold at prices higher than ever before. The organisation of the trade had changed as little as the working conditions in the mills, or the machinery that was used in them. Lancashire presented a picture of an unreconstructed Victorian industry at its peak, with all its solidarity and strength, as well as potential defects.

For families in street after street the day began with a rap on the window.

> We used to have what we called a knocker-up. A man used to come round early mornings knocking up. He had a long pole with a wire on, and he used to knock on people's windows because they used to have to get up at about half-past six in the morning. I had seven brothers, and six of them were weavers.

And my mother used to have all our cups of tea ready in the morning, and then we'd go off to work.

Family and working life were blended together. For over a century children had followed their parents into the mills.

It was a family business, a family thing. There were aunts and uncles and cousins and brothers and sisters and daughters, and they all lived round about. They all knew each other before they came into the mill, and a lot of them had come in from being children, bringing their parents' lunches in. That got them familiar with coming to the factory.

Florence Mortimer was a carder in Bolton.

The biggest majority of Lancashire girls were cotton. They all had to go into the mills. And they were weaving, winding, beaming, reeling, picking the cops. They were everything.

Lancashire had pioneered the factory production of textiles, helped by the combination of local coal to provide power, soft water and a damp climate. With each year more cotton goods were spun and woven in an unchecked growth up to 1914, when the mills produced eight million yards of cloth. In the newer textile industries in other parts of the world one company might buy in raw cotton, and take it through all the stages of production on one site, to end up with a finished roll of cloth, or garment. But in Lancashire the trade was intricately subdivided. Liverpool merchants imported the raw cotton. Spinning mills bought cotton and turned it into yarn. Weaving mills in turn bought yarn and produced cloth, which was finished by independent dyeworks, bleach works, and print works. Finally Manchester merchant houses sold the finished yarn or cloth, and despatched it round the world. It was a system almost guaranteed to find the cheapest source of supply. The merchant would get several quotations for weaving cloth, the weaver would take his yarn from the cheapest spinner, and so on right through the chain. This specialisation was deemed a great advantage. An American trade official sent to study Lancashire before 1914 reported admiringly:

Spinning and weaving are conducted in separate establishments. The manager of a weaving mill frequently knows little, if anything, of a spinning mill or vice versa. Consequently he develops into a more competent man in his specific vocation than the one who is burdened with the superintendence of all the numerous and intricate processes involved in the converting of raw cotton to finished cloth.[5]

The same specialisation existed among the mill workers. Besides the few involved in moving the cotton, or in the finishing trades, almost all were either in spinning or in weaving. Which you did depended on

Above: *Spinning in an Oldham mill. 'Big piecers' helped the spinner and mended threads. This was mule-spinning, where the carriage moved backwards and forwards across the floor*

Right: *The 'Little piecer', who oiled and cleaned*

where you lived. Spinning was the more skilled, and was mostly done by men who regarded themselves as the aristocrats of the cotton trade. But even among the spinners themselves there were gradations, depending on the quality of the yarn woven.

> A fine spinner would go to work in collar and tie. He'd have his hat on, and umbrella or a walking stick. A coarse spinner would have a scarf tied round his neck, or a bit of cotton waste wrapped round his neck.

Inside the spinning mills the heat and humidity were kept artificially high, and the spinners worked in bare feet, tramping up and down behind the mule spinning frames which ran backwards and forwards on wheels, from a central gangway. In the course of a day a spinner could walk up to twenty miles.

> It was noisy, dirty, dusty, oily. Like a prison and very hot. It's about 80 degrees the heat, and that's the first thing that hits you.

> You had bare feet, and a thin pair of overalls. And I used to wear an old shirt that I could take off at night, and put a dry shirt on before I went home. In fact some never wore overalls, just had their long shirt and a piece of string tied round.

> It was very hard work, and it was dirty, dusty, very dusty. Sweat dripping off the end of your nose. Sometimes you didn't have the energy to wash properly, so that you were going out of the mill looking like a snowman, covered in cotton because there was so much floating about.

A strict hierarchy applied within the mills. At the bottom were the boys and younger men who had to clean up, and oil the machines. Because they had to repair the broken threads, which was called piecing, they were known as 'little piecers' and 'big piecers'. They were employed directly by the spinners, who paid them from their own wages. It was a popular axiom that 't'little piecer does all the work and t'spinner gets all the money'. Spinners were chosen from among the older piecers who had proven particularly hard-working, but the promotion took years because there was no fixed retirement age. Once a new spinner had been recruited he might work on until he was over eighty, so that fresh opportunities often came only with death or disablement:

> You waited for dead men's shoes. Now if Gaffer come for me and said: 'Arthur, go on number 12 pair, he hasn't come in, he's poorly', first thing you'd say: 'How bad is he?' If it happened that he will die, then I've got a job, but when he come back, you went back big piecing. You were disappointed.

Conditions were different in the weaving sheds, vast floors with as many as five hundred looms packed tightly between narrow alleyways.

If it was a very big mill you couldn't see across it, partly because of the pillars, but also because each loom had driving belts. With the steam as well, and the slight haze from the cotton, you could hardly see across.

Weaving in Rochdale at the turn of the century: the girl is being taught to run the loom by the older woman behind her

The weaving sheds were not as hot as the spinning mills, but were even noisier. Weavers, who were mostly women, found it impossible to talk to each other with the racket from hundreds of looms and the belts and shafting that powered them.

They used to lip read, and if someone entered the shed all the weavers knew who was coming and what they had come for, because one told another and it flashed across like lightning from one end to the other, just by lip reading.

Young girls who came into the mills were first placed with a more experienced weaver, the 'Missus', who taught them to weave, before they were given looms of their own to run. For the weaver the main problem was to keep the four looms they were responsible for, working. If they stopped for any reason then there would be less pay, for weavers like spinners were on piece-rates. Supervision of the sheds was in the hands of men, the 'overlookers'. If the cloth was not perfect, pay was docked.

Weavers 35 years later: dress changed, but not the machinery. The standard Lancashire looms were so ruggedly built they would last 60 years

When you'd wove it, it went up in the cloth warehouse and a man passed it. He was called the out-looker. If he didn't like it, you were brought up and you were shown the mistake you'd made and he'd fine you threepence. If you had two or three faults in forty yards, he'd cut a piece out and it was a shilling.

For spinners and weavers alike the mills were dangerous. Very few escaped without minor injuries. Weavers went deaf with the noise of the looms. Spinners wore glasses through the strain of watching the threads. There was the daily threat of serious disablement, that could mean the end of work altogether. For the cotton workers these are still vivid memories. Florence Mortimer remembers a young woman being carried down the steps by the manager, with her hand hanging off.

> She started cleaning the waste with her hand brush and she got it fast and it took her arm. Somebody had switched on the engine.

Clifford Hartley's mother was blinded when a steel comb broke a tooth, which flew up and hit her in the pupil of her eye.

> She couldn't see to weave with one eye, and so she was out, finished. She got the magnificent sum of £70 for being blinded. And no health insurance, no disablement in those days.

29

The high accident rate was due to the use of old and unguarded machinery, and to the system of payment by results. It was in everyone's financial interests that the carding engines, spinning frames, or looms, should be kept running. So whenever possible machines were cleaned, oiled and repaired while they were in motion. Once an accident had happened, medical provisions were poor. Home Office figures for the 1920s showed that in industry as a whole nine per cent of reported accidents went septic. In cotton, sepsis occured in 19 per cent of accidents, because of the inadequacy of first-aid supplies and the splinters from rough floor-boards, on which many worked in bare feet.

Apart from the noise and the dust, oil was the principal feature in the life of mills. They smelt of oil. The wooden floors were impregnated and slippery. There was another more deadly hazard:

> You got your feet very oily from the splash of the oil from the spindles on the floor. It used to splash on your overalls, particularly in the region of a man's groin, and this was a serious cause of epithelioma, spinner's cancer.

When the midday break came, men and women sat down on the oily floor to eat. There were few facilities for washing. The single communal sink would be coated with oil. Hands, brushes and tools were all cleaned under the same tap.

All these conditions would have been standard in the factories of Victorian Britain, but after the First World War health and safety levels in cotton textiles were slipping behind, and the industry was so large that it was hard to enforce new regulations. Yet relations between the bosses and the workers were good. Many owners had worked their way from being operatives themselves. They kept close contact with the workforce and understood their problems. Other employers made their sons work in the mill before taking on management responsibilities. For those born into the business learning on the job was taken for granted.

> You obviously had to be put into the mill as an apprentice to the cotton trade. You would have to start at the bottom and work your way up. And you would be expected at the end of your apprenticeship to know something about everything.

The great majority of firms were small family concerns passed on from generation to generation. Some could trace family ownership back to the early days when cotton had first begun to transform the industrial life of Britain. By the 1920s the cotton industry was already 150 years old and was deeply set in its ways. Different parts of the region specialised in spinning and weaving. Fine spinning for fine yarns and sewing cotton was in Bolton and Manchester. The greatest spinning centre for coarse yarns was Oldham. To the north weaving was around Blackburn, Burnley and Preston.

With 90 per cent of their output going overseas, each weaving area tended to work for a particular section of the world market. The biggest trade was in coarse grey cloth, but they also made loincloths and turbans, and saris and scarves. Lancashire manufacturers knew who preferred dhotis with plain borders as distinct from patterned borders. They sent a special umbrella cloth to Japan, and shirtings to Peru. Blackburn wove mostly for India. Burnley wove for China, which took a narrower fabric. The concentration was even greater in smaller centres. In the small hill town of Great Harwood all twenty-three mills worked solely on turbans and loincloths for India. China and India together took half the British production, the Middle East and Africa nearly a quarter. To Lancashire this seemed natural and eternal. A later critic recalled what an old mill-owner had once told him.

> Never again let anybody in Lancashire hear you talk this childish stuff about foreign competition. It's just twaddle. In the first place, we've got the only climate in the world where cotton piece goods in any quantity can ever be produced. In the second place, no foreign Johnnies can ever be bred that can spin and weave like Lancashire lasses and lads. In the third place, there are more spindles in Oldham than in all the world put together. And last of all, if they had the climate and the men and the spindles – which they can never have – foreigners could never find the brains Lancashire cotton men have for the job. We've been making all the world's cotton cloth that matters for more years than I can tell, and we always shall.[6]

This confidence was to prove misplaced. The First World War was followed by an unprecedented boom, in which new mills were built and record sums were paid for yarn and cloth. But in early 1920 the peak was over, and the prices of raw cotton and finished cloth halved within a few months. The first of a series of slumps began, as the delayed effect of the war revealed itself. Four years of dislocation to world trade had changed everything. During the war, when exports from Lancashire had almost ceased, traditional customers had began to make new arrangements. New home industries had been encouraged in Europe and South America, as well as China and India.

The principal gainer was Japan, which started to make her own textile machinery as well as buying automatic machines from the United States. While British cloth was in short supply Japanese exports rose. Once the war was over Japan ordered shiploads of new looms from Lancashire, and the price differences widened. In the 1920s the Japanese cotton industry was expanding rapidly, and as fast as Lancashire's declined. At first the Lancashire mill-owners continued to dismiss it. Sir Charles Macara, head of a large spinning firm already running on short time, said in 1924:

> Too often, alarmist and ill-informed reports get abroad to the effect that this country or that country is doing wonders in the way of cotton cloth production and is sweeping all before it in

foreign markets . . . It is an astonishing thing what credence is given to these things in Lancashire where people ought to know better.[7]

The new Japanese mills were run on two shifts, instead of the one in Lancashire. They employed young country girls, who were regimented by foremen blowing whistles, and who slept in mill dormitories for pay of 8d a day, at a time when Lancashire workers might make £2 a week. Japanese mills were electrified when Lancashire still used coal, and as well as using traditional Lancashire-style looms more efficiently, they introduced faster, automatic spinning and weaving machinery. In just a few years Japan ousted Britain from the Chinese trade and took much of the business in Africa and South America.

The loss of the greatest market of all, India, caused most distress to Lancashire. New mills in Bombay and Ahmedabad produced the cheap grey cloth that India had imported before 1914, and the Government of India protected them with a 25 per cent tariff. Lancashire had already found it difficult to beat Indian prices; now the battle became a political as well as an economic one. The nationalist movement encouraged the villagers to buy from India's own mills, or to revert to handmade cloth. The spinning wheel became the symbol of nationalist resistance, and Gandhi imposed a full-scale boycott on British cloth. India took only a quarter of what she had once taken. In 1931 Gandhi was persuaded to

Gandhi visits Blackburn in 1931, when more than half the mills in the town were closed

come to Blackburn, to see the effects of the boycott on Lancashire towns. One mill-owner remembers his answer:

> He was shown how serious the situation was. In Blackburn alone there were seventy-four mills closed within about four years. 'Well,' he said, 'you come to the villages in India, we're a lot poorer than what you are', and there really wasn't much to say about that.

The effect of foreign competition was traumatic. The output of British cotton goods fell by 60 per cent between 1913 and 1930; exports fell even further, from eight million yards before the First War to fewer than one-and-a-half million yards in 1938. Even though the mills and the unions adopted short time to share out the available work, the dole and the means test came to hundreds of thousands of Lancashire families. Unemployment ran at 50 per cent in some areas. As the younger men left in search of work elsewhere, the population of the cotton towns dropped.

The world depression in 1929 hit almost every section of British industry, and worsened cotton's difficulties because it was the most dependent on exports. Lancashire provided the first great case study in decline. A host of critics turned the investigation of Lancashire's problems into a specialisation of its own. Inquiries commissioned by government, or by the employers or unions, followed one another with increasing speed for the next forty years. The first, chaired by the Home Secretary, J. R. Clynes, in 1930 set the tone.

> The well-being of the cotton industry is more than the concern of Lancashire herself. It is of vital interest to the country as a whole.[8]

Clynes urged the industry to modernise and reorganise. While the rest of the world was expanding output by making standard cloth in large integrated factories, Lancashire had stuck to the equipment and organisation that had served it in the nineteenth century. The Americans and the Japanese were rapidly changing to cheaper 'ring-spinning' to replace the old Lancashire mule-spinning. By the 1930s, the American industry was all on rings, the British only a third. There were now automatic looms as well, much faster than traditional machines. In Lancashire each weaver still worked four of the old-style looms. In the foreign mills equipped with automatics, one operator might run forty looms or more.

Clynes put most emphasis on the divided structure of the trade and called on the industry to put spinning and weaving and finishing together.

> What was probably the best of all systems in more stable times threatens ruin in a time of radical change . . . Lancashire must choose between losing her trade or changing her methods.

THE BOLTON EVENING NEWS, FRIDAY, JULY 4, 1930.

COTTON INQUIRY PLANS TO SAVE THE INDUSTRY.

UP-TO-DATE METHODS AND NEW MILL PLANT ESSENTIAL.

Considerable Fresh Capital Needed for Large Amalgamations.

CO-OPERATIVE PRODUCTION AND SYSTEMATIC MARKETING.

The eagerly-awaited Cotton Report was issued this afternoon. It surveys exhaustively the present depression in the industry, the main and subsidiary causes, and suggests the reorganization and methods essential to the prevention of even greater disaster.

After having enumerated foreign competition, superior foreign technical and marketing methods, lower foreign labour costs, and wasteful home competition in the introduction as the principal contributories, the Report makes the following recommendations:—

TECHNICAL.—Use of short-stapled cotton, high-draft spinning machinery and ring spinning. As to automatic looms, it is stated that these may be a saving in costs, but that the system would be uneconomical on a single shift.

ORGANIZATION AND CAPITAL.—Formations of larger units in the spinning and manufacturing sections, and considerable amounts of fresh capital for re-equipment.

MARKETING AND PRODUCTION.—Co-operative production and systematic marketing of standard lines goods. Government-assisted missions to study Far Eastern conditions. Co-operation between employers and operatives to reduce costs.

"Time Come For Lancashire to Make Her Choice."

The outcome of the appointment on August 1st, 1929, of a sub-committee of Civil Research. The terms of reference . . . were to report upon the present position and prospects of . . . and to make . . . to any action . . . desirable and . . . to improve the industry in the . . .

The committee was composed of: . . . M.P., Secretary of . . . Affairs (chairman): . . . V. Alexander, . . . Admiralty: Sir . . . Joseph . . .

Still more ominous is the fact that this decline in trade has not been arrested. The main losses so far have been suffered in the coarse standard line, which form a very important part of the whole trade. From these Lancashire has already been largely ousted, and the stress of competition is now extending also to medium goods. In high class goods, Lancashire still holds her own, but it can only be a matter of time before Lancashire may have to withstand an attack even in her own high class specialities.

A table gives particulars of the exports of yarn, of grey cloth, and of bleached, printed, and dyed piece-goods in recent years, together with the corresponding figures for 1913. These figures show, in the most striking manner, how widespread has been the fall in the various classes of cotton exports since the war and, in particular, how grave it has been . . .

recently been made in the same direction.

The position in this section is totally different from that in the larger "American" spinning section where the problem is foreign internal competition. It is with the "American" section that we are mainly concerned in this report.

FOREIGN COMPETITION, INDIA, JAPAN AND CHINA THE CHIEF FACTORS.

The manufacturing countries which have made the greatest inroads on Lancashire's export trade are those of the Far East, namely, India, Japan and to a less extent, China. The replacement of home . . . countries had . . . war, but it . . .

CLEARER CHARGES.

Home Office Instructions in Motor Offences.

COMMONS CONSIDER ROAD TRAFFIC BILL

The Road Traffic Bill consideration, in the Col. H— M.P. for claims with a person whose limit or with vehicles should application and payment the particular is based . . .

COST £21,000,000.

Big Increase in G— Road

NEW VICAR.

REV. P. M. DAVIES FOR PETERS—

Left: *The floor of the Manchester Exchange, commercial centre of the trade, where yarn and cloth were bought and sold*

Below: *J. R. Clynes, Labour Home Secretary who led the 1930 inquiry into cotton's decline*

Unions and management blamed each other for the technical backwardness. The real problem was that, by the time re-equipment was most needed, there was no money to pay for it. Michael Grey's family had run a spinning firm for several generations.

We were struggling desperately, financially and commercially, from an appalling depression. There just wasn't the sort of money around, or at any rate the mill masters conceived that there wasn't the sort of money around, to indulge in massive capital expenditure.

The call for amalgamation as a way to raise more capital to re-equip met still greater resistance. Lancashire was the home of free trade where government interference had always been resented. The vigorous competition between hundreds of small firms, each fiercely independent, each highly specialised, was a matter for pride to owners and managers.

As a Lancashire person, I think we were more independent than a lot of people and we wanted our independence to succeed, and it's very difficult to think in terms of a lot of cotton mills getting together voluntarily and forming a combine.

The majority of the bosses in the mills were people who had come up through the trade from being boys, saved a bit of money and put it into the industry. Each knew the particular part of their trade, and they knew it from A to Z, and if they started going into a different part of it they probably wouldn't know how.

Nowhere was the haphazard and divided nature of the business more evident than in the working of the Manchester Exchange, the ultimate expression of the free-market tradition. Producers and sellers came together at the 'Change, bargains were struck on the shake of a hand, yarn was bought for the next week's work, finished goods were sold all over the world. A Manchester merchant remembers the scene.

It was an enormous floor. In the middle was a seething mass of all the people who had to do with the textile industry. One had to know where the people you wanted to talk to stood. There were no labels or anything like that, you just knew that Mr So-and-so wove your particular cloth for you and always stood under a particular bit of ceiling.

Traditional is the word that describes it from beginning to end. They had 7000 members in those days, and it was like going round a crowded dance hall, you could look for half-an-hour for one man and never see him.

The divisions in the system between spinners and weavers, producers and sellers, were to prove unbridgeable for years to come.

Re-equipment was slow. The one response that employers could make most easily was to lower wages and change conditions in the mills. As trade contracted, working life got worse. A spinner remembers:

> I had a Union book where it showed wage reductions, 33 per cent, 7½ per cent, 5 per cent, and it was reduction after reduction after reduction over a period of about six years from 1931 to 1937.

From being among the best-paid workers in the country before 1914 the cotton operatives still in work found themselves pushed further and further down the league table of wages. In 1931 their patience broke and the industry was hit by a rare strike, over manning levels. The employers wanted to increase the number of looms worked by each weaver, to reach the levels in use abroad. To the unions this seemed an unreasonable request on top of wage-cuts and threatened jobs. Clifford Hartley was an Earby weaver.

> The workers looked upon this as one man or a woman doing two men or women's work for one man's wage. Just imagine if somebody comes to you and said: 'Now then I'm going to put up your workload by 30 per cent.' Well, you're going to resist. There's no wonder people resisted.

The More Looms Strike lasted four weeks, and the outcome was a compromise. The weavers agreed to work six looms each, but to do less

Mill workers at the start of the 1931 strike, when employers tried to reduce traditional manning levels

cleaning and maintenance. The strike was the high point of mill-worker militancy. One of the men who helped to organise it explains why there was little industrial action.

It's a well-known fact that if you're working in an industry that's booming and expanding, you can demand and get from employers good wages and shorter hours. But if you're working in an industry that's declining all the time, you've a hell of a job getting anything out of the employers, because they themselves are having to struggle to keep the mills open.

There was also a sense of loyalty among those who remained in cotton. Workers and employers saw themselves fighting the same battles against cheap foreign goods, with little to be gained from confrontation.

By the 1930s it was clear that the condition was not temporary and that the industry was in full retreat. Many companies collapsed in the recession, and other owners owed millions to their bankers. The Bank of England and the clearing banks proved most effective in bringing about change. Together they backed a major new combine, the Lancashire Cotton Corporation, and gave it funds to buy up and re-equip some of the spinning mills, but to close down many others. Later, the government organised another scheme to reduce capacity by scrapping looms and spindles. By 1939 Lancashire had only half the machinery that had been in use in 1920. More government help came in the form of tariffs which helped save the home market but not the export trade.

New machinery in the late 1930s. Re-equipment came very slowly in Lancashire

Some of the more enterprising firms began to make use of synthetic materials and to diversify, but the majority would not or could not change. Refusing to amalgamate, unable to modernise, they had to quote prices ever lower to get work. Some moved overnight from riches to rags.

> There was one family in Bolton that built one of the most modern mills in the town. And this whole thing crashed and one of the sons was selling lightbulbs. Now these were people whose families really had unmitigated wealth. I know one yarn agent, and at one of the Cup Finals at Wembley, I think it was in 1928, one of his local colleagues went down to the match and found him selling matches in the queue for tickets.

Others were more fortunate, and managed to leave the trade before the worst happened.

> Instead of going bankrupt they just closed down and got the little nest-egg that they'd made out of their workers during the years and went to buy a nice little detached house in Lytham St Anne's, and in those days if you went from one end of Lytham to the other end of Blackpool you'd find hundreds of textile employers who had closed down.

The Second World War faced the industry with a new situation. Exports stopped, many mills were turned over to munitions, but a core was required at full capacity to make textiles for the war effort. Production was carefully controlled, and prices guaranteed. The remaining operatives worked long hours.

> We were under great pressure to turn out parachute fabrics, and fabric for air balloons and that sort of thing, and we worked double shifts on Saturdays. I even remember working one Sunday, and on the Saturday night I'd been to the pictures and on the screen it said that employees at such a mill, such a mill and such a mill had to go to work the morning after. That was how they got hold of us, and marvellously we had a 100% turn up. The word had gone round that the mill would be open the day afterward and we all turned up at work.

Though Lancashire was working again, there were difficulties reaching wartime targets. Many of the most skilled workers had left for other jobs in the 1930s. The surviving machinery was as out of date as ever. James Thornber had started at his family's Clitheroe mill:

> When I came into the industry in 1939 we had still got the machinery that my grandfather purchased in 1906. He bought 589 looms for £7 each, so that for something under seven or eight thousand he'd equipped the whole mill.

Peace in 1945 provided Lancashire with a disconcerting challenge.

The mill girl was glorified in government propaganda to raise output after the war. The 1945 caption read: 'Typical of the all-out effort to ensure that the industry pulls its weight in the export battle is Mrs Margaret Colley, seen carrying an outsize load of bobbins to her frame'

Suddenly, the great industrial invalid of the 1930s was being called on to help lead Britain's post-war recovery. In a time of economic austerity and the dollar shortage, reviving Lancashire's export trade became a high political priority. A poster campaign told the cotton workers that 'Britain's bread hangs by Lancashire's thread'. The despair of the depression was replaced by a new hope. Perhaps the decline was not, after all, inevitable.

> At the time there was a great feeling of optimism. Order books were full, there was plenty of work for everyone, wages although relatively low were rising, and there was a great feeling of optimism that at long last there would be a steady textile industry in the north-west of England.

From having too many workers before the war, the industry now had too few. There had been 600,000 in 1920 and 350,000 in 1939. By 1945 there were only 200,000 left. A large-scale recruitment drive was launched to get the cotton workers to return.

> Everybody was encouraged to get back into the mill. People were in a way hounded to get back into the mill, if they'd any past experience. They were going round to find out people who knew how to work in the industry, how to run the machinery. And I can remember seeing notices on mill walls to say that if you could bring somebody in to learn weaving or learn the trade, the firm would pay £1, £2, £3 . . . In fact several of our people did and got paid for taking their relations.

A happy by-product of the labour shortage was an improvement in wages and mill conditions. With their traditional workforce being lured away to cleaner and safer work in modern factories that had sprung up in Lancashire, mill-owners started to run bus services to pick up their workers, and tried to make the old mills more attractive. Canteens and nursery provision had been introduced during the war. The factory inspectors applied an additional pressure. James Thornber made several changes.

> The factory inspector came along and said, 'Look here, you are going to have to make some room in this place, we can't get in.' We had the mill painted and brought in certain other facilities. We had to put in hot water that we didn't necessarily need to have before the war. We had to have a stretcher available for anyone that needed to be carried. We had to have first-aid cabinets brought up to date.

To make more room in the mills, machinery was respaced, and the aisles and alley-ways widened. Machinery was made safer, the oil on the floor disappeared, proper washplaces and lavatories were installed. Payment by results was gradually replaced by a standard wage, which reduced accident rates as well as providing the guarantee of a regular day's pay.

39

Making the mills more attractive was not the same as making them more productive. The industry continued to be hugely inefficient, by the standards of the rest of the world. One of the most damning indictments of British organisation and practice had come from a mission sent to the United States during the war under Sir Frank Platt. It found that American mills were by now two to three times as productive as British mills, where the working day and week were longer, shifts were re-sisted, and the management was less well trained. The mission con-cluded:

> The United States industry is very far ahead of Lancashire in production per man-hour . . . The machinery employed throughout is more modern, and methods about which our industry is in doubt have become general practice.[9]

Only large-scale modernisation could save Lancashire from further decline. Robert Porter was a spinning manager convinced of the need for a wholesale conversion to ring-spinning. He was frustrated at the backwardness he met all around him.

> The attitude of the trade to the Platt Mission was extremely complacent and I was really het up about this. There were a number of letters to the *Manchester Guardian* from employers, and one in particular suggested that if a mill were to be built at that time, 1945, it would be very little different from the mill that was built twenty years ago in 1926, and they did not need to do very much more at all.

More looms and spindles were installed after 1945 but most of them were still the old type. American cotton firms were by now completely converted to automatic looms and ring-spinning. In Britain only a third of the spindles were the modern type, and only 12 per cent of the looms were automatic.

Yet to the individual mill-owners there seemed little need to change anything they were doing. In the years after the war there was a seller's market in cotton as in other British industries. Managers remember the effect this had.

> We were temporarily too profitable. It sounds a strange thing to say but we were so busy, we were making good money, and deliveries were very far ahead for new machinery in those days. A lot of us spent a good deal of money brushing the place up but nothing like the sort of money that would be needed for a massive re-equipment.

> In the good times people are exceptionally busy and the ques-tion of re-equipping is pushed farther and farther into the back-ground, because, let's face it, you are satisfying customers as best you can, and hopefully making a fair amount of profit. As for thoughts of re-equipping, with all that disturbance, and dis-

Ring-spinning: faster and cheaper than mule-spinning, less skill was needed, and teenage girls could be paid lower wages

ruption of production, you just don't want to know about it. Certainly in times like those just after the war, when everyone wanted as much cloth as they could possibly get, to re-equip would have been asking for trouble.

Instead, most of the modern textile machinery being made in Lancashire was exported abroad to Britain's competitors. The difficulty after the war, as before, was that the exhortations for change were general, directed at a mythical 'Lancashire' that did not exist in a collective sense. It was not in the immediate best interests of those who ran hundreds of small firms to get out, or to merge, or to risk re-equipment.

Cotton's problems had not disappeared with the post-war boom but had only been postponed. By the early 1950s the Japanese industry was re-established. British goods were gradually pushed out of export markets. Then, in 1953, foreign cloth began to enter Britain as well. The government had placed import restrictions on certain producers, but the Commonwealth still had free access and cloth poured in from Hong Kong, India, Pakistan. The employers made efforts to get foreign producers to restrict sales in Britain voluntarily, and appealed to the loyalty of their traditional customers. In the mill towns, imports sometimes brought an emotional reaction, as they did from Clifford Hartley.

I remember my wife coming home one day with a jersey, not cotton, that she'd bought for the lad. And I looked at it, and it said 'Made in Hong Kong'. So I threw it in the coal fire. I said: 'Thee don't bring no more of them in England.' And that's the God's truth. That was really the first row we ever had. She said: 'Well, I couldn't afford a British one.' I said: 'Well, he'll do without.'

Old Lancashire looms ready for the scrapyard, in a shut-down weaving shed in the 1960s

This loyalty was wearing thin in the nation at large. Lancashire goods were expensive, and many British producers failed to pay attention to changing tastes in an increasingly fashion-conscious society. Imports penetrated quickly because the same merchants of Manchester, who had bought Lancashire cloth and yarn and exported it from their warehouses for nearly two centuries, abruptly switched to importing foreign yarn and cloth. They concluded it was the only way they could survive, but the danger of having selling and production organised as completely separate activities had now been shown. Mill-owners felt aggrieved.

When it became more profitable for a merchant to suck cloth in rather than pump it out, what had been a highly successful commercial set-up became very damaging to the productive side of the industry. It became apparent that there was more money to be made out of importing Asiatic cloth than there was to be made out of exporting English cloth. The valve blew the other way.

Lancashire had always dominated the home market. It was hard for manufacturers to admit that they could no longer compete even for this.

> Somehow we seemed to think that the home trade was ours. After we'd sacrificed two-thirds of the industry we really felt that the home trade belonged to us. We couldn't quite see that it was anybody else's, and then it seemed to gradually creep in that all these people that had built machinery for their own use after the war, to supply their own market, suddenly found that Lancashire was a sitting duck for them.

Once the merchants had abandoned their own local producers the collapse went even faster than between the wars. The output of cotton goods halved within six years. To many ministers and civil servants it seemed that cotton had been given its chance to change, but failed to use it. Not until 1958 did the government show any willingness to come to the rescue with special help.

> Harold Macmillan came to address the Cotton Board annual industrial conference in Harrogate in October 1958 and in his speech from the platform he said: 'If the industry can come to me with positive proposals for action, I will see what can be done.' Those were the sort of words he used and we took him at his word and we devilled away very hard during that autumn and winter proposing a composite plan for a massive redundancy scheme on the one hand and Treasury assistance on the other, for re-equipment.

The outcome was the Cotton Industry Act of 1959 which empowered the government to close down a large quantity of old plant and offer generous grants to owners who decided to modernise with the most up-to-date machinery. The aim was to reduce the number of spindles and looms by half. Some firms were still operating with machinery installed before the First World War, and these old but serviceable machines were now taken from the sheds and mills and destroyed. To skilled weavers and spinners the abstractions of 'rationalisation' had a shocking reality.

> They broke them all up, scrapped 'em and sold them for scrap, that's all they did, just broke them up with a sledge hammer.

> We were last three mules to be running. The others were hit with a big hammer, and it's heartbreaking to see it being done because you looked after them mules like they were your own child really. You've coaxed them and you've done all sorts, and then the fellow comes along, and you could hit him with bloody hammer . . .

> Unwilling to take further risks with modernisation, a large number of owners opted for the government compensation scheme and pulled out. Even those firms that took up the government improvement grants

43

soon found themselves struggling against fierce competition. By the late 1960s the mills could only produce unwoven yarn at a price that was more expensive than finished Asiatic cloth. When weavers had turned the British yarn into material it was double the import price.

In the face of this arithmetic all the talk of efficiency and re-equipment seemed pointless. But one last effort was to be made to save large-scale cotton manufacture in Britain. For those who organised it the hope was that, through amalgamation on a really large scale, and by putting spinning, weaving, finishing and selling within one firm, sufficient costs could be saved to make British cloth competitive once again. Two rival groups, the one headed by Viyella, the other by Courtaulds, fought to buy up cotton mills that could now be purchased for a song. Lord Kearton was then Chairman of Courtaulds.

> We'd become very concerned by the way in which Lancashire was made up of a number of small firms. We thought we'd try to bring together a big grouping, and formed the so-called Northern Project in which we were going to bring together the five biggest groups in Lancashire to provide a major cotton-spinning combine, much bigger than anything then existing and of considerable strength. We'd no 'Save Lancashire' attitude, as it were. What we were concerned about was making Courtaulds more dynamic and more prosperous and developing its export trade.

For the firms taken over it was a welcome reprieve. But the rest of the trade, remembering the pre-war amalgamation efforts and the similar hopes for the Lancashire Cotton Corporation, remained sceptical. Courtaulds speeded up the modernisation of the remnants of the cotton business and injected new capital. They wanted to assure the future of their own artificial fibre, used alongside cotton. At Skelmersdale they built a brand-new weaving mill, which was one of the most up-to-date in Europe. Much of the new machinery itself had to be bought abroad, but at long last weaving, spinning and finishing were all concentrated together. This was the classic solution for Lancashire's ills offered since the 1930s.

Within ten years the bold experiment and declaration of faith were over. Neither amalgamation, nor re-equipment, nor the three-shift 'continental' work pattern introduced to make the most use of the expensive plant, were enough. As the competition from abroad grew ever fiercer, Courtaulds closed Skelmersdale and began their own retreat. To many in Lancashire this signalled the end.

> We hoped that any venture like this would be successful, but knowing the volume of imports that were coming into this country in the 1960s and 1970s, frankly we couldn't see it. Because, no matter how efficient, how productive, how up to date the machinery is, our wage structure in this country is so

4 a.m.
ph
MANCHESTER. Price 3d.

Bénédictine
DOM
La Grande Liqueur Française

£36m DOUBLE BID BY COURTAULDS

LANCASHIRE COTTON AND FINE SPINNERS

BY OUR CITY STAFF

COURTAULDS, the giant man-made fibres group, took the unprecedented step yesterday of announcing two take-over bids simultaneously, one for Lancashire Cotton Corporation and the other for Fine Spinners and Doublers.

The bids together are worth about £36 million, a figure beaten in the history of the textile industry only by the unsuccessful £180 million bid for Courtaulds by Imperial Chemical Industries two and a half years ago.

If the deals go through Courtaulds, who are already well-established in weaving, knitting and garment-making, will control about 25 p.c. of the spinning capacity in Lancashire.

POLICE CHECK AT MURDER MAN

Desite this, the bids have been ... which ...

1964: Largest of a series of mergers. It was hoped that by modernisation the remains of the industry could survive

much higher than the cheap low-cost countries abroad that we still couldn't see it being successful. And we're sorry to say that this has just been the case.

Big firms started chopping, chop a lump off here, chop a lump off there till you've got a very, very minute textile trade to what it were. Never mind Britain's bread hangs by Lancashire's thread, they'd be lucky to have enough thread to make a pair of shoe laces the way they're going on.

Since 1945 over a thousand mills have closed. The production of cotton yarn and material has dropped by nearly 90 per cent. The number of workers has fallen from 320,000 in 1950 to 35,000 in 1982. The handful of mills that survived the storm have done so by an intense specialisation in goods for which there was not a mass market, including industrial fabrics, cloth for bandages and dressings, and luxury materials. James Thornber and his family run one of the remaining mills in Clitheroe. For a few lines they still use Lancashire looms that are nearly eighty years old.

We have always tried to follow the market. We have always tried to make the sort of cloth that people wanted. We have never expected too much out of the business and we have worked reasonably hard and have managed to keep going.

For many Lancashire people the cotton industry is a memory, but it remains strong because reminders still cover the landscape. The substantial brick-built mills are expensive to demolish, and many of them stand vacant, or have been converted to other uses.

They seem to be doing all sorts of things. Some of them are motor-car parts and electrical businesses. Several of them are set up in little sewing units. All sorts of things. Some of them last a few years, some of them don't last very long. They're not an industry, they're just little bits of things, little bits and pieces.

We were all in cotton, it were our work, and everybody were in jobs, but not today, there's no cotton about now. Not many mills left, it's a shame, because they were all happy in the mills.

Not all the hundreds of thousands who moved out of cotton are sentimental about the jobs they left behind. The friendliness and spirit of the mills did not compensate for the hard work or the low wages.

Cotton was the first great British industry to rise, and the first to fall. If adaptation is inevitable in a modern economy, then in a harsh sense the army of cotton workers were luckier than those in other staple industries which were forced to come to terms with falling demand or international competition later. The cotton towns were not geographically isolated, and for those who left in the 1950s and 1960s there were usually other jobs to go to. Even in the 1930s more of the 'sunrise' industries were establishing themselves in the north-west than in the mining valleys or the ship-building areas. For some there was work in the more successful woollen textile industry, which survived earlier vicissitudes in a healthier state than cotton. Yet, not surprisingly, the virtual disappearance of a trade that still accounted for eight per cent of Britain's exports in 1950 prompted many to ask whether the fall was inevitable, and to consider what might have been. For the owners and directors, many of them now in retirement, it was a political failure. If they blame themselves it is for not lobbying as effectively as other industries for special help and a degree of protection. They feel they were written off in Westminster and Whitehall, where ministers and civil servants, out of touch with the north, let them down.

> There's been a steady decline, which to me, I've got to be honest and say, must rest on the shoulders of the civil servants.

> There was a great deal that could have been done by a more vigorous attack by the government of the day on the problems with the import situation, in detail, which they shrugged off as being outside their will or ability to deal with. In other words, there could have been an orderly retreat rather than the rout which has taken place.

> The feeling was that textiles were an outmoded activity – I think one Permanent Secretary of the Board of Trade in the early days came up to Lancashire and told us, you didn't ought to be making cloth, you should be making aeroplanes up here now. It was regarded as outmoded as making hansom cabs and incandescent mantles. They had no concept of the power the industry had once been, no concept of the opportunity that could have been there if it had been better handled.

It was ironic that the government's help for the new aircraft industry had been much more generous than its treatment of cotton. Yet the government had been giving advice and assistance to cotton for forty years, urging change, but with little effect. The critics of the industry put the blame directly on two generations of owners, after the First and Second World Wars, for being slow to react to changes in the trade, slow to modernise, and complacent when things were going well. Robert Porter was a manager with a technical background, but not an owner:

> I believe that the main reason was the conservative attitude of the men in charge, the employers in general who did not face the issue of re-equipment when all the signs were there that they should have done. Profits were being made on machinery which was completely written off and I think that the main reason was that they should have installed more modern

For its brief life Courtaulds' new Skelmersdale Mill was the most up-to-date in Europe. It closed eight years after it opened

machinery in the thirties, forties and fifties. Not doing that led to the decline and decimation of this Lancashire cotton industry.

The experience of those in cotton had much in common with that of the other great nineteenth-century industries, which also found difficulties in organising and innovating to meet a new era. Cotton's special difficulty was that it was such a mighty export trade, based on a raw material that was itself shipped in from thousands of miles away. In the twentieth century textiles provided for the developing countries a 'first industry' just as they had for Britain two hundred years before.

> Whether Lancashire itself could have done more to help itself by way of introducing shift work at an earlier date or modernising at an earlier date, quite honestly I don't think it would have made a ha'p'orth of difference in the long run, because they still can't compete against low-cost imports.

> It's declined because they took too much abroad, and taught so many people abroad that was getting less wages than we were, and it's that today isn't it?

Lancashire people came finally to accept that developing countries could do their job more cheaply, because wages were lower. They had no choice but to go along with Whitehall's view that a skilled workforce was better employed in new, higher-technology industries, which made complex and higher-value products, instead of the cheapest form of consumer goods. The new aircraft factories at Preston, Blackburn and in Manchester were one sign of this happening, as were the radio and electronics firms which established themselves there. But the final twist is that by the 1980s cotton textiles, too, are becoming a high-technology business, employing a very small number of skilled people. The days of labour-intensive cotton mills, employing thousands of workers to run tens of thousands of clattering looms or spindles, whether in Oldham, Bombay, Hong Kong or Manila, will soon be over, and low wages will count for less.

CHAPTER 3: AIRCRAFT
TAKING OFF

The fascination is working on the frontiers of knowledge, looking ahead, thinking of what you ought to be hoping and aiming for, determined to get into the future.

Sir Peter Masefield, former managing director, Bristol Aircraft

Over the period from 1925 to 1970 I saw speeds increase tenfold, take-off weight a hundredfold, and development costs by a thousandfold.

Sir Archibald Russell, Concorde designer

There's only one eventual way of judging the viability of an aeroplane, just as on any other commercial product, and that is 'Does the profit and loss account look right?' I found it very difficult myself, to take a view that aeroplanes were any different from most other things in this respect.

Sir Arnold Hall, chairman, Hawker Siddeley

On Armistice Day 1918, the hooters blew at 11.00 am at the large Airco aircraft factory in north London, and a cacophony of hammering broke out. A crowd of workers dragged a DH 5 biplane through the streets of Hendon and Cricklewood, down the Edgware Road to Hyde Park. There they abandoned it, among the celebrating crowds. Britain's new aircraft industry had produced fifty-five thousand aircraft, and had grown up almost overnight to serve the war needs of just one customer, the government. A few weeks later Airco were still completing the orders that had been in progress when peace was declared. As they finished the planes and made the final adjustments, the government inspector checked them and sent them back for corrections. Once passed, and stamped, and signed for, the aircraft were taken out to the back of the factory and burnt on bonfires. Dudley Tennet had just started as an apprentice.

> It was a heartbreaking job, because all these machines we were making, we knew what was going to happen to them. Machines were being made on the production side of the works, wheeled through, and destroyed at the other end of the storage area. It was practically a continuous line.

The pall of smoke over Colindale was an early illustration that the relationship between the aircraft makers and their chief patron, the government, would not be straightforward. Though building aircraft gave exciting challenges to engineers, designers and shopfloor workers alike, the close involvement of government did not bring them greater security. Technical progress, jobs, and finance in the industry were at the mercy of sudden changes of government policy. Fifty years after the First World War, the spirit of the Colindale burnings still seemed to survive. After £190 million of the taxpayers' money had been spent on the most advanced strike aircraft ever designed, the project was cancelled and prototypes of the TSR2 were sent to be used as targets on the Shoeburyness gunnery range. Making aircraft combined brilliant feats of inventive engineering and design with examples of wasted effort and economic confusion. It was a high-technology business in which success could be measured in many different ways – in the military strength provided, or in straight commercial terms, or in sheer engineering élan.

In 1918 the new aircraft industry, employing 350,000 people, was the largest in the world, with a clear lead over Germany and the far smaller output of the United States. Yet only ten years before, the making of aircraft had still been at the pre-industrial stage, when flimsy planes were improvised to the instructions of the enthusiasts who would fly them. Making and flying aircraft had been an amateur and eccentric pursuit: in hot weather at the Brooklands flying field before 1914 both pilots and mechanics wore pyjamas. In the speedy development from these informal beginnings to a major war industry, pioneer flyers and designers, including Thomas Sopwith, A. V. Roe, Robert Blackburn, and the Short brothers, found themselves in control of large new com-

At the Farnborough Air Show in 1957, the results of the post-war support for the aircraft industry were on display. Britain had built civil airliners, fighters, and three different V-bombers

Mrs Louie de Havilland sewing the fabric for her husband's first aircraft in a Fulham workshop before World War I. The transformation from these homely beginnings to a full-scale industry took less than four years

panies. New plants were built, and furniture and vehicle factories turned over to planes. Skilled engineering workers in the west Midlands, centred in Coventry, learned to mass-produce aero-engines and parts, but the planes were assembled by an entirely new and largely unskilled workforce. The new aircraft workers benefited from the engineering industry's tradition of payment by results. Dudley Tennet assembled tailplanes.

> There were very few engineers, most of them were labourers, warehousemen, shop assistants, milkmen, tramway drivers, agricultural workers. Anybody who could get themselves into a wartime production job didn't get conscripted. We never worried about money. Always had some money to jingle in our pockets. I remember we had an allowance of half-an-hour for each tailplane to come off. They worked as a gang, and they got a good price fixed at half-an-hour a piece, so they knocked up a bonus on every one they made, and that bonus was divided among the gang.

Over a third were women, brought in to cut and sew linen fabric or paint on the acetate dope. Women also did assembly work, and Frances Farmener helped put fuselages together at the Portholme Aircraft Company when she was sixteen.

> I wouldn't say we got a big wage. We got a small wage and a big bonus, or they thought it was a big bonus at the time. And the others were rather jealous about that. They used to call our foreman 'The Bonus King', 'Tom Ford the Bonus King', and we was 'The Bonus Queens'.

The achievement of the workforce and the designers would not have been possible without the central control and direction of government. If cotton was born in a free market and thrived under *laissez faire*, the aircraft industry was a child of Whitehall. Once the War Office had conquered its pre-1914 hesitation about powered flight, the best scientific brains were brought to bear on an activity it considered too important to be left to private development. When the Royal Flying Corps was formed in 1912 all its aircraft were designed and built centrally at what became the Royal Aircraft Factory at Farnborough. After the war broke out, when more aircraft were needed than the government factory could possibly provide, official designs were sent out to private firms and their production was tightly supervised. Later the new companies were allowed to make their own designs, but the Ministry of Munitions kept a close watch.

By the end of the First World War the firms had experienced both the financial benefits and the frustrations of working closely with the government, many of which were to continue in future years. A Rolls-Royce director complained that the civil servants in the Ministry's contract department had been reared in red tape.

> They have been surrounded by regulations until many of them have become as timid as chickens and obstinate as mules.[10]

Officials, in turn, complained that the companies were poorly managed for producing the planes in the number required. One manager admitted: 'We have good designers in England, but it is no good having good designs without good production.'

When peace came, the government suddenly withdrew. There had been much talk of converting the wartime industry's lead into the civilian field with state help. In 1918 the Civil Aerial Transport Committee recommended a range of subsidies and ways of encouraging passenger services, and warned

> If . . . no steps have been taken in advance to create other markets for the manufacturing industry, the manufacturing industry will dwindle with great rapidity and may well cease altogether to exist. . . .[11]

But the recommendation was largely ignored and civil aviation was left to develop, or not, on its own. Most of the workforce, so recently organised by shop stewards who had unprecedented strength in the war factories, was dispersed back into the trades from which it had come. The young men who had built up the new companies tried to cling on, and stay in the aircraft business on a much smaller scale, or switch over to other products: making cars or motorcycles, sewing machines or kitchen equipment. Dudley Tennet's employers, Airco, tried to make cars and buses, and even experimented with an electric toaster, but were then forced into liquidation like many other firms.

> I was working in the machine shop on capstan lathes. In the ordinary way we would have had labourers coming round sweeping up the floors as we turned the swarf off. But they'd

SATURDAY, SEPT. 11, 1920.

SOPWITHS CLOSED.

Great Kingston Factory Ceases Production.

A SUDDEN SLUMP.

Firm in Voluntary Liquidation.

SALES MANAGER INTERVIEWED.

From yesterday (Friday) the great factory at Kingston of the Sopwith Aviation and Engineering Company, Limited, will be silent. The firm has decided to go into voluntary liquidation through lack of capital.

The Olympia Aero Exhibition of 1920: a multiplicity of aircraft manufacturers, who had started during World War I, still hoped for peacetime orders

sacked all the labourers, so we just had to paddle about in this stuff until it was iron shavings about a foot deep or more. Nothing was cleared until one morning a pay clerk came round about 11 o'clock with a tray full of envelopes and gave us each our money up to 12 o'clock, and that was that, we were finishing at twelve. There was no goodbyes, no thank yous, no 'What are you going to do?' At 12 o'clock they shut down.

By 1920 more than half of the nearly fifty firms which had made aircraft during the war were out of business. Even in the firms that managed to continue, most of the production workers had left and only a small nucleus of engineers was kept on. The surviving firms continued to look to the government which, though it remained blind to the future of civil aviation, at least saw a need to preserve a defence capability. The Air Ministry, realising the danger of a total decline, spooned out small orders for prototypes and equipment to a select list of sixteen firms in order to maintain some competition between them. Norbert Rowe had just joined the Ministry.

The sixteen firms were competing for orders, competing for contracts, and to do something better than was already flying, they always had to introduce something new. So that innovation was the name of the game. This was the challenge of aeronautics, as we knew it, and this was what made the business so extraordinarily attractive.

C. G. Long worked for Geoffrey de Havilland, whose firm stayed clear of the Air Ministry and was the most successful in making aircraft for private and commercial flying.

There was no established data. It was all established on the flying machine. There was usually a fair amount of trial and error. De Havilland would fly all his own aeroplanes himself first, always. Right up to the Dragon and Rapide. And he would come down with various comments on the behaviour of the aeroplane and we would then immediately start to cut bits and pieces off and make them a bit shorter or longer.

De Havilland apart, the story on the civil side became one of failure and misdirection in the inter-war years. Passenger traffic was growing fast in the United States, and the Americans had caught up and developed a range of long-distance planes. Traffic was also growing within Europe, but the British airlines were dwarfed by the German and French services, which received more help from their respective governments and were large enough to support new home-produced airliners. When the British Air Ministry did get involved on the civil side, it was to back the airship programme, which came to nothing, and to support big flying boats for Imperial Airways, which had few uses except on the long Empire routes.

Far left: *Surplus propellers for sale on a north London pavement in 1921 after the slump*

The British companies gained little commercial experience and continued to rely on military orders, although even those dried up still further with successive cuts in defence spending. In 1932, only eighty military aircraft were built. The policy of spreading the work out thinly ensured that the firms in the 'ring' of sixteen companies just survived, but another consequence was that by 1931 the RAF had forty-four different types of aircraft, powered by thirty-five types of engine. Dividing the available work in this way held back technical progress. American, Dutch and German firms were able to go ahead with a new generation of single-wing military planes and more streamlined airliners made of titanium and aluminium. British firms complained that without larger orders they could not afford to re-equip and re-tool to use the new light alloys. Yet larger orders, going to fewer companies, would have put many of them out of business.

Throughout the 1920s and early 1930s the aircraft makers suffered from weak finances and a shortage of steady work on a large scale. Jack Fish had started at Blackburn's in 1930.

> There were not a lot of people about, draughtsmen or anything else. You could say that every six months more would go, because of the lack of work, lack of orders. Most drawing offices were decimated.

But the Ministry policy, together with the government's own research laboratories, kept the military capacity going, and a number of brilliant designers emerged, including R. J. Mitchell, Sidney Camm and Barnes Wallis.

Draughtsmen at Blackburn Aircraft, 1924. Companies tried to keep their design teams intact for as long as they could

The industry was rescued by the growing international crisis. Japan, Italy and the Soviet Union were all rearming heavily. In 1933 they were joined by Hitler's Germany, intent on building up the largest air force in Europe as quickly as possible. In a belated response, from 1935 onwards a succession of schemes to expand the RAF were announced. 'Scheme F' called for 8000 planes to be built in three years. In the midst of this expansion, the whole technology of aviation was changing, away from the frame made of wood or metal and covered with fabric, to all-metal planes that were stronger and faster. Aircraft firms accused Whitehall of technical conservatism, and grumbled that the new orders the Ministry was issuing called for planes with a lower specification than the firms were able to make. Sir George Edwards recalls how the Spitfire was developed by Vickers.

> The specification that was put out by the Air Ministry for that particular fighter was much lower in performance demand than the designers knew they were capable of doing. Sir Robert MacLean wrote to the Air Ministry and said they weren't going to build a fighter to the specification that had come out. They were going to build their own and put their money into building a private-venture fighter, which subsequently became the Spitfire.

With bombers, the Ministry was still asking for biplanes in the mid-1930s, when the designers and engineers wanted to make heavy single-wing types. The Lancaster bomber emerged like the Spitfire in spite of, rather than because of, Whitehall.

With all the new orders and the changing technology, the situation was reversed. Designers and skilled engineering workers were suddenly in short supply. Jack Fish felt the benefit of this, when he moved on to Fairey Aviation.

> They wanted drawings and they wanted them fast. The only people who could do them, that could move from one to another and pick up a job immediately, were the trained aircraft draughtsmen, and they became a kind of élite. The chief draughtsman would come round and ask if you were comfortable, were there any draughts, or did you want to move over there? You were a kind of gold. Consequently it was a very pleasant life.

Draughtsmen were paid £6 or £7 a week. Skilled aircraft workers could command high wages. Welders, toolmakers, lathe operators were recruited away from other engineering work and retrained to make planes. Now it was the turn of the civil servants to become impatient with the firms. Companies that had grown accustomed to hobbling along with orders for individual prototypes and very small batches had neither the management nor technical experience to cope with orders for hundreds or thousands of aircraft at a time. The Ministry nagged

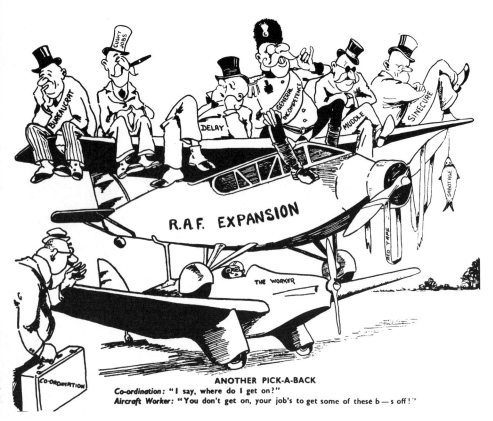

ANOTHER PICK-A-BACK

Co-ordination: "I say, where do I get on?"
Aircraft Worker: "You don't get on, your job's to get some of these b—s off!"

them and took a close interest in their organisations. But to get the planes in the number that would be needed in the event of war, the government turned to the motor industry, with its new expertise in mass production. Under the shadow-factory scheme, car firms built large factories beside the car works, ready for the full-scale output of aero-engines and components. New machine tools, jigs and gauges were ordered at government expense. The accelerating rearmament programme meant that the firms began to make huge profits. A Conservative MP told the House of Commons:

> I do not believe we can go on under the present system with the profits which must automatically come to the great armament firms. The thing is going right off the rails. It is not their fault. They cannot help making enormous profits, and you cannot disguise the fact that a workman who is making armaments for private firms is dissatisfied if profits are too big.[12]

A scheme was introduced to limit profits, but the military orders stayed in private hands, despite talk of the need for national factories.

By September 1939 aircraft production was once again a major industry. Over 700 aircraft a month were being produced and plans were made to work up to 2400 a month by 1942. Once again a balance had to be struck between technical perfection and the need for large

Cartoon from 'New Propeller', news sheet of the radical engineering shop stewards who were active in the aircraft factories, 1938. Rearmament brought the involvement of more officials to 'co-ordinate' the huge RAF orders being placed

The Standard Motor Company's government-financed 'shadow' factory, tooled up to build aero-engines, on its completion in 1937

scale production. Sir George Edwards had started as a design draughts-man at Vickers in 1935.

When you get yourself into a war, one of the basic ingredients is that you've not only got to have something that's a bit better than the other bloke, but you've got to build into the design of every aeroplane, during the war, the ability to build a lot of them and to use labour that previously had very likely never seen an aeroplane at close quarters.

During the war the government and the aircraft makers were inseparable partners, working more closely together than any other industry. The aircraft factories had the highest priority for scarce labour and resources, and for young engineers it was an exhilarating period, in which technical advance was rapid. The retractable undercarriage, stressed metal skins, and variable-pitch propellers were all new. During the war aircraft with pressurised cabins flew at new heights, and the jet engine was developed. The greatest aero-engine success was the Merlin, developed by Rolls-Royce at Derby, where Stanley Hooker was a young engineer.

Rolls-Royce had the biggest experimental facility in the world. Several times larger than anybody else had. This was our great power. We could make a modification to the Merlin engine very quickly, and test it and put it into production very quickly. And so we were able to advance the power of the Merlin all through the war, steadily, from 1000 horsepower to 2000 without basically changing the engine.

The Merlin, for which Stanley Hooker developed the supercharger, was used in the Lancaster bomber, the Hurricane, the Spitfire, and the Mosquito.

The central position of the aircraft industry in the war effort was underlined after the formation of the Ministry of Aircraft Production in 1940. Its first minister, Lord Beaverbrook, involved the public with clever propaganda and appealed to them to give up their saucepans to make fighters. His piratical and anti-bureaucratic approach became a legend. Sir Peter Masefield worked on Beaverbrook's personal staff.

I worked pretty closely with him day and night. He would ring me up at four o'clock in the morning and say, 'Am I ringing you, or are you ringing me?' That sort of thing. He really acted as a suction pump on the industry and pulled out every aeroplane he could get, at long-term expense, because spares

Lord Beaverbrook, Minister of Aircraft Production 1940–1

58

Lancaster bombers being mass-produced in 1943. By the middle of the war 1,700,000 people were engaged in making aircraft

were made into aeroplanes. It worked for the relatively short time during the Battle of Britain when it was critical to get every aeroplane into the front line.

Many felt Beaverbrook's harrying tactics were disruptive and counter-productive, but they had a great effect on morale. Sir George Edwards was sent off on an urgent mission to a factory in the west of England.

> He made my position fairly clear even though not necessarily particularly popular. The bit of paper said: 'This is to introduce George Edwards, who has my full authority to do whatever he wants to do. I don't want him interfered with by anybody down there, least of all by any civil servants or other interfering busybodies.' That was the way to make friends when you arrived.

The greatest difficulty lay in finding enough skilled and unskilled labour for the factories. In 1935 the manufacture of aircraft had employed only 27,000 people. At the peak, in 1943, 1,700,000 men and women were at work, and aircraft building was the biggest industry in the country. Alfred Venables was among those who spent the war at the Chester factory of Vickers.

> People were pressurised into going to work. They didn't necessarily want to come here. They were sent here by the Ministry of Labour whether they wanted to or not. Some wanted to leave. They couldn't go. They were stuck here. They were working very long hours, doing a twelve-hour day and Saturday mornings.

Ernie Jones was also at Chester, where they made over 5000 Wellington bombers.

> You did twelve-hour shifts, eight to eight, days and alternating nights, and then doing fire-watching in between, staying a night in the factory. It was more or less work and sleep all the while. It was only now and again you got a little fed up. I enjoyed myself, and I was there quite some time.

Beaverbrook sent telegrams to all firms asking for work to be done on Sundays, too. Since they were already on twelve-hour shifts, this led to a clash with the Ministry of Labour, which pointed to the evidence from the previous war, showing that when over-long hours were worked for sustained periods exhaustion set in, and production dropped. Hours were reduced again, and conditions improved, after the Battle of Britain. Whereas in peacetime 60 per cent of the industry's workforce had been skilled, management and unions were pressed to try to reduce the percentage to 30 per cent. Women were brought in, and there was a sharp change in labour relations. During the late 1930s unions had spread quickly in the aircraft factories, coming with the new

59

wave of engineering workers from other trades. During the early months shop stewards regained some of the power they had enjoyed during the First World War. They complained about muddled management and poor planning affecting their wages. Union leaders, partly to steal the shop stewards' thunder, took up the cry for committees of management and workers as a solution to factory hold-ups. 'If the employers cannot end the existing muddle,' declared one stewards' meeting, 'then the workers will.' Joint Production Committees, accepted reluctantly by the companies, began in the aircraft industry, from where they spread to the shipyards, mines and other munitions industries. They were used to explain about delays, and to wrestle with specific production problems. Edgar Riley, then a shop steward at English Electric at Preston, recalls how they solved a difficulty with the wing of the Halifax bomber by calling workers from the section into the canteen.

> We told them what the problems were. We told them the necessity for the position, and how the whole of the factory and aircraft production was being held up because of some bottleneck. Within twenty minutes of having the meeting the powers came away with a complete organised method of production that not only gave us what we required, but we found that within fourteen days we had a surplus of labour that we could transfer to other parts of the factory.

The patriotic war spirit was largely responsible for the new mood of co-operation, but there was also a financial spur. Pay was still based on piece rates, calculated on a 'bonus' system when a job was done faster than the time initially agreed by the management's rate-fixer. In the past the engineering unions had accused the companies of cutting piece rates when earnings grew too high, thus negating the incentive to work too fast. But in the war, when production mattered more than costs, the sanctity of piece rates was established, whatever the anomalies. Shop steward Edgar Riley remembers a deal struck with his manager.

> Certain safeguards were made. Mr Sheffield guaranteed the piecework prices, he guaranteed that no matter how much the workers earned there would be no cut in prices, there would be no restrictions on the amount of earnings we could make. Following that meeting, in some cases workers were making as high as 400 per cent bonus.

In practice this meant that some could make £12 a week because the bonus rate for their particular job was generous, while others made £6, before overtime. The very high earnings aroused great jealousy among other war workers.

In the wartime aircraft industry the connection between high wages and high production was officially encouraged. Management was secure in the knowledge that the ministry was paying the bills. The workforce was also secure and had no fear of lay-offs until the last months of war. Unlike the shipyards there were few inter-union complications, and men and women remember the factories with some nostalgia.

> You wouldn't argue about who's going to do this, and who's going to do that. It was just getting on with the job. There was a tremendous spirit on the part of all the people who were doing it, because they all reckoned they were getting fair do's, and this was the great thing to remember.

On the management side, it was an engineer's world. Aircraft companies had been insulated from the market since rearmament began because the government was their paymaster. Most of the great pioneers who still ran the companies, Richard Fairey, Sir Frederick Handley Page, Thomas Sopwith and Robert Blackburn, came from an engineering background, and were in their second war. In wartime the industry found its greatest fulfilment.

In 1945 the lessons of 1918 were remembered. The swollen wartime industry contracted rapidly, and hundreds of thousands left the factories within weeks. The scrapyards filled with damaged and surplus planes. This time there was no doubt in the minds of either the government or the producers that the industry was a national asset, to be maintained and developed. Modern factories had been newly equipped with the latest tools and presses. Major technical breakthroughs had been made. Sir Frank Whittle's jet engine was already flying in the Meteor, with research going on into turbine-propeller versions of the jet. More was learnt from the German research institutes taken over at the end of the war. The relationship with government was as important as ever, and no other manufacturing industry had the same degree of assistance or interest. Personal contacts between Whitehall and the industry were close. Half government research expenditure went on aircraft in the fifteen years after 1945.

What was entirely new, compared with the 1930s, was the government's wholehearted commitment to civil aviation, with a national airline in BOAC, to which BEA was added, and a firm intention that British companies should build their planes as well as sell to airlines aboard. During the war the Americans had continued to make transport planes, while Britain had concentrated exclusively on fighters and bombers. As a result, British companies had a long way to catch up.

It was an indication of how seriously all this was taken that in the middle of the war the Cabinet had set up a high-level committee under Lord Brabazon to plan the civil aircraft that would be needed. Norbert Rowe was a member of the committee.

> It was a visionary gleam. Here we were in the middle of the war, and somebody was telling us to think about the future of the aircraft industry as a whole, when much of it might have to

be devoted to civil aviation. It was a tremendous act of optimism and vision.

At the war's end, some of the initial development work had already been done. The bold intention was that with the five Brabazon 'types' there would soon be a British aircraft for every role, from a de-luxe transatlantic sleeper that would cross from London to New York in twenty hours, to aircraft fit for both long and short Empire and European routes, to a small feeder plane. Brabazon provided a technical blueprint by which the industry could convert itself, and make a concerted assault on the American firms Douglas and Lockheed whose planes were selling to most US and foreign airlines. BOAC was already flying Lockheed Constellations across the Atlantic, in the absence of a suitable British plane. Sir Peter Masefield had served as Secretary to the Brabazon Committee.

> The Brabazon Type 1 was a mistake, but it was understandable at the time. It was for an enormous aeroplane to carry fifty passengers across the Atlantic in full sleeping comfort, with dining-rooms, everyone with a bunk. That really wasn't a concept we could sustain after the war. Brabazon 2 produced the Ambassador and the Viscount, splendid. Britain built 447 of this aeroplane and exported them including 147 to the United States. Brabazon 3 eventually became the Britannia which, but for some icing problems with the engine, would have been a great success. Brabazon 4 became the Comet, a great success in its day, and ahead of the field . . . but we learnt the hard way. Brabazon 5 became the Dove, which is still in service.

As wartime designers turned to the civil models, the success of the Viscount airliner seemed to vindicate all the advance planning. With its jet turbo-prop engines from Rolls-Royce, the Viscount was so smooth,

The Brabazon 1, grandest of the post-war aircraft projects, in 1948. The huge propeller-driven aircraft was abandoned before going into service. It was too heavy and too slow

George Edwards, with the successful Vickers Viscount he designed

quiet and economical that it became the most successful British airliner ever made. BEA liked it, and there were large sales abroad. The plane was built by Vickers at Weybridge and Sir George Edwards was responsible for the design.

> When people said: 'You'll never sell a British aeroplane into North America', in actual fact it was easier to sell a British civil aeroplane into North America than it was into the airlines of Europe. The European airlines used to get themselves very wedded to one or other of these American manufacturers, whereas the American domestic airlines were determined to buy an aeroplane that was competitive, regardless of whence it came, and there was no aeroplane like a Viscount on the horizon in the United States, so that was that.

Yet the success was not to be repeated. No other British aircraft was to sell in such large quantities abroad again, for a combination of reasons.

The early success of the Comet seemed another justification for the Brabazon Committee's foresight. Based on Whittle's jet engine, the airliner was a major advance, leaving the United States some three years behind with plans for a similar plane. Conceived and designed in record time, the Ministry and BOAC were so confident about it that no prototype was felt to be necessary. Fourteen were ordered for BOAC straight off the drawing board. Going into service in 1952 the Comet was operated for nearly two years, to the approval of passengers and the envy of other airlines behind in the queue for orders. Then came two fatal crashes, both caused by pressurisation failures when the cabin split through metal fatigue. The Comet tragedies shook the faith of the government, as well as airline customers, in the industry, and eroded the confidence of a generation of designers and aircraft workers.

The plane had been a complete de Havilland venture. At the Chester factory a fitter remembers.

> It nearly flattened this place. There were people standing around for weeks afterwards. They had no work to give them, but the management just wouldn't get rid of them because they had enough foresight to realise that they would need them again as soon as things picked up. And sure enough they did pick up, when we started on the Mark 4 Comets.

Though de Havilland redesigned the Comet, four years were lost, during which time the Americans caught up with the development of jet passenger aircraft. If the crashes had not happened the whole experience of the British industry might have been different. Instead, there was a cooling of government enthusiasm. Fainter hearts thought designers were entering regions of flight with hidden dangers, and that it would be better to hold back and let others cross some of the frontiers.

One more attempt was made to beat the Americans in the most important market, across the Atlantic. Vickers had brought a much

larger jet transport, ordered as a troop-carrier for Transport Command, almost to the prototype stage in 1955. The company wanted to convert it into a large transatlantic jet airliner that could have been ready before the Boeing 707. But the military version of the V1000 was scrapped to save money, and BOAC pulled out of the civilian version, preferring to get by with the turbo-prop Britannia. In words soon to be regretted, a government spokesman explained at the time:

> BOAC places great emphasis on the superior economy of turbine-propelled aircraft compared with jets. It does not feel that an aircraft capable of flying non-stop from London to New York will seriously damage British air traffic in the early years of the next decade.[13]

An outcry followed, from those who thought the chance of leadership in long-range civil planes was being thrown away. Once the V1000 was cancelled, Boeing and Douglas were ready with their 707 and DC8. Within a year Vickers had the galling experience of being asked by the Ministry if they could revive their transatlantic jet, since BOAC realised they had been wrong. It was too late, for the jigs had been pulled up. BOAC ordered thirty Boeings.

There were recriminations on both sides over the failure of the civilian programmes to take off commercially. Of twenty-three major projects between 1945 and 1960 only seven sold more than a hundred aircraft; only a handful paid their way. Critics argued that the industry was too thinly spread, with too many projects and too many firms. At the end of the war there had been twenty-two aircraft companies and nine engine companies. Government had underwritten the development costs of a series of airliners which had been mistimed, like the Brabazon or the giant Saunders Roe flying boats, or which had had technical troubles, or had been late in delivery. The firms felt that their task of making and selling civil planes was made almost impossible by delay and inconsistency in Whitehall and the government-owned airlines.

The first V1000 under construction, before the plane was cancelled in 1955. Vickers believed it could have been flying the Atlantic before Boeing's 707

Passengers liked the VC10, but it was late in service. Only 54 were ever built, compared with 962 Boeing 707s

The views of the two state airlines kept changing as the passenger market developed. At the same time politicians gave them conflicting instructions. At first they were told to buy British, then encouraged to buy whatever was most economical, then to buy British again. BOAC was said to be more pro-American than BEA. Sometimes the state airlines led the companies into designs that would meet their special requirements, but were not attractive to other prospective customers. The Vanguard was a new turbo-prop that BEA wanted, but which Vickers felt was outdated by pure jets. It sold only forty-four, far too few to recover development costs. The VC10 was designed especially for BOAC's route requirements. Later BOAC tried to cancel it and buy American. The industry, accustomed to looking to Whitehall for orders rather than to the world, complained that their problem was one of scale. Compared with the United States, the British market was too small a base from which to launch sales abroad. When, later on, a British company designed a plane specially for world markets, the BAC 1-11, it was successful. But this required a management with a commercial approach, which the companies had for the most part lacked. At heart the British planemakers had been more interested in making and designing planes than in the techniques of marketing around the world.

To the planemakers' surprise, it was defence work that sustained them in the post-war years. The Cold War period, the strengthening of NATO, and the Korean war brought a call for advanced aircraft in greater numbers than any had dared to expect in 1945. The early jet fighters, the Meteors and Vampires, were built in thousands and sold to many foreign air forces. They were the first in a series of successful designs in the 1940s and 1950s, including the Hawker Hunter and the English Electric Canberra, that brought out the best in the industry. When no less than three different companies, Vickers, Avro and Handley Page, each received orders to develop and build individual bombers that could carry nuclear bomb-loads at great speed and height, the decision represented government defence spending at its most prodigal. But the companies relished the technical challenge. One designer recalls:

> It was the hardest job we'd done. The Valiant was more difficult, technically, than the Concorde.

This was what engineers and shop floor enjoyed most, designing and building aircraft that were among the most sophisticated and difficult in the world. Aircraft jobs were much sought after. Paul Murphy was an apprentice at A.V. Roe's in Manchester where they were building the Vulcan bomber.

> There were a number of engineering factories you could go to but the *crème de la crème* was aircraft, A.V. Roe's, as it was when I joined it. Thousands applied for apprenticeships in any twelve months. And they took who they considered the best.

The defence contracts brought additional jobs. From 1948, when the number was down to 167,000, the aircraft firms were recruiting once again, and by 1955 the number was up to nearly 300,000. Many of the busiest programmes were in the old wartime plants in the north-west, in Manchester, Preston and Blackburn. As in wartime, most of the work was on a 'cost plus' basis, and companies found it hard not to make large profits. Since actual costs were passed on to government, tight cost-control did not receive the highest priority. 'Cost plus' made it less necessary to battle with labour, who still earned some of the highest wages in the country, helped by the piecework system. Fred Moore was a coppersmith at English Electric.

> Once a new aircraft was started, then each particular item had to be priced, and after doing the first five or ten, including the prototype, then the rate-fixer used to come down on the shop floor and he had to argue, or discuss, what the price should be for that particular item, or what number of hours would be allowed for the manufacture of that particular article. Now there were good rate-fixers and bad rate-fixers and quite a lot of arguments were caused through the system.

In the machine shops piece rates could be set precisely. But in the assembly sections, where work was much harder to measure, there were opportunities to play the system when the shop stewards were strong and rate-fixers weak. Paul Murphy recalls the sort of thing that could happen when a price was being fixed.

> If people, for example, worked in a blind hole, you used to tap and bang and the rate-fixer was outside listening to all this banging and tapping. They'd finished fitting this component an hour before, but they'd carry on running the rivet guns and tapping and banging, come out sweating and say, 'It's finished, stop the clock now'. They'd been stopped an hour.

Earnings were very high on the assembly bays because they were very good talkers.

Though the military orders kept them busy and profitable, the relations between the aircraft firms and their chief customer were not much sweeter than on the civil side. As early as 1949 Sir Frederick Handley-Page had replied to a toast at an industry dinner saying 'To hell with government planners'. The firms complained that attempts to produce competitive military planes, in long runs, were made impossible by hold-ups and confusion in Whitehall. RAF officers attached to the Ministry of Defence specified what the RAF needed, but this kept changing as defence thinking changed and others became involved in the decisions. Orders had to be placed through the Ministry of Supply, after the Treasury had had their say. Many of the new designs, for single-seat fighters, subsonic and supersonic planes, suffered expensive delays. Others never passed the prototype stage.

> Every Farnborough Air Show you used to see a great gaggle of new prototypes flying, which you probably saw for the next one, but then didn't hear about any more. They came like leaves falling in the autumn, and suffered the same fate.

There were still twenty separate companies, each with its own design team, in the 1950s. Government became increasingly concerned at the cost of aircraft development. Though £800 million had been spent on aviation projects since the war, the amounts needed to keep pace with developments in America or the Soviet Union were now beyond Britain. It was the increasing complexity of aircraft, and the constantly changing specifications, that did most to make them expensive. Cost estimates, made years in advance, were consistently wrong. Sir Robert Cockburn was Scientific Advisor to the Air Ministry.

> There was a terrible tendency to announce the cost of one prototype and say, 'This is going to be, say, fifty million', ignoring the fact that to develop the aircraft properly you are going to have at least six prototypes just to get through all the testing that was needed. The initial costs bore no relation whatever to the through costs in those days.

The greatest shock to the assumption that military work would always be there to keep the engineers fulfilled and the factories busy came with the Conservative government's review of defence policy in 1957. In a radical look at the future of warfare it predicted that the day of the manned aircraft would soon be over, replaced by missiles. Defensive guided weapons would replace fighters, and ballistic missiles such as Britain's Blue Streak would make strategic bombers less necessary. Research on supersonic bombers was to be stopped immediately. The review said: 'The new defence plan involves the biggest change in military policy ever made in normal times.'

But coming at the same time as declining civil success, the Duncan Sandys' Defence Review spelt an end to the industry's long period of post-war exuberance. The industry which had been the favoured son in 1945 was now looked at far less sympathetically. Lord Zuckerman was asked to help control research and development, and called to see the Prime Minister, Harold Macmillan.

> He asked me across to No. 10 and he started telling me about this process, and his advice to me was 'Well, my boy, what I want you to realise is that these tiddlers become minnows, then the minnows become sprats and the sprats become herrings. You've got to kill them long before they become herrings.'

The government gave the air marshals and the aircraft firms one more major project, when they agreed to the development of a new fast low-level aircraft, for tactical strike and reconnaissance, to be known as the TSR 2. But the order was conditional on the industry reforming itself internally, and ending the competition between small companies which had helped fuel the high costs of the 1950s. To make TSR 2, rival firms Vickers and English Electric came together with Bristol to form the British Aircraft Corporation. Other mergers took place to make a second grouping in Hawker Siddeley. The ground-hugging TSR 2, with its advanced electronics, was to be the most ambitious British military aircraft ever built. Peter Thorneycroft, the Aviation Minister, called it 'the most potent and terrible instrument of military power yet devised'. Twenty thousand jobs depended on the plane, and new methods of cost-control were introduced to monitor spending. After five years, and £190 million, the first test flight took place, fulfilling all the requirements. Seven months later Harold Wilson's new Labour government cancelled the TSR 2, on the grounds of cost. The project had originally been estimated at £90 million. Costs had continued to rise until the likely eventual price was £750 million, before completion. Instead, Britain ordered the American F111 which had not yet flown. BAC made 5000 redundant, but there were further lay-offs at hundreds of supplier and component firms. Sir George Edwards, by now chairman of BAC, lived through another cancellation.

> I must say this was a pretty unhappy moment. Because once more I knew that I was right and I knew that they were wrong and I knew that subsequent events would prove it, and at that particular moment I couldn't. And all the blood and sweat that I had put into it, and all my chaps had put into it, and the hours of work and dedication over the years were carelessly being thrown away by some chap making a speech in the Commons. I rated it as a very unhappy experience.

From the outset, support for the TSR 2 had never been strong, except among those who were building it. The industry argued that the massive increase in costs came once again from the frequent changes in requirement made by the customer, the RAF. Sir Stanley Hooker could see this happening while he worked on the engines.

> I remember saying to the vice-chief of the Air Staff, when they demanded a thousand miles of radius of operation for the TSR 2, 'Why a thousand miles? This sounds like a number just conjured out of the air.' He said, 'It is. It's an objective.' I said, 'Well, that will mean that will cost you a million pounds a mile for the last 150 miles.' And that was an underestimate. The whole thing became a step-by-step increase in everything, and it became very expensive.

Whether the fault lay with the RAF, or the manufacturers, many in Whitehall, including Sir Robert Cockburn, believed the TSR 2 was the epitome of the uncontrolled costings that had been a feature of the previous ten years.

> The contracts were placed on 'cost plus', so there was no inducement whatever for a firm having undertaken the responsibility of developing an aircraft not expanding the back-up roles for it. This system of increasing sophistication of operational requirements was endemic. No sooner had the requirement been established in what we might call its primitive role, than everybody got to work on it to get their bit in, and the aircraft would inevitably get more sophisticated, more and more complicated. It had to land on more difficult airstrips, had to reach higher speeds, had to carry more bombs.

Defence Minister Denis Healey cancelled two other aircraft projects around the same time as the TSR 2, on which another £42 million had already been spent. He felt the aircraft makers had been living in a fool's paradise.

> They tended to get the government on the hook by giving cost estimates and delivery dates which were far too optimistic and then were quite content when the aircraft was cancelled. The previous government had cancelled thirty major aircraft projects in about ten years at a cost to the taxpayer of £250 million, without ever actually getting an aircraft off the ground.

In the factories and design shops it was an unsettling time. Unions and management both campaigned together against cancellations. When they came, redundancies were negotiated in sorrow rather than in anger. Many felt nationalisation was the only measure which could stop the wasted effort. Young draughtsmen and technicians who were discouraged by the general pessimism left for the aircraft factories on the west coast of the United States, where Boeing, Douglas and Lockheed were thriving.

The aircraft companies felt bitter at their treatment by the Labour government. Britain's most technically advanced industry was plunged into a depression almost as deep as that which some of the oldest sectors, including cotton and coal, were suffering in the 1960s. But in the process Whitehall and the aircraft makers were forced to confront fundamental questions, always dodged after previous cancellations, about the appropriate size of the industry, and the criteria by which it should be judged. The case for a large air industry rested on the strategic argument that there could be no political independence if Britain had to buy the RAF's planes abroad. It was also contended that aviation was a 'lead' industry, a pump-primer stimulating technical development in other fields including metallurgy, electronics, and machine tools. The case against was that too many resources had been taken up, and the costs were no longer bearable.

When Harold Wilson announced a full enquiry into the future of the industry, the aircraft bosses were cynical and suggested it was for 'the direction of the funeral'. During his evidence Sir George Edwards compared the relationship between the British and American companies to David and Goliath. He accused the politicians of taking away his pile of stones and giving them to Goliath. Lord Plowden's report told the government what it wanted to hear. There was '. . . no predestined

A prototype of the TSR2 on the Shoeburyness gunnery range, after the cancellation. The plane was the most ambitious all-British military aircraft ever built, and the most expensive

place for an aircraft industry in Britain'. The state support should be reduced until it reached the level of help given other industries. In future the most sophisticated military planes should be bought from the United States, where longer production runs would always make them cheaper. Civil aircraft should be built in collaboration with other European countries.

Well before Plowden, the plane-makers were adjusting to the new situation. The greatest change came after the grouping into two firms in 1960. They altered their assumptions about government help, as they realised a new commercial yardstick was being applied to them. New military aircraft would have to appeal not just to the RAF but to other governments, so that export orders could help pay for the development costs. Civil planes had to be conceived with the world market in mind, and sales efforts were overhauled. The attention paid to aircraft projects had hidden the shift that was taking place from aircraft to aerospace work. Electronics specialists were more in demand than engineers, and Hawker Siddeley separated off Hawker Siddeley Dynamics to work on missiles and space projects. Other firms diversified into electrical and mechanical engineering.

Even while a new atmosphere of commercial realism was being established, there was one project that predated it which was so huge that for more than ten years it dominated not just the aircraft industry, but the government's entire policy towards science and technology. Plans for a British supersonic airliner had originated in the 1950s with the enthusiasm of civil servants at the Farnborough research establishment as much as the plane-makers themselves. Sir Archibald Russell recalls the thinking behind the plan for what became the Concorde.

Sir Archibald Russell, British designer of the Concorde

> We had failed on every attempt to break into the world's long-range markets, and the general view was that we should have at least one more shot. And the ministry set up a research investigation. After they'd been working for two years they asked the industry to undertake feasibility studies to see what may be possible. At the beginning there was no idea what type of aeroplane it would be, whether it was swept-back wings or swept-forward wings or triangular wings. There was a completely clean sheet of paper, that the whole industry and the whole of the official research establishments combined together to solve.

In acknowledgement of the high costs involved, the scheme became a joint one with the French, and politicians supported it when it seemed a key to Common Market entry. When de Gaulle eventually said no to British entry, Britain was nevertheless committed by treaty to building the aircraft. The project required technical collaboration on a scale never attempted before. Sir Archibald Russell was the British designer.

At the beginning, with the frequent meetings we had, with

A French centre section of the Concorde arriving at Filton from Toulouse, for incorporation in one of the planes BAC were building

> French officials, British officials, British airframe firms, British engine firms, French engine firms, at any discussion all the French people would take one view and all the British would take another.

The French and British learnt to co-operate closely, but the cost estimates rocketed upwards, so that the plane was by far the most controversial public-spending project. Several attempts by the British government to cancel it failed because of the binding nature of the agreement with France. When the plane flew, it was a technical triumph. After the first flight the British test pilot, Brian Trubshaw, said, 'It was wizard', and BAC looked forward to sales of hundreds. But the huge development costs, taken with the objections to the noise and a tenfold rise in fuel costs, had turned Concorde into a commercial catastrophe, expensive to buy and expensive to operate on the limited routes over the sea where it could fly supersonically.

Concorde and TSR 2 were the last examples of the older, more adventurous, less cost-conscious industry. A project which started with every sort of government encouragement had ended in recrimination. The engineers and designers, who had produced something no one else could do, felt misunderstood once more. Sir Archibald Russell retired in 1970, having joined the Bristol Aircraft Company, working on piston-engine biplanes, in 1925.

> I'm sure that the only charge you can make against the Concorde is that it was destroyed by inflation and the cost of fuel. If the cost of fuel had remained where it was, and we'd been able to build the airplane at our original price, we would have made 500 Concordes without any doubt. They would have been making Concordes at Filton for another ten years. I don't think you can blame the engineers for Concorde being a financial fiasco.

Yet many did blame the engineers for being overoptimistic about the building costs. After the Concorde their position within the companies was further reined back, by a new type of management. Sir Stanley Hooker, who had worked for Rolls-Royce and then Bristol on engines, saw the difference as a change for the worse.

> The tendency today is to have engineers controlled by administrators or project directors. In my younger days we weren't controlled that way. I told them. We used to start an engine by saying, well what's the engine got to do? That much. How long does it take to draw it? That much. When can they put it into production, and how much will it cost? So we start with 'Is it any damn good?' That was the number one question. Now it's the other way round. How much is the damn thing going to cost? It's all gone round the other way. And people are so much more interested in this so-called management side of it. It used not to be that way. It used to be the other way. When we did our most successful work it was that way.

But the engineers' inventiveness still produced examples of sales success that went against the trend. In a lean period after a cancellation in the mid 1960s, Hawker Siddeley needed a plane to build. Roy Chaplin was Assistant Chief Designer.

> What do you do with a design department with something like 400 people with no real work to give them? The success of the firm depends on producing a design. At that time we realised there was another thing which was interesting and that was a vertical take-off plane.

Produced not to a government specification but at the company's own initiative, the jump jet that resulted was highly successful and sold to the American Marine Corps, as well as to the RAF and foreign air forces. It proved what the industry could do when innovation and commercial skill were combined.

The independently-developed Harrier was an example of a calculated risk that paid off. But for the most part companies, and government, became more cautious than ever before and insisted that pre-sales were obtained before work commenced. An all-British replacement for the successful BAC 1-11 airliner was turned down because so many resources were already going into Concorde. The industry came to accept that if expensive aircraft were to continue to be built at all, it would need to be in cooperation with plane-makers in Europe.

Foreign collaboration has become the standard procedure for major projects in a smaller and more compact industry that was nationalised in 1977. Paperwork has multiplied, decisions are slower, and British designers and engineers commute to Toulouse, Munich or Milan, for technical meetings they would once have crossed a corridor for. At Preston, British aircraft workers who once made the Canberra and the

TSR 2 in their entirety now build only the nose and tail of the Tornado strike plane. The wings come from Italy, the centre fuselage from Germany. Because the Tornado will go to equip three air forces, a run of over 800 can be built, rivalling the economy of scale of the Americans. The gain is in security, at all levels. It is only through collaboration that Britain remains involved with a large civil airliner, building the wings for the French-controlled Airbus at Chester. To give them the old satisfaction, of seeing the plane fly, completed Airbuses are flown in periodically, so BAC workers can see them in their entirety. For most who worked on aircraft, whether craftsmen or designers, it has been a rewarding life. Paul Murphy is a supervisor at BAC in Manchester.

Tornadoes being made at BAC near Preston. With the joint British, German and Italian project a military aircraft can be produced in numbers to match the Americans. Each one costs £13 million

> People who work in the aircraft industry, there's no question they consider themselves an élite, and they probably are. There's some magnificent tradesmen. There's also a real mystique around aircraft. I admit that I still look up at aircraft when I hear them in the sky, and I've worked on them all my life.

Sir George Edwards, the engineer who built many of the most successful post-war planes and became Chairman of BAC, describes his feelings about the job.

74

When you are designing an aeroplane, if you get something wrong, and go and kill chaps who are your friends, you have to go and talk to their widows afterwards. If you're doing a big programme, if something goes wrong, you can put a whole factory out of work, and all the people and their dependents. It's a trying game, but by gosh, the rewards when you really do something are worthwhile. When you get your hooks on it and you fly it yourself, and you wheel it around and there you are sitting in it and it's going like you thought it would when you first drew the lines on a bit of paper – wouldn't have missed it for anything.

The enthusiasm of those involved helped make the aircraft industry unlike any other, and in the twenty years that it enjoyed a unique and privileged position, the technical achievement was outstanding. The pure jet, the turbo-prop, the first jet airliner, the swing wing, the vertical take-off plane and the Concorde all showed the ability to innovate and lead. Encouraged by the Air Ministry who wanted competing design teams for military planes, and who backed the civil ambitions after the Second World War, engineers and designers were given their head and produced results over a long period. Other industries were deeply jealous of their advantages. They lacked little in machinery or equipment, the workforce was co-operative and well paid, and new technology was introduced easily. The industry was run by brilliant technocrats that other industries were said to lack. They had the government's ear, and huge development funds were made available.

But the cost of government interest was also high. Constant military work on the 'cost plus' system, almost from the very birth of the industry, meant that keen financial control was not a tradition. Because so many dealings were with civil servants and the military, few commercial managers and salesmen emerged in the 1960s, though some small firms provided notable exceptions. The industry complained that Whitehall did not understand what it was trying to do technically, and envied the more far-sighted and technically-informed civil service, and steadier government support in France.

A smaller but profitable British aerospace industry now employs 190,000. Over 90 per cent of the work is military and over half the production is exported. Britain's concentration is on equipment and engines, and helicopters and smaller aircraft, while France has become the dominant airframe builder in Europe, as the senior partner in the Airbus consortium. Though they feel that stability has been achieved at last, the planemakers believe that in the years after the Second World War the inconsistency of government was the greatest penalty. In the words of Sir Stanley Hooker,

Over a period of years we were in, we were out, we were in, we were out. It was more like a boat race than a policy to follow.

CHAPTER 4: STEEL
THE INHERITANCE

The work to be done to reconstruct our industry on modern lines is enormous, as the final aim must be nothing short of a complete replacement of the majority of existing plants by very much larger and more efficient units, and learning to manage and operate such plants in accordance with modern methods and practice.[14]

Charles Atha, 1917

To the nations and financiers who first developed it, iron and steel meant power. Steel brought railways, bridges, ships and armaments. It was the giant of industries. The people who worked in the melting shops and mills sometimes felt dwarfed by the dark, awesome surroundings in which they laboured.

In the old heavy bar mill they rolled railway lines and billets, and if you can think of a fifteen-year-old boy going into an atmosphere like that, with this huge building and several hundred yards of glowing red-hot railway line, and all the noise and the smoke, and the smell and the shrieks and clatter of the rollers. It was terrifying, on the first day.

It was frightening the first time I experienced it. I was working when I was aged eleven and in those days there were no canteens, so you took your family's breakfast to them and as you opened that small door into the works you would see rows of flame flashing round you, hissing of steam from the big engines and the banging of the steel bars being rolled through the mills.

Iron and steel involved production on an epic scale. But even in an industry that grew up with modern capitalism there was a limit to what machinery could do. The key processes of steel-making were only automated in the 1960s. Until then, however large the plant, production depended on the closely guarded skill and judgement of the men who ran the furnaces. In the intense heat of the melting shops, wearing flannel shirts and sweat towels, they fed the furnaces and controlled the temperature, and watched until the metal had bubbled its impurities into the slag. Then the steel was ready to pour. The senior melter was the 'first hand'.

It was an art not a science. It was termed black magic because of the knowledge they had. There was no instrumentation at all. No textbooks. They had to do their work by the eye. The eye was the important thing. You had to know the colour of the steel, the flame.

There was no more responsible job than a first hand. He controlled the whole output of the steelworks. He made the steel. And he controlled everyone's pocket.

The experience required was terrific. Management couldn't take over a furnace. Only the first hand could do that job, with an apprenticeship of twenty-five to thirty years.

Few of the melters knew what was happening chemically, or could explain quite why they were doing what they did. They learnt the job from others, and were part of steel-making's tradition and mystique.

The legacy of the past was strong in the iron and steel business. For

Melters fettling the open-hearth furnaces at Shotton in the 1930s

77

many years the industry was the largest in the world, playing the major part in Britain's nineteenth-century growth and predominance. British iron output soared, demand seemed unlimited, and Henry Bessemer and other engineers made the breakthroughs that allowed cheap steel to be made in large quantities. But by 1900 iron and steel had become the first major field in which Britain had lost its lead and confidence. First the United States and then Germany had overtaken British output and seized much of the export market. Their success was partly due to tariffs, but also to lower production costs. Large steel combines had built entirely new plants run by energetic and trained managers, who made use of the processes developed in Britain, but put into practice more slowly at home. British steel-makers went to North America to study their progress, and some brought over American managers to run their works for them. One of these, A. J. Reese, who became the General Manager of the Cardiff works of Guest Keen and Nettlefold, gave an unflattering description of what he found in 1916.

> I have observed in this country that there are a great many very antiquated ironworks in existence and operation: they are plants the design of which represents a period many years out of date.
>
> There are blast furnaces which in the United States would have been done away with years ago as being absolutely in-efficient and not suitable for operation in competition even at that time. Those furnaces are all much too small. The outputs are really ridiculous.[15]

At the war's end a Government enquiry recommended a 'radical re-construction' of the old iron and steel industry. What was needed, as a matter of great national importance, were 'large and well designed new units for cheap production upon modern lines', and they had to be on new sites and close to raw materials and transport, with space to develop. It was only the first of many such calls to rebuild the industry, for an end to hallowed traditions and old-fashioned methods, and it provided the central theme in the story of steel. Men were aware of the need to change, and they attempted change, but they were frustrated by vested interests and the deadweight of traditional practices, in a busi-ness whose enormous capital costs made it hard to start afresh. So instead of radical change there was 'patching in', changing enough to avoid collapse, never enough to take the lead. Only a few new works were ever built, and most of them involved political compromises that made them less effective than they could have been. Fifty years later, critics and steel chiefs were still talking about 'restructuring' and 'relocation' to restore the industry's flagging fortunes. They echoed in the 1960s and 1970s phrases and appeals which had been first used in 1918.

The root of the problem lay with the steel industry's nineteenth-century heritage, which dictated who owned the works, their size, and

Dowlais Steelworks, 1920: a centre of the Victorian iron industry, Dowlais had once made railway rails for the United States and Russia, but was now out of date and isolated

where they were situated. The Victorian iron masters had been fiercely independent. There had been some mergers to form more powerful groupings, like Dorman Long in the north-east, and the Sheffield-based United Steel Company, but even in the 1920s most firms were still small and dealt with only one stage in the total process. The cheapest way was to take iron ore and coal through to finished steel all on one site, never allowing the metal to get cool. But in the majority of cases in Britain the ironworks, steelworks and rolling mills were not integrated, but separate, even though the same company might now own them. As well as being small and divided, many works were in places that had ceased to make economic sense. In the nineteenth century they had been built in south Wales, Scotland and the north-east, on the coal fields where ore was also found. By the 1920s many of these original supplies had been exhausted, or far cheaper ores were available from elsewhere, but the plants were trapped. In south Wales, Dowlais, once the greatest ironworks in the world, was on a hillside at the head of a valley. To feed it, imported Spanish ore had to be brought from Cardiff docks.

The effect of the First World War had been to make matters worse. To meet the munitions crisis, and with no time to build from scratch, money had been spent on upgrading and enlarging old steelworks, many of which ought to have been scrapped. These extensions had increased capacity by a third, just when demand was falling, especially with the post-war slump in shipbuilding. As British costs were high, imports rose. Steel-makers complained they had no capital for new plant. One critic said, 'The British industry turns out steel as a by-product, its main product being self-pity.' Though there were some efficient plants, their scale was still far smaller than in the United States, or in the newly-reconstructed German industry. The average British blast furnace was half the size of the American, and each American blast-furnace worker could produce over three times as much iron per year as his British equivalent. Rolling mills were smaller and slower. Heat, an expensive commodity in steelworks, went to waste. As a young engineer, Fred Cartwright arrived at Dowlais in 1928.

> The first thing that struck me was the steam engine driving the biggest mill, which was called the Goat Mill. I estimated it was about half a turn before it took up the slack, when it reversed with a terrific crash. And then the waste heat boilers, which I knew should take the last of the waste heat out, had flames coming out of the chimneys. So I had a shrewd suspicion that the thermal and mechanical efficiency was not of the highest.

Tom Craig, a member of a Scottish steel family, travelled to France as a young man.

> I remember writing home to my father, who was the Chairman of Colvilles, that having seen what the French could do, the only thing for our works at Motherwell was to blow them up.

Another steel manager, Edward Judge, described his first impression of the Dorman Long works at Middlesbrough.

> Most of the equipment was very old indeed, and it is difficult to appreciate that the very high class steel that had to be produced for all those bridges round the world was rolled in mills driven by great big steam engines snorting and huffing away. And the rolls were adjusted in many cases by a fellow with a sledge-hammer knocking a wedge on one side of the rolling mill to tighten it. But these men made a marvellous product out of the very poor machinery they were operating, and they kept the very poor machinery operating for many a long year.

Outdated plant meant that working conditions were even tougher than they needed to be, in an industry in which the work would always be very demanding. Muscle and physical endurance were still as important as skill. Old blast furnaces had to be opened up by three men striking at the clay bung with a heavy iron pole. In the older melting shops pig iron and scrap were still charged by hand, rather than by machine. With a shortage of cranes, labourers spent their days heaving sticks of pig iron weighing over a hundredweight into wagons, or pushing materials in heavy barrows. Even in new works a spill of slag or

Dorman Long's at Middles-brough, where the structural steel for the Sydney Harbour Bridge was made in the old rolling mills

metal could mean long periods of strenuous work clearing up with crowbars and sledgehammers. In the normal routine of the open hearth furnace melters used long-shafted shovels to throw lime and manganese or chrome ores accurately into the furnace door from many feet away. The heat was intolerable to anyone who had not grown up with it.

> Conditions were very hard for us. I think in the early days as a young melter I drank about a gallon of water a day. Sweat used to pour off us. Our boots were full of salt, white and very hard.

> The temperature was 1700 degrees, a biting heat. Every melter perspired freely. If he didn't perspire he would burn. Unfortunately I didn't perspire as much as most people and therefore I lost the pigment of my skin.

Accidents were routine, with the risk of crippling burns and explosions.

> It was very simple for a man to go on fire at the back of a furnace, because he was standing very near molten metal or molten slag. The heat is so terrific, you didn't even know if your clothes were on fire, until someone else told you or came to put you out.

In more modern plants water cooling at the front of the furnace could reduce the heat levels significantly. But there was little spending on improvements that affected either working conditions or efficiency.

> It was the wish of every melter to have water cooling to make the work more tolerable. There were only one or two plants in Britain that had water cooling, but not anywhere in west Wales. Thirteen steel plants and no water cooling at all.

Despite these conditions the workforce was committed and loyal. Patrick Mcgeown, a steelworker who wrote his autobiography, thought the management got away with a lot in his melting shop. 'The melters got absorbed so often in their steel-making that they didn't bother to complain about many small legitimate grievances.'[16] Traditionally, labour relations in the steel industry had been good and wages high. There was a well-established conciliation procedure. Pay was linked to the price of steel on a sliding scale. In the 1920s a blast furnaceman could be on £3 a week, three times what a farm labourer would get. Strikes were almost unknown, and even the General Strike in 1926 met with a mixed reception in the steelworks. Managers complained, in a rather general fashion, about restriction of output, and about the number of trade unions who represented the various crafts. But they accepted the rigid divisions and hierarchies, and many of the steel bosses were liked and respected. Ivor Jones says he was proud of working for the Summers family at Shotton.

> There was a family atmosphere. They would be out in the plant and they knew people individually and they used to talk to them very intimately. Anything that developed at Summers made an impact on the locality. There was a great deal of pride felt amongst everybody.

Patrick Mcgeown wrote: 'Ours wasn't a hating trade, steel-making in Britain has never been a hating trade. The end products are tough but its practitioners are mild.'

Hand rollers in South Wales: steel sheets had to be made on hand mills before the introduction of the continuous-strip mill

Steelworkers suffered as much as anyone except the miners and shipbuilders as the depression worsened. By 1929 unemployment was already running at 25 per cent. Three years later a total of 90,000 men were without work, and steel output had halved. When the old Dowlais works closed local unemployment reached 73 per cent. At the worst point only one out of twenty-two blast furnaces in south Wales was working, and in Scotland only one out of eighty-nine. Many plants closed down never to reopen, but in the tinplate areas the mills tried to share out what work there was. G. W. Phillips remembers.

> A works would be idle for a month, and the men would be on the dole. Suddenly the news would come round, 'D. R. David's is going to start, don't know how long'. And they would start producing tinplate again for maybe two months. Then they closed down again. We called them 'umbrella plants' in that they were opening and closing.

Taff Evans, a melter at Shotton, felt the extra physical stress of working a week on, two weeks off, intermittently.

> When you have been off two weeks, and you go there into that heat again, you are not ready for it. After half the week has gone you begin to get acclimatised again. It used to knock us about that way, especially on the mills and furnaces.

If the industry was to recover there had to be a major change in the way it was run, or in the outside factors that affected it. The steel unions, seeing what their members were living through, came out for nationalisation. They argued that central planning was needed, since private ownership and nineteenth-century individualism had shown themselves incapable of running the industry in the country's best interest. They called their study 'What's wrong with the British Iron and Steel industry'. Many were asking the same question by now, including the steel companies themselves, the banks to whom they owed millions, and the government. The heavy steel-makers' answer was that foreign steel producers, paying low wages and gaining from the high value of the pound sterling, could dump cheap steel in Britain. Edward Judge saw the trade.

> Iron was brought into Middlesbrough from the continent and unloaded there to be used to supply the engineering industries in this country, and was being delivered at a cheap rate which the local iron-makers couldn't match at all. The amount of steel and iron that was coming into Middlesbrough docks from overseas at low prices was a very depressing sight.

In 1931 bars of steel from Belgium were being sold at £3.15 a ton while the British-made ones were £5 a ton. The companies demanded tariff protection, as they had through the 1920s. But tariffs would not make the industry more efficient, and the banks and government talked of the need for drastic rationalisation. Even after several enforced amalgamations there were still around twenty major British steel companies, but they were pygmies compared with their foreign competitors. When added together their total output was about the same as just one German company, the Vereinigte Stahlwerke, and only a third of the output of the United States Steel Corporation.

Once again the radical talk of 1918 was repeated. A government committee and Brassert's, the American consultants hired by the Bank of England, recommended a regrouping and concentration of the industry in five or six 'pivotal' plants. *The Times* promoted the same approach. 'The whole steel industry in this country needs re-planning and laying out afresh. Five big units, say one in Scotland, one in the Furness district, one in Sheffield, one at Middlesbrough, one in south Wales . . .' could supply the country's needs. All these grand schemes would take years to implement, even if they could be financed and organised. Meanwhile unemployment was reaching levels unacceptable even by the standards of the time. In 1932 48 per cent of the men in heavy iron and steel were without work. When the National Government finally introduced tariffs to protect a range of British industries, iron and steel was given special treatment. The general level of tariffs to be placed on imported goods was 20 per cent, but on iron and steel products it was set at 33 per cent. For this there was a price. The duty was said to be temporary, and conditional on the industry reorganising and modernising itself. The deal was a straightforward one, as Robert Shone remembers:

> The deal made with government was that they would provide a tariff on the industry but in return we accepted supervision of the industry by an independent authority, at that time the Import Duties Advisory Committee, the supervision of our prices, and a supervision of our development plans.

The industry was to be allowed to co-ordinate its own affairs, through a new industry-wide organisation, the Iron and Steel Federation, under the energetic Sir Andrew Duncan.

Protected by the high tariff, and helped by the devaluation of the pound in 1931, the steel industry's recovery seemed at the time to be one of the brighter stories of the thirties. Unemployment fell, and demand rose again fast, helped by rearmament. Steel price-levels were much higher, and Britain elbowed its way into the European steel cartel in order to reduce foreign competition further. But though many steelworks were modernised, and working conditions improved as a result, the most radical solutions were put aside again. Most development was 'patched in', to extend the life of existing plants, wherever they might be. 'Relocation' for the sake of the future, on entirely new sites, usually threatened the interests of existing steel companies who felt there was too much capacity anyway. In 1934 one steel manager, Henry Summers, complained about the schemes that the Federation had encouraged so far.

The Brassert report in 1930 recommended a radical rationalisation of the iron and steel industry

The main objects which the authors seem to have had in view were to bolster up redundant and obsolete plant, and by rings and quotas to put up the cost to the consumer. Anything which could help us to make our industry more efficient and more capable of competing with the markets of the world is lacking.[17]

In Scotland, a plan for a big new integrated works at the mouth of the Clyde was abandoned. A scheme to place an entirely new works on the site of the old Palmer's Shipyard at Jarrow, on the Tyne, was also dropped. It would have produced steel 25 per cent more cheaply, but the neighbouring steel companies in the north-east who were most threatened managed to strangle the project. In another case it was political pressure that prevented a new works being built in the most economical place. Richard Thomas wanted to erect the country's first continuous strip mill in Lincolnshire, close to the cheap ore and the motor industry the mill was designed to serve. But after much lobbying it was built on the site of the old steelworks at Ebbw Vale, in south Wales, where jobs were desperately needed, but where building costs were expensive and transport costs would always be high.

Demolition of the old steelworks at Ebbw Vale, to make room for the first continuous-strip mill in Britain, 1936

The most impressive development of the 1930s, which had been planned before the days of the British Iron and Steel Federation, was at Corby. A Scottish steel company, Stewarts and Lloyds, built a brand new steelworks right on top of the cheap ore of Northamptonshire. It was the textbook relocation, away from a 'high cost' area to a low one, and it was highly profitable. Brassert's, the firm of American engineering consultants, conceived and built the plant, and since the giant Bessemer converters which would use the low-grade ore had been developed in Germany, German engineers and foremen came to start the works up. A Scottish steelworker who was one of the thousands to make the trek south from Glasgow remembers working with them.

> Germans came because they were coming to teach us something we didn't know anything at all about. But I must say that if you riled them, which you could do quite easily, then you were in trouble. If the place wasn't clean enough and you thought you'd made a good job of it they would come and make you do it all over again. This really got us going.

After the completion of Corby, Henry Brassert went off to build an even bigger new works, using the same basic Bessemer process, for the Germans themselves. The plant at Salzgitter was designed to be the largest in Europe.

At the new plant at Corby in Northamptonshire, steel could be made more economically than anywhere else in Britain

During the Second World War British steelworkers turned out seventy-two million tons of steel. The forgings, plates, sheets and the whole range of steels they made underpinned the war effort. Steelworkers grew used to the disciplines of the Essential Works Order and the black-out measures which attempted to conceal the night-time glare of the steelworks. Huge sides were put on each end of the melting shops, and every crack of light was sealed. Patrick Mcgeown recalled:

> The black-out not only kept the bright lights in but it kept the dust and gas fumes in too. It had been thrown up in panicky haste and with no regard for ventilation or the welfare of the workmen. Many times we worked in a grey haze which was sometimes thick enough to blot out the furnace next to us. We were all in it, furnacemen, pitmen, scrapmen, cranemen, and all the maintenance trades, and it ruined many a good chest.[16]

Steel managers coped with the shortage of coal and ore, and the strict wartime control imposed on the industry through the Ministry of Supply. But unlike the First War there was almost no expansion of plant. The existing furnaces and mills, many of them already worn out in 1939, were run as hard as they could go, with little time to stop for maintenance. Plans for post-war reconstruction were laid for steel as for almost every other industry. Critics saw the effectiveness of government control as strengthening the case for nationalisation. The industry itself was forced to a truer appreciation of its fundamental problems. Its own report admitted,

> There are a number of works which due to age, location, or change in demand ought to be replaced or abandoned altogether.

But neither the industry nor government plans immediately after the war, when there was a chance for a clean start, were as radical. There was an overwhelming demand for steel of any kind, from plant of any kind, and a major rationalisation seemed unnecessary. Instead, after the Labour victory of 1945, the industry was plunged into an ideological debate over public ownership. At first this was just a threat. The railways, coal, and electricity were taken over before a reluctant Labour government, under left-wing pressure, came round to steel. George (now Lord) Strauss was the Minister of Supply who introduced the legislation in 1948.

> The steel industry was in a bad way. It was disorganised. It consisted of a large number of independent and warring units, no co-ordination, no effort to ensure that the work was done in the most efficient plant. Something more drastic we felt had to be done to make this industry really efficient and to meet the national needs.

Once Labour had made up its mind to go ahead, every effort was

STEEL
IS POWER:
THE CASE FOR
NATIONALISATION

BY WILFRED FIENBURGH & RICHARD EVELY
of the Labour Party Research Department

"A most valuable contribution
to the current controversy
on the socialisation of.
Britain's iron & steel industry"

—from the foreword by Morgan Phillips,
Secretary to the Labour Party

net **3/6** net

made to get the industry to co-operate with their plan and accept the inevitable. But Sir Andrew Duncan, Chairman of the British Iron and Steel Federation, mobilised the industry to carry on fighting. Of all the state take-overs, steel provoked the most bitter political battle, and at the second reading of the nationalisation bill in the House of Commons, Winston Churchill used the industry's good labour relations as an argument for leaving it alone.

> There has been no serious dispute or stoppage between the employers and the employed during this tumultuous century. It has been one of the islands of peace and progress in the wrack and ruin of our time. Yet this same steel industry is the one which the Socialist government have selected for the utmost exercise of its malice . . . this is not a bill, it is a plot. It is not a plan to help our patient struggling people, but a burglar's jemmy to crack the capitalist crib.[18]

'I suppose we'll 'ave a lot of those chaps in black coats and striped trousers 'anging around 'ere if they nationalises steel.'

(1948 cartoon)

When the bill was through, and the shares of two hundred companies were taken over by the new Iron and Steel Corporation, it was found that state ownership made little difference. The central control of the Corporation was weak. Ivor Jones remembers the brief period of the first nationalisation, at Shotton.

> It didn't mean anything to anyone except the Chairman. The Board of Directors was left exactly the same. I heard Richard Summers say, 'I am the only person who knows we are nationalised because I get all the bumph, and I throw it in the wastepaper basket.'

Almost as soon as it had begun, it was over. Fifteen months later the Conservatives were back in power, and kept their promise to denationalise. Yet the steel industry remained under close government scrutiny and an Iron and Steel Board was set up in 1953 to supervise the industry at a national level. As in the 1930s the owners were left in no doubt that they were expected to set their own house in order. In return for government help the slow process of modernisation was to continue.

The capacity of the industry expanded rapidly. From the 11 million tons produced at the end of the war, production had risen to 27 million tons by the early 1960s. Many of the targets had been met, greater fuel economy, larger blast furnaces and mills. But as in the 1930s there were limits to what the steel industry would do of its own accord. Nothing like the relocation and expansion, that had been advocated before the war, was achieved. Instead, there was more grafting of the new onto the old. In 1950 the combined profits of the biggest steel producers were £48 million. By 1960 they had risen to £167 million. There were years when the industry could not produce enough. Although in the special steels largely based in Sheffield the reputation for quality remained second to none, in other cases the pressure of demand affected the quality of what was produced. Don Owen was a melter.

Our job was to make steel. We made it to the specification we had on our charge sheet. Well, if they wanted the steel in a hurry, and the shift manager or sample passer said it was OK, then as far as I was concerned it was on his shoulders and out it would go. I know my brother and father would not have done this. They would have said, 'No, I am not tapping this steel, it is not to my satisfaction.' I was a different breed. I thought, 'You are the managers, if you say it is OK I will tap it.' Things went from bad to worse. Steel was being turned out too fast. I didn't like it.

Managers could see the same trend, but were more concerned with quantity. A strip-mill manager in south Wales remembers how material of second quality could be sold as easily as first.

There was a fifteen-year run in the world steel industry when we used to say that, provided it looked reasonably flat, we could sell everything that came off a strip mill at full price.

Ronald Towndrow was a works manager for Colville's in Scotland.

It was a producers' world. The customers were queuing up for products. The boss rang you up every morning and said, 'You didn't make very much yesterday, could you do a little better today?' It was a tremendous boost to morale, working in those exciting times when there never seemed to be any limit to the demand for steel.

The call for steel sheet, for cars and refrigerators and tin cans, continued to rise fastest of all. After Ebbw Vale, a second mill to meet this demand had been built at Shotton just as the war began. The third mill was to be the major post-war development, and gave another opportunity to get things right from the start. Abbey Works at Port Talbot was the largest and most technically advanced steel plant in Britain when it was opened by Hugh Gaitskell in 1951. The new melting shop and rolling-mill buildings stretched for miles, and their rectangular outline looked quite different from previous steelworks. The cavernous interiors were no longer dark because there were glass windows in the roof. The steel furnaces had four or five times the capacity of the old ones. Don Owen moved there, to work as a melter.

We were making fifty tons of steel in twelve hours in Duffryn steelworks. And when we were in the Abbey we were making four hundred tons in seven hours. And excellent steel, better steel.

But though much of it was newly built, the Abbey works was not an entirely new site. It used an existing dock, which was too small for large ore carriers, and was linked to two old works in Port Talbot and Margam. The coke ovens were in the middle of the town, and the railway

lines crossed a busy main road. Fred Cartwright had been involved in the development from the start, and became general manager.

The most ambitious post-war steel project: the Abbey works of the Steel Company of Wales (foreground) was linked to old Margam steelworks (rear). It cost £60 million, much of it from Marshall Aid

> Nobody would have laid out a brand-new works exactly as it was laid out. We had the rump of the old works. If we had enough money the best thing to have done was to say, 'Out with the old entirely, and start with a clean sheet of paper.' But we didn't, and so you had a good deal of stuff left there, and that was a pity because it introduced labour practices as well as mechanical and other practices.

Both managers and men recall the arguments and the high level of manning that marked the early days. There was a long wrangle over who should drive the locomotives on the internal railway system that linked the different parts of the steelworks complex. Management fell out with the bricklayers over the method by which they were paid for repairing furnaces. Demarcation lines between the different craftsmen, represented by separate unions, were strictly drawn. Some steel-workers found these agreements frustrating in their daily work. Gerald Pollard was an electrician.

We were talking about a workforce approaching 18,000 people and a lot of them had come from redundant hand mills in west Wales and had to be slotted in. Every craftsman had a mate. You think of the number of craftsmen, electricians, fitters, boilermakers, welders etc. within the works and multiply it by two and you have an idea of the excess of labour that existed at that time. It was an inefficient system because for quite a lot of the time the craftsmen had to think of jobs to give the mate to do. If I worked at the top of the ladder I would have my mate hold the ladder for perhaps the whole eight hours, and that was all he had to do.

Thomas Daniel, a locomotive driver in the works, found he could no longer do everyday repairs in the cab that he had always carried out in the past.

We had been taught as drivers to change our own gauge glasses. We carried a spanner or two in the loco for that purpose. Well, our fitters from our local shed removed all tools from the locos and said it was their job. They were demanding the right to be the only people that used the tools, you see.

Thomas Daniel also saw how the numbers rose on the staff side, in the Steel Company of Wales offices.

The personnel department in the old plant was the personnel manager and his assistant and one young lad and the typist. But in the Abbey, every section had its own personnel department. It increased from about half-a-dozen at Port Talbot to well over a hundred in the Abbey.

But like many at the time he felt the cost of labour was a small factor in the total arithmetic.

Our plant at one time made £47 million profit in one year. What did they have to worry about in those days when wages were about five or six pounds a week, about carrying a few extra men?

Nevertheless some did worry about the manning levels. Fred Cartwright sent two young managers to the United States in 1955 to compare productivity at Port Talbot with a roughly similar American plant in Chicago. They found that, although the Welsh works were the more modern, the output of steel per man was 60 per cent lower. In some specific areas the comparisons were even more alarming. The Steel Company of Wales needed ten bricklayers for every two in Chicago. In the maintenance departments, one craftsman in America could do the work that would have to be done by three separate trades in Wales. The report was equally devastating in its assessment of the comparative failure of British management to train, organise, and communicate with the workforce. When the report was read by the chairman of the Steel Company of Wales, he ordered it to be destroyed, as being far too provocative. Sir Campbell Adamson was one of the authors.

> It was a very good time for the steel industry. They had no problems selling their steel. Growth was high. So the great thing to do was to make a profit. As the labour cost per ton was comparatively small, somewhere in the region of 17 to 20 per cent, I think the very top management felt it was not worth closing the plant to make your point, or to hold out against a strike, because this would destroy far more profits than they could see it fulfilling.

The same situation applied at almost every steelworks in the country. There was a belief that labour costs could be comfortably absorbed. Managers did not want to antagonise the unions, with whom they had shared the hard times of the early 1930s, by attacking custom and practice in the prosperous 1950s. This meant that there were very few strikes, but Sir Robert Shone, who was with the Iron and Steel Board, felt that managers were not firm enough.

> United States Steel were very impressed with the British labour record because we had had no strikes for fifty years. So they sent their Labour Director over to examine the British situation. And he reported to the United States Steel Corporation: 'Yes, indeed, excellent relations there, but for God's sake don't follow their example, the only reason they have had no strikes is they face no issues.' And this was the reason we hadn't got the efficiency, because we hadn't faced up to the issues. It was this 'live and let live' attitude between management and unions.

In 1950 there were 296,000 steelworkers, in 1960 326,000, even though much of the new equipment was supposed to be labour-saving. The long-term penalty was to be reaped in the 1970s. The short-term penalty was low wages. Fred Allen was a blast-furnaceman at Port Talbot.

> At one time we were practically falling over each other, but we were lowly paid at that particular time because the management used to turn down all our wage claims, and rather than give us money, give us extra men, and this is what the result was, overmanned and lowly paid.

Sir Campbell Adamson lays the blame on the way employers approached the whole question of pay and productivity.

> The thing that particularly struck me, and other young men in the companies I got to know, was this backward and unconstructive look that the Iron and Steel Employers' Association

had in the whole of their wage negotiations. They were always arguing about halfpennies. They were never trying to make a constructive advance and say, 'If we get more efficiency and more productivity we will give you more money'.

Manning, and the way in which the advantages of new plant were sometimes wasted, was a problem internal to the industry. But before the prosperous 1950s ended there was another example of direct political intervention, beyond the steel men's control, which had a deep effect on their future. With demand still rising, yet another big strip mill was felt to be necessary. The favoured site was at Llanwern, near Newport in south Wales, a genuinely new location with room to build a plant that could make three million tons a year, using the basic oxygen, or LD process which the Americans and Japanese had already adopted in their big new steelworks. But as with Ebbw Vale before the war, there was intense effort by other parts of the country to secure the £100 million project, with particularly strong political pressure to bring it to Scotland instead of Wales.

In 1958 the team already planning Llanwern heard the news that the Conservative government, with an election imminent, had decided in response to the lobbying to build not one strip mill but two. One plant would go to Wales, and the second to Scotland. In an instant all the calculations of cost and demand were upset. Three million tons a year was reckoned to be the minimum economic size, but each plant would

now be half this, and each would cost proportionately more to construct. Harold Macmillan called the decision 'the judgement of
Solomon'. At Ravenscraig in Scotland Colville's reluctantly set to building, with government help, a huge new plant that never paid for itself.
In south Wales, Richard Thomas and Baldwins built Llanwern, which
could never benefit from the economies of scale they had hoped for
because it was only half the size planned.

Although a nightmare for the directors and accountants, it was an
exciting project for the engineers.

> Llanwern was the first major works in Europe which was
> totally based on top-blown oxygen vessels for steel-making.
> That was a very bold decision. The other big technical develop-
> ment which was in its early stages then was continuous cast-
> ing. There again the United Kingdom was well to the fore. If
> you turn to rolling-mill technology we were well up. The
> Llanwern strip mill was as modern as any in the world when it
> was brought in.

On a new site, many of the jobs went to men fresh to the industry, as
well as to experienced steel-makers who moved from other steel areas.

> We thought our future was bright. We were the tops in steel-
> making, or were going to be anyway. We had all brand-new
> equipment, we had a new workforce, good management and
> the future was very bright.

But Llanwern and Ravenscraig were being built just as the confident
predictions of an ever-expanding demand were turning out to be
wrong. What might have been the first step towards the reconstruction
of the steel industry became a financial disaster, and in the 1960s the
easy attitudes of the 1940s and 1950s received their due correction.
Profits collapsed to only £23 million by 1967, less than half the figure for
1950. Home steel production stagnated, and imports increased.

Apart from the new 'green field' site at Llanwern there had been no
major relocation of the industry since the war, and no elimination of
older small-scale plants. Planners continued to advise that an efficient
industry should have just a few large works, producing at least a million
tons a year. But by 1965 there were still forty-one steel plants in Britain,
thirty-one of which produced less than a million tons, twenty-three less
than 500,000. Many of the firms were still in the wrong places for cheap
ore supplies.

There was also a technical lag. By 1965 only 20 per cent of British
steel was made by the LD-oxygen or BOS process, the new method
which offered phenomenal savings. The old open-hearth furnace might
produce 300 tons of steel in twelve hours. The new method produced
300 tons in thirty-five minutes. In a large plant BOS steel might cost only
one-third the price of open-hearth steel. Yet many steel manufacturers
spent small sums to update the open-hearth plants and remained

Llanwern's new strip mill made strip steel at up to 30 miles an hour, but demand was falling off as it opened

sceptical of the claims made for the large plants abroad. With the private owners facing increasing criticism, the Labour Party committed itself to renationalisation. Many of the managers felt that their industry had become a political football and that this restricted development. Sir Campbell Adamson had become General Manager of the new Llanwern works, and a director of Richard Thomas and Baldwins.

I was in the steel industry for twenty-three years, and only for the first year of that twenty-three years was government not arguing about nationalising or denationalising or renationalising. The whole way through, right up until the final nationalisation in 1967, we were under this awful cloud that we never knew what would happen. This inevitably had an effect on the investment in the steel industry of Britain during the fifties and sixties, a very bad effect.

The second nationalisation in 1967 was a clean sweep. This time the old names disappeared, and deliberate attempts were made to lose the old identities and organisation, and achieve a fresh start. Richard Marsh was the Minister who brought in the bill. At first a doubter, he had been converted to renationalisation by the attitude of the private owners.

> When I came into office I found that, apart from a report, they had actually done nothing, and were doing nothing, to re-organise the industry. And from that moment I became convinced that the only way you would get the industry re-organised and restructured was by taking it over and doing it.

Under Lord Melchett as Chairman, the new British Steel Corporation was one of the largest steel producers in the world. But apart from the few new plants, its inheritance still owed much to the nineteenth century, and the new regime was harsh in its criticism of the old plant, and of the old attitudes they encountered. As on many occasions in the previous seventy years, the reformers looked abroad for inspiration. They found it not in Germany or the United States, however, but in the enormous new works constructed on coastal sites in Japan. Japan's steel output had risen ten times since the war. The Japanese steelworker in 1969 produced three times as much per head as his British equivalent. None of the new Japanese works produced less than six million tons of steel a year. In Britain only one works produced as much as three million tons. To Lord Melchett and his Chief Executive, Sir Monty Finniston, what the Japanese were doing seemed entirely appropriate to the British situation. If a small number of new plants could be built, on the Japanese scale, the same economies could be achieved. To try to get the workforce to see this, they sent groups of trade unionists and steel workers on the journey of discovery they had made themselves.

> We heard a lot about Japan from the British Steel Corporation. Every time you went in, it was 'They're doing this in Japan', and 'This is happening in Japan'.

When Billy Booth, a blast-furnaceman from Llanwern, made the trip in 1973 he was impressed by what he found.

> Everything that I had been told was absolutely true. Their furnaces were much bigger. They were just years ahead in front of us as far as steel-making was concerned.

The technology was not the only thing that interested the steel-workers. They found that working conditions were cleaner, cooler, and less dusty. To prove that pollution levels were low, the Japanese had aviaries and ponds full of goldfish and carp close to the furnaces. Stan Thomas from Port Talbot found that the arrangements for the management were less elaborate, however.

> When I saw their offices I was rather amazed. They had one very large room. The manager of the plant would be at one end with his three-piece suite with coverings in white calico. Behind him he'd have his assistant manager. Then he'd have

*First meeting of the new
British Steel Corporation,
April 1967, with Lord Melchett
as Chairman (centre).
Sir Monty Finniston is on his
left; Sir Peter Parker, later
Chairman of British Rail, is on
the extreme left*

his secretary and clerks. Down the room you had various
metallurgical and maintenance departments. The offices were
not as palatial as ours.

Back at home, the tantalising example of Japan raised many questions. Hundreds of millions of pounds of new investment would be
needed to rebuild on a similar scale, and the human consequences of
rationalisation were as socially and politically complicated as they had
ever been. The productivity problems had stayed on through the 1950s
and 1960s. Even when a totally new plant had been built, as at Llanwern,
the old demarcations were introduced into it and the union rivalries were
greater than ever. Billy Booth remembers.

> In the early days it was terrible. Craft unions wouldn't sit down
> with production unions and the different production unions
> wouldn't sit down together. I've known on many occasions
> where a meeting has been geared up by the management that
> included craft unions and production workers and as soon as
> we walked into the meeting the craft representatives would get
> up and walk out.

In the pressure to get the new steelworks opened without hold-ups,
there had been many concessions on the number of men needed. Raymond Sharpe was a foreman at Llanwern.

> In the end there were too many. You had to find work for the
> fitters. Where you would normally put one on a job, you would
> have to try and slide two onto a job, which was making the job
> cost twice as much. You'd have to send out a gang where you
> would normally send four. You'd then have to find work for
> eight men. In the end they were all in each other's way. There
> were too many men there. It applied to the staff as well.

Manning comparisons with Japan seemed to be too extreme to be relevant. But BSC also produced comparisons with Europe. One study compared Llanwern with a similar plant in Belgium, built at the same time with the same capacity, but operated with 45 per cent fewer men. The unions contested the comparison.

Numbers apart, the effect of nationalisation, and several reorganisations, had been to weaken the morale of the foremen and middle management. Val Maybury ran the open-hearth furnaces at Shotton.

> Decisions that we used to take on the shop floor, as management running the works, had to be referred to the headquarters of BSC. A lot of our man-to-management relationship was badly distorted by virtue of having to work through a third party, who were faceless people with whom we had no contact at all. So you felt you were on your own, fighting a losing battle. You were very scared to do certain things. You tended to back off, particularly on discipline.

While their existing steelworks were operating with increasing difficulty, British Steel's high command were looking ahead. They argued about whether it was really best to pursue large-scale super-plants on the Japanese scale, or selectively to improve the better works already in existence. Those who thought big won, and in 1973 the Corporation finally published a ten-year development plan which envisaged spending £3000 million to reshape the industry. Production would be concentrated on five existing major steel plants. Port Talbot would be expanded to six million tons. A giant new steel complex would be built at Redcar on Teeside. Over the next ten years they expected to double the average productivity level and reduce the number of steelworkers by about 50,000. The plan's most optimistic feature was the estimate of the amount of steel that would be needed. It predicted that in 1980 production would be up to thirty-six million tons.

The ambitions of the nationalised British steel industry reached their high-water mark with the 1973 plan. But the timing was unhappy, and the estimate of future demand was disastrously wrong. The 1974 OPEC oil price rise, and the recession that followed, saw world steel demand collapse. Fred Cartwright describes how the dream went astray.

> The multiplying of the oil price by four upset the whole world. It wasn't just the British steel industry. We didn't realise that suddenly people were going to start buying smaller cars, and that everybody was going to start being frightfully economical, almost overnight. Instead of building a new power station every so often, people said 'We've got too many'.

In the recession of the 1970s it was the big steel producers with the lowest costs who survived most easily, and even in the shrinking home market BSC lost out to imported steel. Imports of foreign steel rose from five per cent to 20 per cent between 1970 and 1977. At first BSC tried to keep to the grand plan, but to speed up the closures of the old plant with open-hearth furnaces. But closures that might have been made less painfully in the 1960s, when the Coal Board had shed its greatest numbers, now met fierce resistance when steelworkers had little hope of other jobs. The managers of what was professed to be a new-style nationalised concern, whose brief had been to produce an efficient modern steel industry that paid for itself, found themselves at loggerheads with a Labour government, which was reluctant both to hand out more money for modernisation or to accept the social cost of mass closures. Sir Monty Finniston describes his relationship with the minister to whom he answered when he was chairman of BSC, Tony Benn.

> He wasn't allowed to interfere in the operational day-to-day activities of the Corporation but on occasions he did, and then there was a great battle, and to a large extent I think the difficulty was with him, because he was looking at the Corporation as a social activity. He didn't want anybody to be rendered redundant, he wanted them to be well paid, he wanted them to be kept in business, even with an obsolescent plant. How are you expected to make a profit and how you were expected to gain markets, I don't know. Whereas we were still trying to make a commercially viable organisation.

But the collapse in orders was so great that Sir Monty's plan was put aside, and with new political masters the pace of closures and redundancies was speeded up. In 1970 there were 255,000 steelworkers, in 1980 only 166,000. BSC made higher redundancy payments than had ever been paid before, and started BSC Industries to try to create new jobs in the steel areas, but the workforce that remained was shaken and insecure, and management–union relations reached their lowest point. In 1980, facing a loss of £500 million, BSC refused to pay their men a wage increase that kept up with the cost of living, and prompted the first national strike for seventy years. For steelworkers like Billy Booth, it was the breaking point.

> You had Glengarnock, Hartlepool, Shotton, Corby, Bilston, Shelton, Ebbw Vale, East Moors in Cardiff, it seemed every week there was a plant closing down. Men were getting disillusioned and people were afraid that we were going to be the next one. During all these plant closures, redundancies and cutbacks we'd fallen behind in the pay scale. And I think everyone then had come to the conclusion, well, enough is enough, and if we've got to fight them that was the time to fight.

After thirteen weeks, the unions lost the fight. New working agreements were forced through, and in the space of the next three years the number of steelworkers was halved again, from 166,000 to around 70,000. Among the works where steel-making stopped were the showplaces of the thirties, Corby and Ebbw Vale. Steel was now a small

employer compared with electronics with 500,000 jobs, or retailing with 2,000,000. Many redundant steelworkers were forced to hunt for jobs in the new sectors which offered an entirely different type of work from that which they had known.

What happened to iron and steel in the late 1970s and early 1980s approached an industrial holocaust. It was the steelworkers who were paying in a very short time for the earlier failures in planning, in government, and for the comfortable consensus between union and management in the years of the sellers' market after the war. In many cases management had been misguidedly benign back in the 1950s, when new machinery was introduced. Ivor Jones remembers the John Summers company at Shotton.

A blast furnace comes down at Shotton, 1982

> I must admit we were overmanned at times, particularly when we put these new modern mills in, because they didn't require the same number of people to operate them, and having to shut down forty-one old handmills could have put a lot of men out of work. The company said, 'No, no man will be out of work. We guarantee to find every man work.' This we also did when we put in the coke ovens, the blast furnace and the new melting shop. They had this feeling of responsibility to the workforce who had been so loyal to them over the years.

But now Shotton has been closed too. Taff Evans was a roller in the hot strip mill.

> I just can't bring myself to go over there because I am afraid I would come home deeply upset to see all that has happened. Everything has been dismantled. It's a sad affair, like making a reservoir out of a village and filling it up with water. It breaks my heart to look at it. I can see it from a distance here. All the old chimneys have gone, it's very sad.

Seven years after the 1973 plan which predicted an estimated 1980 demand for thirty-six million tons of steel, the actual figure turned out to be twelve million. BSC argued that the contraction was inevitable. The unions pointed out that other countries had not made such severe cuts, that world demand had begun to rise again, and argued that instead of surgery there should have been lower prices and better marketing. Sir Charles Villiers succeeded Sir Monty Finniston as Chairman.

> It was a conviction that we had too much capacity, and that the old capacity had to be closed, and that the men in it had to stop making steel and learn to do something else. If you have an intellectual conviction that what you are doing is right, and it isn't just something off the cuff, you can go about it with more certainty.

Yet during the period of British contraction Japanese steel output had risen from 93 million tons in 1970 to 111 million in 1980. The effect of the

Control cockpit for the Basic Oxygen System of steel-making, at British Steel, Port Talbot. BOS made better steel far faster, but with fewer men

closures was to achieve by force of circumstance what rational planning had failed to reach, the concentration on five big steelworks proposed as the ideal solution ever since 1918.

In the smaller, slimline steel industry that survives there have been extraordinary changes in the working lives of men and managers. BSC say their productivity and manning levels are now as good as any in Europe. In the peak years the old Abbey works at Port Talbot employed over 17,000. In 1983 the figure was down to 5000. Gerald Pollard started at the works as an electrician in the 1950s.

I find more job satisfaction than I have had for many years. We are a smaller workforce now and yet more integrated. There are no craftsmen's mates within the works now, and the various craftsmen help each other out. Even the production workers help the craftsmen out as well, so there is a greater sense of purpose about it.

Many steelworkers now say they feel isolated, working almost alone in plant that is larger than ever. John Horton is a production manager at Llanwern.

People have got more to do. They're more responsible for their jobs. The foremen have been cut by almost half. There's no shift manager, no assistant manager. They're all gone.

Cyril Jenkins has seen many of his colleagues go. He runs a BOS converter, making 38,000 tons of steel a week at Port Talbot. His father worked in steel before him, and he is an enthusiast for his job. But he has had to accept that his own son will not follow him, which had always been his expectation in a town whose whole economy relied on the steelworks.

Sons can't follow fathers because we are in a situation where you can't employ new men. Once you break the chain that's it, you don't restart it. My own son's on the dole, and it's heart-breaking for me that I can't get him a job in the steelworks. I can't get him a job alongside me now.

CHAPTER 5: RETAILING
TURNING OVER FAST

We thought that packaging was going to take our jobs away. We had it that we were selling loose things, weighing them out, and that was our labour you see. We used to weigh everything out that there was, currants, raisins, pepper, salt, tea, coffee, cocoa. We used to make these cups, tuck it in, turn it up and present it. We thought if it came in packets there wouldn't be any jobs.

Rochdale shop assistant

I remember a judge's wife at Purley swearing at me and saying I had no right to expect the customer to do the work the assistants had done in the past. In another case a woman threw a wire basket at me, because she thought self-service was all wrong.

Lord Sainsbury

For the people who owned or served in shops, history was seldom an encumbrance. The past could be thrown away quickly, with a new shop-front, or a change of management, or a move to a new building. Since 1918 retailing has seen a succession of rapid shifts and almost continual growth. When the jobs that service and support it are included, retailing now employs one-eighth of the working population and has become the biggest industry in the country. In one sense economic success was unavoidable, because the prosperity of the retailer has been bound in with the rise in the national standard of living. Other industries might expand or contract, but so long as there was more to spend overall, people were bound to spend most of it in the shops.

Eighty years ago, the working man used up most of his wages on food and the bare necessities. Most shops were food shops. But with rising prosperity came a call for carpets, furniture, ready-made clothes, radios and refrigerators – 'consumer durables'. When the house had been furnished and the family clothed, there was a rapid expansion in shops dealing in books, records, sports equipment, cameras and a succession of new products. There has been a parallel change in the way that goods are sold and in the whole organisation of the trade. Retailing has become a large-scale business, where once it was dominated by the small independent shopkeeper. The chain store and the supermarket now account for half the custom. For the majority of shopworkers these changes have meant that less skill is needed, either to prepare goods or to persuade customers to buy. Rita Greendale worked in shops in Hull:

> When self-service really got going I didn't feel such a complete
> person. I didn't have the job satisfaction that I'd been having as
> a counter assistant or a store assistant.

Though shops are larger, their total number has increased. There were 300,000 on the eve of the First World War, 350,000 in 1980. Those in the business talk about the 'retailing revolution'. The way in which the revolution occurred and the effect that it had on the lives of the participants show how different retailing was from much of the rest of British economic life. Competition was fierce, unions were weak, and entrepreneurs had unusual freedom of action, though in this free market there were costs to be paid as well.

The principal characteristic of retailing has always been its diversity: the great differences between types of shop and the way they are run, from the market stall to the department store. In 1918 the trade was still dominated by the small independent shop, each with its narrow specialisation. There were haberdashers and drapers, shoe shops and hardware merchants, but the majority of shops sold food, usually prepared and packed on the premises. Butchers slaughtered their own animals, bakers made their own bread, and provision merchants sliced their bacon and cut butter and cheese from blocks. In the grocer's shops, which sold dry goods, shopworkers had to know how to deal with the

*Branch shops in Amersham
High Street, 1937*

103

range of goods, – rice, salt, flour, biscuits – that came loose or packed in kegs or sacks. One shop assistant remembers having to come to terms with dates:

> We used a long crowbar to undo the dates. We had to dig it into the box and it got very sticky, so you had to plunge it into a bucket of cold water. And the dates were very sticky and eventually you'd prise up a lump, and they'd go all over the place. The crowbar would be sticky again. Back into the cold water. Then we'd break them up into 3 or 4 pounds, and gradually half-pounds and pounds. Every last thing was sticky including your hair.

For the grocery trade there was a six-year apprenticeship in which the range of commodities sold and the use of the different scoops and knives were learnt. Many shops were family run, which meant that children started at an early age. Miss Mott was born into the bakery business in London.

> My mother was in the shop all day long from about eight in the morning to eight at night, and on a Saturday night she used to keep open until twelve o'clock. I used to work in the shop. I used to pack bread on the shelves and help serve customers. As soon as I could add up I was able to serve, and of an evening time I would allow my mother to go upstairs for a few minutes.

Before 1914 there were already signs of change. The first 'multiples' had appeared, chains of grocers, shoe shops and chemists which won new customers with their low prices and good quality. By the 1920s Liptons', Home and Colonial, Maypole, Freeman Hardy and Willis, and Boots, were established in many high streets. Independent traders complained that the competition was unfair because the chains could make special arrangements with the farms and factories who supplied them.

Left and right: *Small independent shops had most of the trade at the time of World War I. Family-owned, they kept long hours*

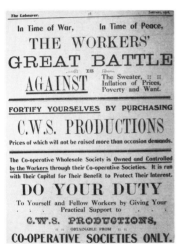

An advertisement for the Co-op, 1916

Another and older form of competition to the small shop came from the Co-operative movement. Begun in the nineteenth century as a means to provide cheaper food to their members through profit sharing, Co-ops had spread rapidly, particularly in the industrial areas of the north and Scotland. By the 1920s they had ten per cent of the retail market, and there were over four million members who not only shopped with the Co-op but could save, insure themselves and be buried through the Co-op. Servetus Hartley describes the loyal following the Co-op had in one of the movement's home towns, Rochdale.

> A lot of people had their money in the Co-op, and they were intensely loyal. You would go a quarter of a mile to get it at the Co-op rather than go around the corner and buy it at the local grocer's. You would have five hundred people at a quarterly meeting to hear all the dry as dust statistics.

The middle classes shopped at the department stores, which combined a high standard of service with a wide range of goods. Department stores brought consumerism to the well-off before it came to the country at large. Most big provincial towns had their own local version of the shop that Irene Sutton served in.

> Pendlebury's was a beautiful store. It had a ground floor, first floor, second floor, and the centre of the shop was a big well. You could stand on the ground floor and look right up to the roof, and it had beautiful balustrades which were dusted every morning by cleaners who never stopped. The customers were the élite of Wigan.

Wide differences in the types of shop were matched in working life as well. In the big department stores, men assistants wore black jackets, striped trousers and spats, and the women had to wear black dresses. Jobs were coveted because conditions were better and the hours

SHOPPING AT SELFRIDGE'S
A Pleasure—A Pastime—A Recreation

WE aim to make the shopping at "Selfridge's" something more than merely shopping. We would like to think that everyone who spends an hour or a day beneath our roof is better for the experience, has seen many "things different," has gathered some new point of knowledge, has discovered a way to do something better and revealed the thought to us.

Such suggestions we will welcome very gratefully and act on to the best of our ability, for by this friendly criticism we can more readily accomplish the work that we have set ourselves, that is, to do every day some one thing better than we did the day before.

This is part of our ambition, and what we know will come about by cordial "entente" between Customers and ourselves.

SELFRIDGE & Co.,
OXFORD ST.,
LONDON, W.

Gordon Selfridge (above) had brought American showmanship to British shopkeeping when he opened his London department store in 1909

generally shorter than in smaller shops, and some stores had their own doctors and welfare arrangements. The Co-ops also had a reputation as good employers. They gave greater job security and paid higher wages than the average. Some gave their employees a forty-eight-hour week long before this became standard. Servetus Hartley remembers the prestige that went with his job.

> Compared to working with textiles, you were like Royalty. Everybody in the street knew that you were working with the Co-op. If you worked at the mill you were three a penny, but not at the Co-op.

But as a group, shopworkers were victims of the highly competitive nature of the business. This was apparent in the long hours that most shops stayed open, and in employers' attempts to pay wages as low as possible. One of the most extraordinary survivals was the system which had been standard in much of the trade before the First World War whereby more than 400,000 still 'lived in'. There was no job unless assistants accepted a regime under which wages were paid partly in

THE LIFE OF A SHOP-GIRL

PATHETIC SIDE OF AN OCCUPATION WHICH SPELLS DRUDGERY AND HOPELESS OUTLOOK ON LIFE FOR MANY THOUSANDS

kind, through the provision of accommodation and meals. As a result they were totally beholden to their employer, who could impose fines and make arbitrary rules about how they spent their off-duty time. Small shops had dormitories above, in which from six to twenty young men or women might share a room. Big stores had separate hostels. The practice was widely criticised, but employers defended it on the grounds of respectability. As one factory inspector explained,

> One of the main arguments put forward in favour of the 'living in' system is that it is absolutely necessary for the protection of the women and the discouragement of immorality.[19]

Arguments against 'living in' were based not only on the fact that shopworkers were exploited and exposed to appalling conditions but that their very lives were endangered. When fire destroyed Barkers department store in Kensington in London in 1912, five shopgirls who lived on the premises were burnt to death. 'Living in' still lingered on into the

107

1920s, but by then, after a long campaign, most workers had won the right to choose between taking board and being paid a full wage.

The long hours put in by shop staff had been identified as a scandal at the turn of the century, when seventy-five to ninety hours a week were regularly being worked. A Shop Act of 1912 imposed a half-day closing, but there was still no statutory limit to the working week. In the bigger high street shops hours were coming down, but there were great variations. As a young girl in the early 1920s, Rita Greendale remembers hours that were not at all unusual for small traders.

> We normally started about seven in the morning, unless it was a market day. You had to be at the early morning market at five o'clock. Get the stall out before half-past seven. And we used to have a snack on the counter at about twelve o'clock in the shop. Then at five o'clock you had a sandwich or a banana, and then you just went on working, and on a very early night we might close at 9 or half past. Mostly we were open until midnight.

Legislation in 1923 and 1928 brought in a general closing time of 8 pm, but there were many exemptions and the hours were almost impossible to enforce. It was a subservient and hierarchical workforce. Youngsters started at the very bottom, running errands, delivering parcels, cleaning up, watching the more experienced clerks and salesmen. Each branch of retailing had its own pattern of work, but common to all was the power enjoyed by the managers and chief assistants, or in the department stores the buyers. When Servetus Hartley had graduated from flour boy he was allowed to fetch groceries to the counter, where an assistant totted them up. Then he had to pack them in the customer's basket.

> You had to produce a neat bag which would pass the scrutiny of the manager before you were allowed to pack it on your own. That was a great day, you thought you were somebody then. If you did it wrong he'd say, 'You're missing today. You made a shocking mess of that bag and you'll do without lunch.'

In the small shop the discipline was arbitrary. In the multiples and department stores it was more formal. There was a scale of fines and deductions. Admittedly there was a small commission of 3d in the pound for sales made, but there could also be a penalty if a customer did not buy. In some shops it was only necessary to fail to complete a sale on three occasions to be dismissed. Even when successful, the junior salesman could find himself pushed aside at the moment of sale by the first assistant or floor manager who would then claim the commission. No one could risk complaint. Lionel Harrisson joined a London department store in 1926.

> The shopwalkers were always in morning dress. They were very particular, very erect, real martinets in a way. The junior

IMPORTANT NOTICE.

You are requested to observe that all Employes are engaged subject to Dismissal Without Notice.

HARROD'S STORES, *Limited.*

February 18th, 1891.

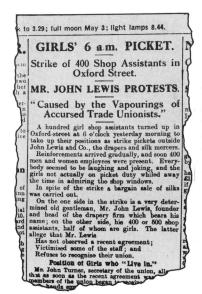

GIRLS' 6 a.m. PICKET.

Strike of 400 Shop Assistants in Oxford Street.

MR. JOHN LEWIS PROTESTS.

"Caused by the Vapourings of Accursed Trade Unionists."

A hundred girl shop assistants turned up in Oxford-street at 6 o'clock yesterday morning to take up their positions as strike pickets outside John Lewis and Co., the drapers and silk mercers.

Reinforcements arrived gradually, and soon 400 men and women employees were present. Everybody seemed to be laughing and joking, and the girls not actually on picket duty whiled away the time in admiring the shop windows.

In spite of the strike a bargain sale of silks was carried out.

On the one side in the strike is a very determined old gentleman, Mr. John Lewis, founder and head of the drapery firm which bears his name; on the other side, his 400 or 500 shop assistants, half of whom are girls. The latter allege that Mr. Lewis

Has not observed a recent agreement;
Victimised some of the staff; and
Refuses to recognise their union.

Position of Girls who "Live in."

Mr. John Turner, secretary of the union, all, that as soon as the recent agreement was members of the union began

shopwalkers were approachable, but the head shopwalker was a god. We were all scared stiff of him because if we put a foot out of line we got ticked off and that might mean the sack.

In this atmosphere, there was little union activity among shopworkers apart from those who worked in the Co-ops. In the 1920s the shop assistants' union had only 30,000 members, a tiny fraction of the total workforce. Recruitment was difficult and hazardous and the risks which a shop assistant ran by joining a union were considerable. Between 1919 and 1939 there were just nineteen small and local strikes for the whole trade. Some of the shopworkers were strongly anti-union themselves, but in most cases they were too frightened to join, too isolated and disorganised to present a united front. One shopgirl recalls what happened at her Woolworth's branch, when it was found that she had attended a meeting.

Next morning I was called into the office by the manager and he said, 'Miss Ramsbottom, did you go out last night?' I said yes. He said, 'Where did you go?' I said the YMCA. He said, 'What was on?' I said a union meeting. He said, 'Miss Ramsbottom, had you not been one of my best girls you would have been out of here this morning.'

The rapid turnover of staff was a further discouragement to the unions, who found it difficult to keep regular track of membership.

Though few shopworkers earned high wages, and though the hours could be longer than those in offices and factories, there were at least jobs to be found. Between the wars retail distribution became one of the great growth areas of the British economy, at a time when the old staple industries were in crisis. The percentage of unemployed in the country at large was high. But those who had work found that, with prices standing still or falling, they could afford to buy goods that would have been beyond their reach in the past. Shops selling furniture and electrical goods spread quickly. The number of confectionery shops grew two and a half times, and the number of chemists trebled, in twenty-five years. Though many individuals managed to open their own tobacconists or sweetshops, the growth was accompanied by intense competition in which the independent shopkeeper was often squeezed out. It was the chain store, the multiple, that adapted most rapidly and successfully to the growing mass market. Those that had been in existence before the war, including the grocery chains, continued to expand. The American-owned Woolworth's already had 280 shops in Britain when Alexander Taft started as manager of a north London branch in 1928.

The chain store firstly gave you good value for money. Also they gave you an excellent variety, your haberdashery, your hardware, your range of toys, biscuits, sweets. The variety was much bigger than you could have in smaller shops.

An entirely new set of multiples sprang into existence, including chains selling men's and women's clothes. They challenged a new set of small independent retailers. Jack Rose was a salesman for one of the new multiple tailors.

The solid appeal of the Chelmsford branch of Sainsbury's, with the manager, Mr McGovern, by the cashiers' windows. Grocery chains had been among the earliest multiples

> The thirty-shilling suits in those days were bought by the everyday working man. They were a cheap line, something they had not been able to get hold of before, because at that time there were so many private tailors charging fancy prices. And Weaver to Wearer got in on the ground floor, until everyone else had to follow and the smaller tailors had to go out of business.

Alan Farmer worked to establish the Dorothy Perkins chain of dress shops in the 1930s, when their top price for a dress was five shillings.

> Women were able to buy things they couldn't previously afford. A lot of shop girls, and even mill staff and all those sorts of people, suddenly found they had got prices that enabled them to buy things.

The multiples had the money to advertise and to carry a wide stock, which they displayed well. The old draper's shops had kept their goods in packets and boxes piled high. The new chains had glass-fronted fittings, and attractive shop fronts. The new shops clustered together in the high streets, paying high prices for prime sites next to each other. But their principal strength came from the prices they were able to charge, by cutting out the middle man and dealing direct with manufacturers. At first the manufacturers resisted, out of loyalty to the wholesalers, but what won them over was the great size of the orders the multiples could place. Michael Hornby was a director of W. H. Smith between the wars.

Dorothy Perkins branch at Sutton: in the 1930s new chains, selling men's and women's clothing, spread fast

Our buying was done centrally for the shops and bookstalls, so that a book department manager could go to a publisher and give him a very large order, and expect to get better terms than one little bookshop would get. It's the buying power you've got by being a multiple that puts you in a better position than the individual shop.

In the first round of a succession of high-street battles that were to come, the vigorous new multiples doubled their share of the market within ten years, at the expense of the department stores and independents. When in 1930 a teashop and food chain made record profits, its chairman boasted: 'In these distressing and doleful days the House of Lyons stands out as a beacon on the industrial horizon.'

During and after the slump the new retailers were held up as paragons for the rest of British industry. One of the leaders was Marks and Spencer, who had progressed from their penny-bazaar origins to being one of the most efficient businesses in the country. In a broadcast in 1934 Israel Sieff, one of its founders, criticised those who looked to the government for help.

If trade is bad, if men are on the dole, if profits are not being made, it points to the absence of thought and imagination, of the power to co-ordinate industrial and financial processes, and to the lack of a forward, courageous sales policy by a strong marketing organisation for the industry. It is almost pathetic to listen to those businessmen who look everywhere else but to their own lack of imagination and understanding for the cause of their ills.[20]

Politicians felt ambivalent about the rise of the multiples. There was no doubt about their popularity with the customers, but in the mid

Assistants at Woolworth's in Liverpool. Selling everything at 6d or under brought profits for the firm's senior managers and executives (opposite), celebrating in the ballroom at the Savoy Hotel in London. By 1931 they had 434 branches

1930s the distress calls from the small traders became so frequent, and their lobbying so powerful, that it looked as though government might try to put some limit on the growth of the chains. The mere talk of this served to accelerate the process of change. Worried about what might happen, the Dorothy Perkins shops expanded even faster. Alan Farmer remembers.

> I had this hunch that they would stop the multiples really creaming the trade, and that made me frightened, and I thought, 'Well, I'm jolly well going to get as many shops as I can before the thing is stopped.'

But the threat was never fulfilled, and the free market continued to operate. Small dairies, butchers and bakeries suffered badly. Maud Mott remembers what happened to the family baker's shop she had worked in as a child.

> There was a multiple firm of bakers, A. B. Hemmings, they had over 100 branches in London, and they offered bread cheaper, and at the end of every week, if you'd had so many loaves, they would give you an extra loaf free. Well, we couldn't compete with that, and my father eventually sold out to this firm.

With the rise of the multiples came changes in the nature of shop work. For ambitious young managers there were opportunities that hadn't existed before, to take charge of new branch shops springing up. Woolworth's, Marks and Spencer, British Home Stores were each open-

112

ing branches at a rate of one a week in their period of fastest growth. Alexander Taft's career with Woolworth's moved quickly.

> I did terribly well. I worked very hard. In two years they moved me to a bigger store which was Richmond. I had that for a couple of years, increased the sales, increased the profits. I was rated as a pretty good operator so they gave me Kilburn. I was there for two years, I did the same thing. The great thing was to beat the average and be better than anyone else.

For the managers of the stores the pay, linked to the turnover of the branch, was good. Jimmy Bubear also worked for Woolworth's, starting his career as a manager in Bangor in North Wales.

> We reckoned that a Woolworth's manager was the highest-paid manager of any retail store in his town. We weren't able to prove that, but we could live well, we could bring our family up well.

When Mr Bubear progressed to become manager of one of the biggest branches in the country, in the centre of Liverpool, the bonus system brought sizeable rewards.

The manager of a super store would have a very nice house. He would have a very nice motor car. We had some managers with Rolls-Royce motor cars. I always had a saloon and a sports car. I could send my children to good schools and could dress very well. I could send my children to north Wales for six weeks in the summer with my chauffeur and my cook and nanny, and my wife and I could then go away on a fortnight's cruise.

The new shops, and the manufacturers who were behind them, were making the job of the salespeople simpler all the time. On the food side, more goods came prepacked and labelled from the factories, reducing the time-consuming work of preparing, weighing and packing in the shops. When branded goods had simply to be taken off the shelves, many of the skills learnt during the long apprenticeships were redundant. Like many other changes in retailing, the customers resisted packaging at first.

These porridge oats came in packets, and people didn't like it at all. We'd been used to weighing it out for them. They had to buy a packet, and they wouldn't buy a packet. They didn't want so much. They only wanted enough for perhaps two breakfasts, small portions.

Surprisingly, the coming of packaged goods was one of the factors that helped preserve the small shops. Many manufacturers who were producing the new branded provisions insisted that they be sold in as many places as possible, and at a standard price. The small shops benefited most from these conditions because the chain stores could not undercut their prices. Only a few discounters, like Tesco, challenged the resale price maintenance agreements that were concluded for a wide range of products. By 1939 over 30 per cent of goods were sold at prices fixed by the manufacturer, so that competition in the late 1930s was based on service and convenience, rather than on price.

One way the small shops could compete was by continuing to provide traditional opening hours. Customers expected them to keep open till late into the evenings and at weekends, when the multiples would be closed. Efforts by small shopkeepers to achieve earlier closing often broke down because of the fear that a competitor would stay open longer and steal the trade.

The boss I worked for came up with a wonderful idea. If all the other fruit shops would fall in with it, we'd close early, at nine o'clock. After a lot of performance everybody, except one man, said they would fall in with this early closing and we got very excited about it. But he said he'd always closed at midnight and midnight he was going to close at, and so it all fell through. Because if everybody wasn't going to do it then you'd just lose your customers.

The Second World War did much to improve the conditions and hours of shopworkers. Other industries had to do more overtime and raise output. Because of the shortages, shops did their patriotic duty by doing less. To save heat and light and labour, compulsory 6 p.m. closing was introduced. There were other improvements. Some efforts had already been made in the 1930s to introduce minimum standard wages. Shop-owners had accepted these changes in only a few areas and trades. When the war came the government, in the person of the Minister of Labour, Ernest Bevin, insisted that conditions and pay should be arranged across the industry as a whole. Wage Councils were established to set minimum pay levels, so undermining the commission system. As so many of the men were away more women were taken on, and in the big stores managers could no longer be so particular about what employees wore. Morning suits and black serge dresses disappeared for the duration, and in most cases forever.

> It was marvellous for us, because they relaxed so many rules. You see, the clothing rule had gone, the hat business had gone, the back door had gone. We came in through the front door.

The change was felt most keenly by the smaller shops, whose hours had been longest before the war. Some shopworkers found the new leisure time that was suddenly available took some adjusting to. A shop-girl recalls.

> It was a big come-down really. It was ever so funny at first because you didn't know what to do with yourself in the evening, being so used to going home in the cold and dark and not doing anything. Then suddenly you could go to dances, or to the pictures without seeing only half the film. The bosses weren't very happy with all this free time and were absolutely sure they'd go bankrupt because of closing so early.

Price controls and quotas froze the competition between shops and held up the advance of the entrepreneurs. Shortages also changed shop assistants' attitudes towards their customers. Some of the old servility went.

> Before the war we really had to sell goods. When the war came along it put the customer in the position of asking, 'Would you happen to have such a thing?' We were calling the tune really. They were calling the tune before the war. That's when I think shop assistants started not to care as much, because it was no use the customers getting shirty, because they just couldn't get anything.

During the war years the only area in which enterprise really flourished, and where the laws of supply and demand continued to operate without inhibition, was the illegal world of the black market. These conditions survived into the period of economic stringency that followed victory in 1945. Though goods began to trickle back into the shops many government regulations were kept on. Rationing did not end until 1953. Price controls and the allocation of goods on a quota system continued, and so the large multiples increased their share of sales by only one per cent between 1939 and 1950. But some of the major companies began to amalgamate and to take over smaller chains or shops, so that when controls were eventually lifted they would be in a more powerful position.

From the austerity of post-war Britain retailers took a close interest in what was happening in the different circumstances of the United States. Larger shops, where customers helped themselves and paid at a check-out desk, were transforming American shopping. In Britain there were far fewer goods with which to stock the shelves, but labour was scarce, government was preaching the need for greater efficiency everywhere, and the retailers saw a way to increase their productivity. Unlike some other industries they grasped it quickly, for the potential of self-service was seen by large and small shops alike as a way of saving costs. The Co-op made early and unsuccessful experiments. Tesco opened its first store in 1947. Daisy Hyams was working for Jack Cohen, Tesco's founder.

> At that time we were not permitted to spend more than £100 in altering a store, and we altered our first store at St Albans. And it wasn't a success for the simple reason that the products were in short supply, the clients were in short supply, and there was still rationing, and so it wasn't a success and we turned it back into a service store in 1949.

Tesco, like others who started self-service early, met much resistance from customers. The shop where Rita Greendale was working also changed over.

> The customers hated it. They wouldn't pick up a basket. They were very suspicious. They didn't want to buy very much, and they felt belittled, I think, at having a basket with perhaps two Oxos in, and a small bread loaf. And people hated the way there was nobody to talk to them. People didn't feel they'd done a proper morning's shopping, if they hadn't had all these conversations which took up the assistant's time. And so the boss tried it for about a year and then it had to be closed and he reopened it later on.

An angry customer at the first Sainsbury's self-service store threw a basket at the proprietor. But whatever people's initial reaction self-service had come to stay, and though some grocery chains held back for a while, all followed eventually. As rationing ended, and the general level of prosperity rose in the 1950s and 1960s, the supermarkets grew bigger, and the multiples selling clothes, bicycles, radios and other goods adapted their own versions of self-service. Those who were slow to do this withered, or were driven out of business.

Detailed instructions to guide customers who might be confused, at a shop which converted to self-service in 1950

As this transformation in the nature of shops was taking place, a further change was on the way in the pattern of ownership. Retailing became very big business, speeded by the rising values of high-street property. This brought fresh injections of capital from new sources. In 1952 financier Charles Clore had bought up 850 shoe shops, not because he was interested in selling footwear but because investment in prime high-street sites offered potential profits if he were to sell them again. In practice, once he had acquired the shoe shops and the factories that went with them, Clore set out to buy up all the other shoe chains, and stayed in retailing for its own sake. In every branch of the trade the more powerful and financially successful groups swallowed up those that were less effective. By the 1970s the grocery field was dominated by three large companies which between them had over half the sales. The multiples as a whole raised their share of total sales from a quarter in 1950 to almost half by the mid-1970s.

The rapid expansion of the chains continued to be at the expense of the independent department stores and individual shops, although those with good managements were able to find a new role for themselves. The most marked decline was in the fortunes of the Co-op, which had been the first of the large-scale retailers at the turn of the century and was now paying the penalty. As early as 1958 a report prepared by the movement observed that the customer was 'a great deal more exacting than her predecessor of even two decades ago'. She was demanding clean, well-laid-out modern premises, attractive windows and bright lighting. The new multiples had given first priority to these factors, but

> If we ask what is the 'image' of a Co-operative shop in the public mind, the answer will not be a supermarket or new department store. It is more likely to be a ponderous, unrestored and unimaginative grocer-cum-butchery-cum-drapery cluster built in the early 1900s, still operating counter service, the window display old-fashioned, the exterior clumsy and badly in need of paint, the interior frowsy.[21]

The Co-ops made several attempts at renewing and defrowsing themselves. But in the late 1960s large-scale rationalisation was necessary,

117

and the number of shops fell by 40 per cent in five years. All other factors apart, the dividend system had ceased to be attractive in the new era of straight price-cutting that had now overtaken the retailers.

Like the rapid advance of the multiples in the thirties and the arrival of self-service in the fifties, the era of discounting in the sixties brought a fresh dynamic to retailing. Up to then the alliance between the manufacturers and the majority of retailers, under the system of resale price maintenance, meant that the price charged was the same whatever type of shop you bought in. The way to attract customers was still through choice and ease of shopping, not better value. There had always been a few discounters, led by Sir Jack Cohen and Tesco, who fought continual skirmishes with the suppliers. It was competition from these early discounters that eventually forced other large chains to cut prices on branded goods, and brought pressure for the removal of RPM to benefit the consumer. In 1955 the first legal battle was won by the large stores, and in 1964 RPM was finally ended altogether by the Conservative government. Once started, the price competition did not stop. The way to cut prices still lower was through discount or warehouse outlets with small overheads and few trimmings. In food, KwikSave and ASDA led the way. Peter Asquith was one of those who set up the ASDA chain. Rather than competing in the high street itself, where property costs were high, they bought up old factories or mill buildings. Their first shop was in a cinema in Castleford in Yorkshire.

> People thought we were a bit round the twist. We had got to draw people maybe thirty yards from the main street, which to many seemed impossible. We did this, so much so that brother Fred used to stand by the door saying, 'Five more, please.' They used to queue to get in. The aisles were so crowded we used body heat to keep the store warm. We'd no heaters.

After the end of RPM, discounters emerged to compete with established shops across almost the whole range of goods, from carpets to car tyres and electrical appliances. At first many of them were buccaneering and independent operators. As they forced prices down generally, discounting was itself institutionalised and produced its own new multiples. Some of the shops, both large and small, which continued to offer the traditional degree of service felt aggrieved by what was happening. Norman Beale ran the department store that carries his family name in Bournemouth.

> We were being set up, as it were, by the price-cutters as the shop window, the nice people to deal with. The customers would come in to us and learn all about X, Y, Z and then go around to the cut-price operator, the discounter, and make her purchase, us having done all the work.

Fred Burgess ran a small electrical shop which sold refrigerators, washing machines, radios and televisions. He suffered from the discounters.

The thing that surprised most people in the retail trade at that time was the number of wholesalers who were supplying us in the past, who suddenly switched their tactics and started to supply direct to the public. We were in the silly situation of having to go to a supplier for certain goods who was already supplying direct to our own customers.

There was little room for sportsmanship or sentiment as the discounting wave swept through. Politicians had allowed *laissez-faire* to reign for the benefit of the customer. The consumer had to make his own judgement about whether he wanted traditional service or the cheapest possible prices. Peggy Hinxman had run a small village shop in Pudsey from before the war, and felt she provided a community service over and above the practical business of shopping.

> People used to come in with all their thoughts, their difficulties. They used to sit on the chair and tell us, and we listened and we tried to be sympathetic. And this was part and parcel of our way of life.

When a discount store opened nearby, Mrs Hinxman found they were selling many goods to the public at prices which were the same as she was charged by her own wholesaler. Many of her customers deserted, or only bought small orders.

> We noticed that a lot of people were coming into the shop with various ASDA goods and yet asking us for an ounce of yeast, and bits and pieces that you didn't make a profit on. It was very grieving to a person who was trying to give of her best and at the best price they could afford, to be confronted with such things. We thought about joining the enemy and having our own little supermarket, but it was a matter of retraining and restandardising everything, changing our whole mode of life.

Time and again in retailing it was a case of survival of the fittest. The abolition of resale price maintenance had an equally direct effect on many small shopkeepers, who considered themselves as much a part of the fabric of British society as, for example, the small farmer. But whereas small farmers engaged the public sympathy and had their interests cherished by politicians, small traders did not. Their lobbying was ineffective. When RPM was abolished Mrs Hinxman said she felt let down.

> I often thought, our recommended selling price is our wage. I wonder, if price maintenance stopped with the miner, the bus driver, anybody like that, how they would like their wage cutting because there was a man who was prepared to do it for less money. This was a very bitter pill for us to swallow. Our wage was not guaranteed as a private business person. We were having to cut our wage in order to stay in business.

In other countries in Europe small shopkeepers were treated more sympathetically. In Britain governments would not interfere with the free play of market forces in an area which was so close to voters' pockets. Though Mrs Hinxman's shop closed down, hundreds of thousands of similar independent shops survived by converting to self-service or by leaving the grocery trade and selling something else. A new force in retailing came with the arrival of thousands of Asian traders expelled from Uganda in the 1970s. With whole families working together, and putting in hours of the kind that the shopworker's union had been fighting since the 1890s, many managed to make profitable businesses out of small corner shops otherwise threatened with closure. Ramijid Patel opened a shop in Dulwich.

Left: *Village shop, Sussex. The spread of car ownership and the end of RPM threatened many country shops*

Above: *Closure in Tottenham Court Road, London. As property values rose, retailers had to maximise the return from their floorspace*

> When I took that shop the hours were short. I decided that if I wanted to make the business viable I must have long hours because it was a residential area. My wife and I worked 100 hours each per week. Besides that I had help from my children. That shop I kept for four years and I didn't have any holidays for four years.

Mr Patel's family now has three shops.

> Refugees have nothing to lose in their life so naturally they are the hardest working people. After ten or fifteen years I might be like an Englishman, or any shopkeeper.

As retailing continued to expand, the nature of the job continued to change. Even after prepackaging came in it was still necessary for shop assistants to know the stock and the prices. With the coming of self-service, the main task was filling the shelves and running the tills. They still had to read the prices and key them onto the cash registers. With the newest electronic point-of-sale equipment cashiers simply pass an electronic beam over a price tag, and the computer not only adds up the bill and calculates the change, but notifies the warehouse for stock-control purposes.

To an older generation of managers, many of the changes are for the worse. Jimmy Bubear thinks that retailing, as he understood it, has gone.

In retailing we had to fight for sales. And we had windows. You advertised your merchandise through your windows, then you backed up your windows with specialist displays on the counters. You had service. If a woman came in for curtain rail on the hardware, you would have a girl trained who could tell her the length she wanted, how many runners, how many bits and pieces. Today there is nobody there to serve you. Our girls had to know their merchandise. Today it's all hanging up. You have to work things out for yourself.

Managers no longer have the freedom in multiples that they used to have. Daisy Hyams of the Tesco group describes the firm control that large companies now apply from the centre.

You cannot leave it to a manager's ingenuity to lay out his store. You have to give them directions as to how each fixture is laid out, how much goes on each particular commodity, each particular product. So a manager becomes an administrator today, he doesn't have to be a trader.

To the old-style managers it was the trading that provided much of the appeal of the job. Jimmy Bubear sympathises with the people in charge of modern supermarkets.

I don't think they are getting the same kick from it. I think they are automatons. All they seem to do is fill up the shelves and then a customer comes along and helps herself with a basket. He may be specialised and have a bigger display of baked beans, or cosmetics but he doesn't sell it, he doesn't serve it, he doesn't tell the customer which colour of face powder a girl wants.

The number of women employed rose to far outnumber men. Before the second war the multiples had forced girls who married to resign. Now many married women work part-time or temporarily. Though the constant turnover of staff remained a problem for the unions, the rise of the big groups helped them. One large store could employ several hundred. Tom Cynog-Jones was an USDAW organiser.

As the stores got bigger they became in a sense small factories, and therefore they became strong trade union units, and that is true today. The large supermarket is normally well organised, as a closed shop. This was not possible with small shops.

The further increase in the size of shops provided yet another stimulus for change in the 1970s, with the coming of superstores and hypermarkets. Big groups who had once jostled for sites in the city centre now competed for developments on the by-pass, or out in the country. The barn-like shops were up to 100,000 square feet in size, when 1500 square feet had been regarded as spacious before the war.

121

They were run with mechanised warehouse handling and computerised ordering systems. The only new factor was that retailers, used to un-restricted and virtually unregulated conditions, met growing planning-permission difficulties when they tried to find sites for hypermarkets. Otherwise, the most distinctive feature of retailing remained: change came easily, helped by readily available finance, good business brains, and the absence of entrenched attitudes and practices.

A photograph taken at regular intervals over eighty years of the same stretch of high street in any British town would show how frequent the changes have been. Particular types of independent shops disappeared. The big multiples of another generation, like Timothy White's or Woolworth's, fell behind. The old chains that did survive were the ones which were most flexible in what they sold: having started as a railway station newsagent, and become a high street book-seller, W. H. Smith took itself into selling computers. Marks and Spencer began selling books. It was possible for completely new busi-nesses like Habitat, Bejam, Laura Ashley or Mothercare to mushroom just on the energy or vision of founders who spotted a new need. Laura Ashley began as a textile designer working from home, and opened her first shop in 1968. Now she and her husband have sixty shops, 4000 employees and a turnover of £60 million a year.

> We have really just specialised in our own field, and what we
> have done is from our first success we have noticed what sells
> best, and when we have brought out new collections we go in
> that direction. It always has to be something we love ourselves,
> we never produce anything tongue in cheek.

The same responsiveness to the customer's changing interests marked the independent shops that did best. Thousands of new specialists opened up, selling everything from antiques to health foods.

Though many retail businesses were huge, their managements were very different from professional managements in other areas. There was no textbook way of running shops, and the most successful depended on the flair or taste of one person, or remained under the domination of families that established them in the first place. The

Mothercare grew up in the 1960s when its founder, Selim Zilkha, saw a gap in the market that was not being filled. The group was bought by another new chain, Habitat

Sieffs, the Lewises, or the Sainsburys continued to pursue particular business philosophies and their own well-tried formulas. Some concentrated on quality, some on a particular ambience or target customer, some simply on price. Discounter Peter Asquith explains his own philosophy.

> Take as little as you can as often as you can. As much as you can get at the lowest possible margin. It's very tempting to go for that extra one per cent but once you do that the other fellow next door can knock that one per cent off and he's better than you.

Lord Sieff, a grandson of a founder of Marks and Spencer, has a different, but equally profitable, approach.

> We are rarely the cheapest, but we hope in our particular field we are offering the best that money can buy at that price. Unless it's good enough for us and our families and our executives, then it's not good enough for any customer.

The efficiency of British retailing is hard to measure against that of other countries because it faces no foreign competition. But on any account there has been a most dramatic rise in productivity and earnings. As in farming, the other instance in which a great increase in productivity was helped by a co-operative but divided workforce, shopworkers shared few of the gains. Though profit ratios of the big retail companies were among the highest in the country, the general level of shop wages was low. But unlike cotton, aircraft or steel, and other industries which have been periodically rescued or protected by government, retailing has been left almost entirely to itself – to sink or swim.

CHAPTER 6: SHIPBUILDING
DIVISION OF LABOUR

It was all in the work. You had your shipwrights, your platers, you had your riveters, you had your engineers, you had your blacksmiths, you had the joiners, you had your caulkers, your drillers, electricians, and many more small trades, and of course there was the labouring man. He was out of the question really.

Shipwright

In shipbuilding I think you've got to appreciate that things went wrong in the last century, and got progressively worse as modern technology came in. Attitudes got more and more entrenched.

Scottish manager

Shipbuilding was mass unemployment in the thirties. Poor working conditions. It was a hard industry. No pensions. You could be laid off at an hour's notice so naturally you didn't love the boss.

Shop steward

The success of the shipyards in their greatest days at the turn of the century was based on an intricate division of labour. Specialist craftsmen in Britain had skills no other country could match. At the heart of the shipbuilding process were the riveters, who were paid for each hundred rivets they knocked down. High up on wooden planks beside the hulls on the building berths, the riveters worked up to ten hours a day, in all weathers. When the wind was too high they tied themselves on to the staging with ropes. The fusillade of hammer blows ringing along the shipbuilding rivers, and the flying sparks, were the principal sound and spectacle of a prosperous industry. Bert Barry began as a riveter.

> First of all the job is prepared by the shipwrights and the platers. The plater shapes the plate, the shipwright files it, and then we come into it. The riveting squad was comprised of two riveters, one holder up, and a heater. There was one left-handed, one right-handed riveter.

The 'heater' kept a small coke fire going and heated the rivets until they were red hot. He tossed them to the 'holder up', who bumped the rivet into the hole, and held it there with a long hammer. From the other side of the plate the two riveters knocked it down.

> They do alternate blows, left, right, left, right, until that rivet is flattened right into the hole. They have got to get it nice and tight you see. Now that is basic riveting. The harder job for the hand riveters was the bottom of the ship. When you were under the bottom you were twisted over, with the men inside putting the rivets down the hole, and you were underneath knocking them in. It was a difficult job.

The riveters earned the highest wages in the shipbuilding areas. In the north-east, and down the Clyde, as well as at Belfast and on the Mersey, there were hundreds of small family-owned shipyards which before the First World War built the most advanced steamships at the lowest prices. At the peak they were responsible for eight out of ten new ships in the world. Between 1900 and 1914 they were still producing six out of ten of the world's ships in a domination based on frugal management and craft skill. But as the First World War ended it was clear that world markets had changed for the shipbuilders as for everyone else.

Methods were also altering. In 1917, as Bert Barry began his apprenticeship as a hand riveter, he was learning a skill that was already becoming redundant. Pneumatic riveting hammers were coming into British yards after their much faster introduction in America and Germany. They could be worked by untrained men after a few days, and could put in rivets much faster. Today the power tools have long since been replaced by welding, and there has been a revolution in shipbuilding methods. But as the technology changed, the British shipbuilding industry declined. Of all the readjustments which old British industries had to make, that of shipbuilding was the most painful. For

When the Mauretania *left the Tyne in 1907, she was the pride of Britain's shipbuilders*

125

most of the twentieth century it was held back by attitudes and conflicts rooted in the conditions of eighty years ago.

When the *Mauretania* was launched in 1906 she was the biggest ship ever sent down the Tyne. From her steam-turbine engines to the electric passenger lifts that ran between her nine decks, she was also the most mechanically efficient. The system of shipbuilding that produced her was highly efficient, too. It was calculated that, at a time when there were 122,000 British shipbuilding workers, their average output per head was twelve tons per year, twice as much as the American shipyard worker, and four times as much as in Germany. The *Mauretania* took eighteen months from signature of the contract to launching, and the speed at which it was built was largely due to what was called the 'squad system', of specialisation. Skill was broken down in such a way that managers could employ, on different days, at different stages, precisely the right number of men they needed, drawn from the pool of thousands of shipyard craftsmen who lived in the back-to-back houses that lined the river banks. Hiring was done through the 'market system'.

> The market system is where workmen went each day in the mornings and stood in a crowd hoping the foremen would come out and offer them a job. Foremen actually felt men's muscles, and said, 'Ah, you seem a good strong lad, you can start.'

Pairs of riveters working from the wooden staging beside a ship's hull. They belonged to the Boilermakers' Society

Shipyard workers coming up the bank from the Wallsend yard where the Mauretania *was being built*

The men who worked for the family-owned shipbuilding firms were employed casually with no security. They spent a 54-hour week in yards where icy winds blew off the water, and worked with heavy steel plates, red-hot rivets, and unfenced punching and bending machines.

Conditions were primitive. When you walked about and it was raining, everything was all mud. And it was manhandled. 'Armstrongs Patent' the men used to call it. You know, arm strong, a lot of heavy work particularly for the platers' helpers, and it was dangerous in the yard.

I saw a boy killed right beside me one day, a boy who lived right next door to me. I was working on the bottom of the ship on the rivets and outside they were hoisting a big heavy shell plate up, and I heard a hell of a clatter and I went out. I wish I hadn't went out. The boy was only 14½, and he was lying there.

You'd be walking on two planks, about 60 or 70 feet up. They used to put this staging right around the ship, and you had to stand on that. The ends of these planks were put through wooden uprights, tied with what they call grass rope. Secure so they shouldn't slide. But if somebody wanted a bit of rope it was nothing for them to take a knife and cut it off. That left a danger for someone else. One day, I went along a plank and fell off, and it was a bit of grass rope hanging that saved me, because I grasped it.

More than half the men who routinely endured these conditions had served five-year apprenticeships. They did not identify themselves as shipbuilders, or as employees at particular yards, but as members of a particular craft. They were platers, riveters, caulkers, burners, ship-wrights, drillers, blacksmiths or plumbers; or they were joiners, car-penters, cabinet-makers, upholsterers, french polishers. Most of the trades were represented by a union, sometimes more than one, which guarded entry jealously, as well as protecting the 'trade rights' of the work their members performed. 'It is our duty', said the Amalgamated Society of Engineers' rule book in 1891,

> to exercise the same care and watchfulness over that in which we have a vested interest as the physician does who holds a diploma, or the author who is protected by copyright.[22]

The semi-skilled were almost as specialised in the work they did, and clearly identified themselves as plater's helpers, rivet heaters, or riggers. The hierarchy was plain.

> The manager was a man that was remote. He'd never think of coming and having a word with you. It was like the Indian caste system. If you were a craftsmen he might give you a nod if he happened to look at you. But if you were just a poor labourer he would just walk past with contempt. Some crafts-men would treat labourers with contempt, too.

The industry was characterised by insecurity. For the men there was the fear of lay-offs, but the managers were afraid too, haunted by the spectre of foreign competition even before the First War. They knew that their grasp of the world market rested on cheaper prices. But ship-building was the most 'unsheltered' of trades, and international ship-owners could easily switch their orders elsewhere, and there were signs that the technical lead was beginning to slip. Germany had built a new navy, and fast new passenger liners to which the *Mauretania* was a response. While British marine engineers still concentrated on the further perfection of steam power, European engine companies were far ahead in developing the patents of Dr Rudolf Diesel, for internal com-bustion engines that burnt oil.

However, the principal concern of the British builders was not with design, but with the fact that many foreign yards paid lower wages and worked longer hours, and might at some point undercut their prices. At the time when the industry was at its very strongest, a British naval architect, David Pollock, blamed most of the problem on the workers.

> There is now much which British shipbuilders must not disdain to learn from their foreign competitors. This is especially true in matters in which the employed as well as the employers are concerned, viz. the working methods and the time worked . . . The greater steadiness and tractability of workers in Germany

and America form one important reason for the progress made in recent times. There is not the same time lost or wilfully squandered, nor are the same objections raised by workers in either of these countries to the introduction of new and labour-saving tools.[23]

Allegations that unions imposed restrictions on new equipment and output were often made in British industry. But shipbuilding had a particular difficulty and it was the major snag of the single-trade 'squad-system' from which the employers otherwise gained so much. Demarcation disputes went back to the time when wood was replaced by iron and steel as the material for ships, and the old shipwrights and carpenters found their work taken by boilermakers and engineers who could deal with metal. As ships became more complicated, other new skills were introduced, until over twenty unions were represented in the shipyards and arguments between them were constant.

Debates about the nature of tools and materials were conducted from the 1880s, as they were for years to come. Platers fought with shipwrights about who should erect sections. Fitters battled plumbers about their historic rights to handle iron pipes as distinct from lead pipes. Carpenters and joiners argued over the thickness of wood that each should deal with, citing earlier craftsmen all the way back to Noah. An exasperated Scottish shipbuilder said:

> Whether a plumber may join a 2-inch pipe, but not one of $2\frac{1}{4}$ inches, whether a joiner may dub a plank or a shipwright may plane a rail, must appear to a disinterested person tremendously trivial.[22]

But such questions were not trivial to skilled men, who were barred from changing their craft, and whose livelihood was at stake. A set of procedures for dealing with demarcation disputes gradually evolved. Tribunals of other trade unionists were established, and printed lists were produced to mark out the boundaries between different trades. But nothing more fundamental was done to solve the problem itself. Demarcation practices proliferated into every part of the shipbuilding process, ossifying custom and practice, and preventing changes in equipment and deployment. The few who worried about the long-term health of the industry found little support in figures, however. It was calculated that Britain had built 61 per cent of the world tonnage in 1914, a slight increase over the 1900 figure.

In the First World War the shipyards became a centre of national attention, as they struggled to replace the merchant tonnage sunk by German submarines and to build warships. The emergency brought some dramatic changes in the way they worked. The Admiralty took control of all merchant shipbuilding, and decided what was to be built and by whom. They controlled costs, and the necessity for something approaching mass production meant that many techniques were learnt, only to be lost again. 'Standard' ships, taking seven months to build, were turned out in five designs.

The changes for the shipyard workers were equally radical. With the Treasury Agreement, union leaders were persuaded to suspend demarcation rules and other restrictions and to allow 'dilution', which meant that the unskilled could do the work normally done by skilled men. In return firms' profits were limited, and there was a promise that the old ways would be restored after the war. Women came in to heat rivets, and paint, and work as labourers. Alf Senior remembers how they helped the shipwrights.

> I had about twenty women working with me on the launching ways. All they did was just labour. They went across and got the wood, what they called the slivers, that was pieces to go in between. It was packing really, for the launch-ways, and they used to go over with a big barrow, maybe four of them, and bring it over. Then we would just have to pick it up and do the job, which saved us from going there. It was all right for us.

Whatever the union leaders said, the rank and file were not con-

vinced that the surrender of rules and customs was necessary; instead they wanted the return of all the skilled men from the army. Nor did they believe that the promise of restoration would be kept, and they were frightened that if work was allowed to go faster their piece rates would be cut. After a while the agreement was given the force of law by the Munitions of War Act, which forbade strikes and provided for special tribunals to prosecute offenders for absenteeism or bad time-keeping. The tough policy exacerbated unrest in many areas, particularly on Clydeside. A Board of Trade Committee, set up to study the industry's post-war prospects, reported:

> Many witnesses have told us that, in their opinion, the policy of labour (particularly as regards the restriction of output, which they allege is adopted throughout the trade concerned) and the relations between capital and labour have a more intimate bearing on the future of the industry than any other matter.[24]

Victory in 1918 saw an enormous boom in the shipyards. Nearly 1700 British ships had been sunk during the war, and owners hurried to replace them. No ships had been built for foreign owners either, so they also queued up with orders. Yards were recapitalised. In 1920 a record two million tons were launched. But the boom did not last. There were too many ships at a time when world trade was down. Hundreds of confiscated German ships added to the surplus. As with the steel industry, the wartime expansion made things worse. By the war's end Britain had the berths to construct up to four million tons a year, just when foreign countries had also built up their yards. Warship orders almost stopped after an international agreement to limit naval armament. Many yards closed, including some that had only just been extended. As the shipbuilders began their long ordeal between the two world wars, they realised that, though fewer ships were being built in total, their own share was falling. They had lost their pre-war lead in price. Though British owners mostly stayed loyal, Norwegian or Greek or South American ship-owners, whose orders for tramp shipping had been the bread and butter of most of the small yards, particularly on the Tyne, Tees, and Wear, took their business to newer firms in Germany, Holland, or Scandinavia.

Conditions for the shipyard workers were almost unchanged from before the war. Only a few covered yards had been built. There were now more electric cranes, and so there was less lifting and winching, but it was still heavy, cold, dirty and dangerous work. Plater's labourers had bleeding hands from manhandling steel plates with rough edges. Falls were common. Inside the ship there were poisonous fumes from red lead. In one respect conditions had actually got worse. Noise had always been bad in shipyards, and shipyard workers shouted into each other's ears or used sign language. The pneumatic hammers were noisier still.

Women labouring in the yards, 1916. Only a few did more skilled work, because of the controversy over 'dilution'

131

As the pneumatic machines got stronger in power, and more of them, the racket was terrific, especially working in enclosed spaces. You came out of the job you were working on to where it was more open to get a bit of relief. After about a fortnight or three weeks it didn't seem quite so bad. Then when you'd been there two months you said, 'It's getting great, I can stand that noise now'. And when it got to years it sounded quieter still. Until one day you were talking to your wife and she would say, 'Don't shout'. And I said, 'I am not shouting'. And she said, 'You are. And I am shouting to you so you can hear.' You didn't realise you were deaf.

Owners of a new ship and managers of the yard that built it, at a launch ceremony in 1921. As the post-war slump set in, there were few replacement orders

The major post-war improvement was a cut in the working week from 54 hours to 47, but there were more disputes and strikes over differentials and pay, and the work was now even less secure, because there was less work to go round. Men were taken on for a week, or two or three days, and then let go.

When in 1926 a substantial order for five ships for Furness Withy, a British shipping line, was placed in Germany there was an outcry. Unions and employers agreed to hold a joint inquiry into the nature of the competition they were up against. Their findings confirmed that the Germans and the Dutch were working 54 hours a week and not 47 as in Britain. Foreign yards were often better equipped, with more and better cranes, complete electrification and more pneumatic tools. The inquiry also tackled the thorny question of demarcation, asserting that it was possible to 'secure greater elasticity and interchangeability without infringement of the broad principles of craftsmanship'.[25] There was no agreement about how this might be done, but the employers insisted on

TIMES, FRIDAY, MARCH 6, 192

ORDER FOR GERMAN SHIPYARDS.

FIVE MOTOR VESSELS

RESULT OF LOWER PRICES.

(By Our Shipping Correspondent.)

A great deal of discussion is certain, properly, to centre round the placing by British shipping interests of a contract for five large cargo motor-ships with a German shipbuilding company. It may stated that the contract has been on behalf of one of the lin

Drillers, who belonged to a section of the Shipwrights' Association, photographed together. Each trade was proud of its identity

listing more than fifty flexible practices they would like to achieve. For instance,

> Hole boring: Any trade may bore and tap odd holes as they require them in their work . . .
>
> Water testing: Caulkers may carry out the whole operation . . .
>
> Cutting out rivets: The trade that drills or burns the rivet may do their own centering, punching back and re-countersinking . . .

The loss of orders to foreign yards also brought into question the traditional way in which managers dealt with customers. Freddy Hopper remembers the close contacts between the shipowners and particular shipyards.

> They knew if they went back to them it wouldn't be quite such hard work thinking things out. They knew what to expect. We had lots of firms that came back to us. If we thought it was time they had a new ship we used to just pop in and see them, tell them what it would cost. At that time it might be £85,000 for a 10,000-tonner. 'We'll think about it. Thanks ever so much for calling.' And you got it that way.

Harold Towers, whose grandfather and father and uncle had run the firm which he eventually took over, also saw this informality.

> I can remember my grandfather coming back from London with an order on the back of a matchbox, and not even a contract was signed. An exchange of letters was quite good enough, good faith between two people.

133

In the late 1920s before the full force of the slump struck, British shipbuilders were more obsessed with foreign competition, and mutual recrimination about the reasons for it, than ever before. The old family managements were accused of an amateurish approach to business, poor salesmanship and a poor record with science and research into ship design. They had been slow to convert from steam to motor ships, though this had more to do with the conservatism of ship-owners. Investment in the re-equipment of the yards was proceeding faster abroad.

When criticised for not buying more modern machinery a Scottish shipbuilder, Sir James Lithgow, replied:

> The real fact is that the invention of pneumatic tools has been a blow to British shipbuilding, looked at from an insular standpoint. It has converted many operations in which our men were specially skilled into purely unskilled jobs, for which all our foreign rivals have an ample supply of suitable labour.[26]

Lithgow complained that British workers wanted to be paid the skilled rate, and then to run new machinery at a speed which made it impossible to reduce costs. But neither he, nor any other shipyard manager, questioned the system of institutionalised insecurity which lay behind those attitudes.

A few years later the grass grew high on the building berths, birds nested in the steelwork of the cranes, and over 60 per cent of a once great industry's workforce was on the dole. The slump of the early 1930s was so severe that for a time all the fears about foreign competition seemed irrelevant. Shipbuilding all over the world was at a standstill. The greatest casualty of the depression in world trade was shipping. There was no call for new vessels so long as millions of tons of serviceable ships were laid up in ports and estuaries, waiting for the cargoes to return. In 1932 when 20 per cent of the world's merchant shipping was idle, only 307 new ships were built in the whole world. At one point only two out of 72 berths on the Tyne were occupied. The post-war increase in capacity was blamed. There were more shipyards than could ever be needed. But though yards were idle, only a few went bankrupt and were eliminated by market forces. One manager explained this tenaciousness at the time.

> Shipbuilders die hard. They hang on in the hope that competitors may go under and that things will get better . . . It is common to find the third, fourth or even fifth generation at the helm. Family pride and prestige are at stake. Some of these men would prefer to fight on and go down fighting rather than surrender. Intense individualism is in their blood.[27]

The shipbuilding managers could live off their reserves or family fortunes accumulated in better times. The unemployed riveters and platers, joiners and plumbers were not so well placed. Bert Barry was unemployed for much of the thirties.

Palmer's shipyard at Jarrow went bankrupt in 1933, and was sold to National Shipbuilder's Security Ltd in the following year

I got to the point where I was going looking for work in the shipyard and I really didn't mind if the foreman didn't see me. I'd lost my confidence. It was an insidious feeling that you didn't think you could manage again after being away from it for a year or more. Some men got into a very low way. Others went on a fiddle. Where I lived they went and stole coal. That was their fiddle. Some people went away to Australia. Some went down south.

When the companies did come up with a plan to 'rationalise' the industry, their solution brought added bitterness. National Shipbuilder's Security Ltd was formed in 1930 in a collective move by all the shipbuilding companies, backed by the Bank of England. By putting a levy on the sale of those new ships that were built in yards still working, NSS would use its funds to purchase and then close down other yards. Whole firms disappeared, as well as individual yards within bigger groups. By 1937 a million tons of capacity had gone, a reduction of a third. In their own words NSS 'sterilised' the yards they closed, and their lawyers drew up covenants preventing shipbuilding from ever taking place there again. In a town with almost no other industries, such a closure removed the last hope of better times returning for the unemployed. NSS argued that their sacrifices were necessary, for the greater good of the industry at large. For the workers there was no compensation.

> I remember NSS came up and we discussed it. 'Oh,' I said, 'that's very good, and what percentage do the retired men that have been thrown on the scrap-heap get? Is there any fund to recompense some of them?' Only the employers were getting the benefit, you see. The workers were getting nothing.

In Britain 'rationalisation' was a scrapping process alone. In Germany mergers and re-equipment, and closer link-ups with steel-works, made it a more positive process. As other industries looked increasingly to the government for support, shipbuilders complained that foreign countries subsidised their merchant fleets, and gave direct aid to their yards. Signs of a government change of heart came with the aid given to Cunard in 1933, when Cunard and White Star agreed to merge as the price for a cheap loan to finance the building of two new transatlantic liners. The return to work on Ship 534, which became the *Queen Mary*, was greeted as the beginning of better days, and a pipe band played the shipworkers back through the gates of the John Brown yard at Clydebank. More widespread government help came with the 'Scrap and Build' scheme, and new subsidies for tramp shipping.

Though there was a trade revival, rearmament finally did most to save Britain's shipbuilders towards the end of the thirties. Naval ship-building had stopped almost totally for a while, but in 1935 the Admiralty put forward a plan to spend £245 million over five years on building up the fleet. Awareness that a war would require a strong British merchant navy also made the government pay more attention to shipbuilding.

Driller at Clydebank, 1934

Work began again on the Clyde on the large Cunarder Queen Mary *in 1933, after government financial help*

When war broke out, every usable building berth was occupied. But though there was work again, many problems had just been postponed till the end of another war, or until the end of another post-war boom. Once the country was at war, foreign competition over price could be forgotten. The demand for the greatest possible tonnage, in both navy and merchant ships, itself revealed the rundown state the industry was now in. Sufficient berths were available despite all the closures, but the skilled men needed to work them had gone. Only half as many were attached to the industry as there had been in the peak years. Though unemployment still continued, many of those on the register were old and in poor health. There were not enough young managers either, and the intake of students to the Institute of Naval Architects had fallen by three-quarters. Hardly any apprentices had been taken into the yards in the depression. Electricians, fitters, and turners were in particularly short supply. Many had been drawn away to the better wages in the new aircraft factories.

With no time to increase production by modernising the yards, the Ministry of Labour scrutinised the way men worked in shipbuilding, and investigated the sensitive areas of craft skill and demarcation. This time an Act of Parliament did the work of the Treasury Agreement of 1915, and guaranteed the restoration of all trade practices after the war. But though the introduction of unskilled men and women to do work normally done by skilled union grades went fast in other war industries, the shipbuilders were highly suspicious. Less real progress was made than in the First World War, when the same problems had arisen.

On several occasions war work was stopped by strikes and demarcation disputes. On the Clyde, the boilermakers struck when members of the Constructional Engineering Union were allowed on the ships. On Tyneside boilermakers went out over who should operate a new American flame-planing machine, which had to be withdrawn from use. Ernest Bevin found both sides of shipbuilding stubborn. On two occasions he tried to get the whole industry transferred to direct government control, so that the work could be carried out as a 'public service and not limited by the pre-war conceptions of private interest and limited individualism'.[28]

The only new factor in labour relations was the start of Yard Committees, as part of the Joint Production Committee movement that had begun in the aircraft factories under shop steward pressure. By the end of the war all yards had committees so that management and unions could discuss ways of increasing production and pass on information and suggestions. For the workers this recognition was important.

> You could talk to them, put your cards on the table and criticise them, where before you were wandering round the yard, a lot of individuals grumbling about this and that and the other.

The committees brought a new sense of power to the workforce, strengthened by the acute labour shortage. Bert Barry remembers.

> When we were sitting in the air-raid shelters for our dinners, and we got on about politics, they were unanimous that they would not put up with things after the war that they had suffered before. If the management came messing them about then the management could just go to hell.

Welding was replacing riveting during World War II

Among both shipyard workers and managers the new technique that brought most controversy was welding ship-plates together instead of riveting. Before the war Britain had been slow and cautious with welded ships, and many more had been built in the United States and Germany. For a long time Lloyds held back from classifying all welded ships as 'A-1'. They doubted their reliability after some spectacular accidents in which welds fractured, and ships broke in two. These accidents intensified continuing argument in the yards, as one foreman remembers:

> When I was walking round the ship the men would say, 'Look at the welding.' I'd say, 'You're going to tell me it's no good.' 'Yes.' He'd be a machine riveter that was talking. I'd say, 'Do you remember the hand men, how they used to attack you when we changed from hand work to pneumatic riveting?' The handmen used to say, 'You canna go to sea in a ship like that. Built by machines.' Well, when the welding came out, the pneumatic riveters would say, 'I wouldn't go to sea in a welded ship.' They had no confidence in welding at all, the riveters.

The Admiralty was also suspicious. Sir Leonard Redshaw was working at the Vickers yard at Barrow-in-Furness.

> We were struggling to build submarines as fast as we could. We wanted to weld them in part or in full, but the Ministry

would not agree. Then one day they brought into Barrow a German submarine they'd captured, plonked it in front of us, and it was all welded. Then of course there was a tremendous change of attitude, but the irony was that I had worked on all welded submarine parts in Germany in 1935 but they wouldn't listen to me.

But with the shortage of riveters and with growing experience, more welding was done and new techniques were developed. Welding made its greatest impact on shipbuilding methods in the United States, which took the main load of allied merchant shipbuilding. Thousands of standard Liberty and Victory ships were built in newly laid-out yards. With the space available for assembly-line production, and no burden of folk history to inhibit them, the Americans used previously untrained labour to prove that there were other ways of shipbuilding, which might count after the war was over.

British shipbuilders achieved astonishing feats during the war, especially with ship repairing. But many of them were triumphs over difficulties of equipment or organisation that were part of their own particular inheritance. War removed the normal commercial concerns for the managers. There was no need to worry about competition or salesmanship. Sir John Hunter was in the family yards, on the Tyne.

> We really only had two customers. One was the Admiralty and the other was the Ministry of War Transport. And all the work we did was allocated to us from these two sources.

After 1945 the forecasts that there would once again be a quick boom followed by a slump seemed to be confounded. For the next ten years the rivers were busy, jobs as plentiful as they had ever been, and firms made profits. For a few years, immediately after the Second World War, Britain again made over half the ships in the world. Outside the dry docks long lines of ships awaited repairs or reconversion back to civilian use. As these were cleared, owners pressed for replacements for the liners or tramps that had been sunk. The demand was immense as world trade began to revive again, and the British position was all the stronger because the German and Japanese yards had been reduced to rubble.

Some shipbuilders saw this as a moment of opportunity and warned of the competition that would arise soon:

> The race will be to the swift . . . we must apply our minds to the evolution of original and constructive ideas, and of advancing methods of production.

Robin Rowell of Hawthorn Leslie appealed for more co-operation among the firms, in research and practical matters.

> Individuals and small detached groups cannot progress far alone today.[29]

Nevertheless individualism remained the principal feature of British shipbuilding. Over thirty independent companies were still in business, many of them still controlled by family dynasties.

The Labour government was preoccupied with the nationalisation plans for coal, the railways and steel, and the shipbuilders were left to themselves. However keen they were to meet demand, they were frustrated by shortages of timber, fittings, paint, and above all steel. One of the effects of the shortages was to reduce the extra capacity for export and 'new' work. Yards wanted to give priority to their old customers. Most avoided standardisation on one type of ship, and prided themselves on their traditional versatility and ability to make a cargo liner, a naval ship and a tanker beside each other in the same yard. But some large yards went back to concentrating on passenger liners and expanded their facilities for these, just at the time when aircraft were about to take the passenger traffic.

The other way of meeting the demand for ships, once the steel was coming through, was by renewing the yards themselves. But most yard owners, remembering what had happened to their fathers when demand slackened after the First War, steadfastly refused to expand capacity or to make major changes. They made some improvements, but there was no great injection of new capital. Financial caution apart, they were so busy that they did not want to disrupt production. Ken Douglas was working at Pickersgills.

> With the need to replace tonnage after the war we had to keep what yards we had going full blast. We simply couldn't shut building berths down and delay deliveries to owners. They wouldn't wear that. So we had to put up with what we had.

Welding spread only slowly, partly because yards had to be reorganised to make best use of it, and partly because many owners still resisted it. There was almost no industry-financed research into the best ways of organising shipbuilding, and not much advance in the design of ships themselves, despite major progress in the war. With pressing demand, commercial attitudes were not to the fore among shipbuilders. Little selling skill was required when customers had no choice but to wait their turn in a queue. Little cost control was required when jobs were not done to a fixed price, but customers agreed to pay 'cost plus'. Labour and other charges were simply passed on to the purchaser of a new ship with 5 to 10 per cent on top for profit. Sir Leonard Redshaw remembers.

> In a place like Vickers in my time you could get a job where you might say you had a blank cheque to paradise . . . you were paid on costs plus profit, and immediately you had that in your establishment, you had inefficiency developing in those particular sectors. It was obvious to the thinking man.

Sandy Stephen came into his family shipbuilding firm in Scotland around this time.

Everything was very easy. People were able to make ends meet, we were able to make money. We could more or less within reason ask what we liked for our ships. Altogether it was a very happy time. There were underlying problems, which while we were making money didn't really rear their ugly heads till later.

The problem was that because it was cost-plus we weren't worried about keeping costs down, and because the ship-owners were making a lot of money, they developed expensive habits too, with the net result that we both became very in-efficient and un-cost-conscious.

The post-war boom lasted so long that even the old threat of foreign competition began to be forgotten. Employers who had remained con-scious of it still identified the problem in the same way that it had been seen before the First World War or in the 1920s. They believed that even if they did modernise, the unions would not allow them to use the new equipment. Managers had a catalogue of examples:

There were occasions when machines were bought and the men would not use them and they were laid in cold storage. I remember some welding machines, and it was two years before they were allowed to use them.

They wouldn't man the planing tables. We had them and for fourteen months they stood idle.

We got a one-man punch and we got a lot of opposition over this, because there used to be a plater and four helpers punch-ing with the old machine. We got it going eventually, produc-tion increased, and it became part of the establishment. There was opposition to any new machinery that they thought would possibly cause them to lose jobs.

Despite the years of plentiful work and the improvements that had taken place in hours and holidays and safety, the mistrust between the employers and the men was as great as ever. The employers had made no effort to change the casual nature of shipyard work. One shop steward recalls:

Even with full employment in the fifties and early sixties there were different building-cycle times, and if a major contract had been launched many of the black squads, which was mostly the boilermakers, were laid off until the next ship had reached a certain stage, and could employ all the boilermakers. So they moved from yard to yard, but in a sense whilst no one in that period ever suffered a long period of unemployment, it still bred insecurity in the minds of the workers.

Men were still kept on two hours notice, and could be let go for a week,

even when the yard knew there would then be work again. Only a few employers saw that this insecurity prevented workers from identifying with the firm, and kept the craft group as the focus of loyalty.

Union leaders made constant references back to the 1930s. Ted Hill, the General Secretary of the Boilermakers' Society, had been unemployed himself in the depression. He feared that once demand fell the private shipbuilding companies would close down yards again and the shipyard workers would be 'slung on the industrial scrapheap'. He wrote to his members, 'You cannot have forgotten the early 1930s when you lived on bread and margarine, a few potatoes and perhaps a scrag end of mutton now and again.'

Though a few managers fought battles to change methods, and paid the cost in disputes, in the years after the war the unions reached a *modus vivendi* with most companies. Even though they were making good profits there was little attempt to reform or buy out the same practices that another generation of managers had listed when foreign competition had been felt so keenly in the 1920s.

As welding spread and materials changed, there was a rash of new demarcation disputes. Some of the most publicised were at Cammell Laird's in Birkenhead. In 1955 the joiners and the sheet-metal workers fell out over who should have the right to fit aluminium sheets, instead of plywood, over insulation in a refrigerated-fruit ship. After a five-week strike a settlement was reached, by which the sheets would be cut by the sheet-metal workers, and fixed by the joiners. At this point the

Belfast shipyard workers building the liner Canberra *in 1958. They were still employed casually. Disputes were on the increase, and the boom was ending*

drillers, belonging to the Shipwrights Association, entered the affair with a claim of their own. The dispute brought strikes and lay-offs for seven months, followed by a Court of Inquiry. There were similar hold-ups over the drilling of other holes, and about who should make a chalk line on plates to show where cutting was to be done. At the base of all the disputes was the same real fear, that certain work once lost would be gone forever, since there was no transferability between crafts. As a result of the arguments, British yards gained a reputation for slow and delayed deliveries. But order books were still full. For every order that was cancelled there was another waiting behind.

Nevertheless, the effect of these hold-ups was to draw more attention to what was happening in the rest of the world. In six years of the greatest demand ever for new ships, British yards had managed to increase their output by 16 per cent. Over the same period ships launched in the rest of the world had risen 300 per cent. Though it was natural that other countries should recover, the figure that gave most concern related to Britain's share of the 'export' market. Though Britain still made most ships in total, by 1954 Germany had overtaken her as the leading builder for foreign owners. The greatest blow to morale came after 1956 when it was calculated Britain had been overtaken by Japan in total output, losing a lead she had held since records began. Two years after that the Germans went into second place, and Britain's share of world output had sunk to 15 per cent.

At the same time it became clear that a revolution had taken place in the method of constructing ships. Welding had made the traditional way of building them, on a slipway, obsolete. It was best done under cover in sheds, where plates and sections could be turned over by powerful cranes to present the easiest positions for welding. Making blocks of the ship away from the berth required a major reorganisation of yard lay-out, including new sheds and storage areas and more powerful cranes. All this needed money and space, and more staff to do the necessary pre-planning. Sweden had pioneered prefabrication, and Holland and Germany had been able to rebuild on these lines after the war. Japan had constructed new yards on new sites with a flow line that allowed the rapid building of large tankers. Some British companies, with a newer style of management, achieved considerable modernisation. On the Wear, Austin and Pickersgill used additional space from an old adjoining yard that had been closed in the thirties to build fabrication sheds. But in most yards geography as well as tradition mitigated against modernisation plans, with small sites closed in by high river banks or housing.

In the late 1950s, the shipping recession that had been feared all along arrived. It was caused by the collapse of freight rates after Suez, as shipping was laid up again. For a time the British yards could live very well off the backlog of orders but they could see that they were now exposed to the full wind of foreign competition that they had talked about but never really encountered over so many years. The Japanese

were the most damaging. Sir John Hunter was the managing director of Swan Hunter.

> Most of the time the Japanese seemed able to quote prices which were anything from 15 per cent to 20 per cent lower than those we could quote. I always used to feel we were competing with Japan Limited, and the Japanese as a whole, rather than in a straight fight between shipbuilders.

As the international tanker business began to be monopolised by Japan, and the market for liners and more traditional types of shipping shrank, the industry argued that the competition was unfair, that the Japanese were subsidised, and that the quality of their ships was not comparable. But the Swedes and Germans also took many orders. By 1963 the great British industry that had dominated the world until so recently was sinking fast. Ten yards closed that year. Twenty-eight were working on their last orders, or were without work altogether. The number in employment had dropped from 215,000 in 1958 to 160,000. Britain's share of world launchings had reached a new low. Most orders that were taken were at a loss. Government, which had left the ship-builders alone since the war, became concerned. Lord Hailsham, the Minister for Science, asked the Institute of Naval Architects:

> Are British yards doing enough to apply new techniques of shipbuilding compared with some of their rivals? Are we satisfied that our yards are making the best use of space – and are there not too many of them? Are we spending enough on research?[30]

Welding prefabricated ship sections under cover made for faster and cheaper shipbuilding. At Sunderland, Austin and Pickersgill produced the SD14 standard cargo ship, and were highly successful when other yards were failing

Newly-produced figures were convincing evidence that Britain could no longer make ships at a competitive price. Productivity had increased only one or two per cent since 1946. For a typical tanker British prices were £5 per ton above Swedish prices, and £10 per ton above Japanese prices. Even British shipowners, who had remained loyal for so long, were now placing their orders abroad. By 1963 40 per cent of all the ships being built for British owners were coming from foreign yards.

For the rest of the world the recession passed and shipbuilding began to grow again, with output rising three times over the next ten years. But Britain took no part in this expansion, and output stayed at around the same level. It would have been much lower, and the industry might have been wiped out, if Whitehall had not started to intervene on an increasing level. From 1963, the year before a general election, a series of special grants and credit schemes were announced, and helped to keep orders coming in, though yards continued to close. Politicians vowed to look after the depressed areas of the north-east and Scotland better than had been done between the wars. When the large and modernised Fairfields yard went bankrupt in 1965, Harold Wilson's new Labour administration moved to the rescue, with a generous formula that provided joint ownership with the state. Fresh management attempted to deal with productivity, demarcation and manning problems through greater involvement of the unions, and giving secure contracts of employment and better pay. The experiment angered the private yards who saw the large subsidy as unfair competition with their own financially stretched companies. Oliver Blandford was the managing director of Fairfields.

> They hated our guts. We were trying to do things that they'd set their faces against doing, like actually talking to our chaps, and getting to know our shop stewards, and general persuasion and talk.

Sir John Hunter, like others, was sceptical.

> I don't think they got any reaction from their workforce that a lot of people hadn't already had, and were continuing to have. When it came to the crunch, Fairfields was one of the first to go bust.

Shipbuilding became a major preoccupation of the Labour government, and a full-scale inquiry was completed shortly after the Fairfields rescue in 1966. The Geddes Report listed the underlying causes which had brought the industry down. It alleged that the old managements' attitudes to markets, men and money had been short-term. Individual firms were too small to deal effectively with customers and suppliers. But its central analysis was the now-standard historical one.

> The past is very much alive in the minds of the workers in the industry and coupled with the general lack of confidence in the

future of the industry it has bred a deep feeling of insecurity which is at the root of most of the demarcation disputes and practices in the industry which are commonly known as 'restrictive', but which the workers regard and describe as 'protective'.

Geddes recommended new procedures on disputes and demarcation, which were established. The report also urged fewer unions, which was harder to achieve. But the main proposal was 'restructuring'. A concentration of the industry into five big groups would allow much greater management strength with strong new sales departments, better use of labour between yards, and specialisation in particular kinds of ship. Warships would be built in three yards, not twelve. In return for agreeing to these amalgamations the industry would qualify for state aid, then reckoned at about £30 million.

A few large firms stayed independent but the majority yielded to the plans the government had made for them. They formed four new groupings. In the north-east, Swan Hunter Shipbuilders became the largest firm in the country, taking in John Redhead, Hawthorn Leslie, the Vickers Naval Yard, and Furness. On the Clyde two groups were formed, Scott-Lithgow on the Lower Clyde, and Upper Clyde Ship-builders, which absorbed John Brown and Yarrow, as well as the

John Brown's had lobbied to get QE2 built at Clydebank. By the time the ship was launched in 1967, the large passenger liner was a thing of the past. Other countries concentrated on tankers and newer types of ship

Jimmy Reid, leader of the Upper Clyde Shipbuilders' work-in, 1972

troubled Fairfields. Another group was established in the east of Scotland. But structure and organisation were easier to change than the fundamental attitudes.

For a period the industry seemed to revive under the massive injection of public cash, then staggered as the world demand for ships collapsed after 1974. The shipbuilders stayed in the headlines. When the Conservatives, who were committed to non-intervention and to a more ruthless attitude towards what they called lame ducks, let Upper Clyde Shipbuilders go bankrupt in 1971, the long and defiant work-in forced them to reappraise industrial policy. The work-in, at yards where the Queens and other great liners had been built, caught the public imagination and inspired trade unionists who faced closures in other declining industries. Jimmy Airlie was one of the shop steward leaders.

> Without our struggle there'd be no merchant shipbuilding left on the upper reaches of the Clyde. And it would not have been a central plank of the Labour Party manifesto in 1974, to bring the shipbuilding industry into public ownership. I think they would have avoided that commitment if it hadn't been for the struggle at the UCS works.

Even before full nationalisation the old economics had ceased to apply. The industry had failed to pay its own way, and in six years over £160 million of government funds were pumped into it. In this new situation the shipbuilders had a chance to escape the constraints of their own history. Some yards were closed, management was strengthened, and new effort was put into the criticised areas of research, training, and marketing. Late in the day, the industry moved into the new types of ship, like the VLCC super carriers, and container ships, which had previously been produced by the Japanese.

Shipyard workers had gained security of employment back in 1965, and now, with a new national procedure on disputes and demarcation arguments, some flexibilities were at last achieved. But in one sense government support made a reform of practices more difficult. The Commission on Industrial Relations concluded:

> There are grounds for believing that financial assistance has in some cases had an adverse effect on industrial relations by encouraging the belief that public support would be forthcoming whatever difficulties the companies got into . . . In no such cases was the provision of aid made conditional upon any changes in the conduct of industrial relations.[31]

Though the unions had always campaigned for state ownership as the one true guarantee of job security, it was only after Labour had nationalised in 1977, that the major redundancies began to be .made. British Shipbuilders lost £106 million in their first year, and though the figure dropped for a while, still lost over £100 million in 1982. Employment stood at 86,000 in 1977, and 66,000 in 1982.

After nearly twenty years of heavy state support, shipbuilders now speak quite candidly about what went wrong, and their attitudes are as polarised as ever. The management still make their old diagnosis. Sir Leonard Redshaw, who ran the Vickers shipyards, said:

> It was the British disease, the trade unions. Their attitudes towards progress were really lamentable. Simple things – the Swedes invented a small portable hand-welding machine where one man could easily work four machines, and in Sweden four machines were worked by one man, ditto in Germany, ditto in France. In Britain one man to one machine and that took a long time, because the fact that it was automatic was objected to.
>
> There were plenty of good managers, have no doubt. But the atmosphere under which they had to work was demarcation and restrictive practices. I decided to pull my company out of building tankers, because they could build tankers on the continent with twenty per cent less man-hours than we could build them, purely because of British trade union practices.

John Chalmers, who was General Secretary of the Boilermakers, the strongest of the shipyard unions, retorted:

> That is an old-fashioned Victorian rhetoric, you know, always blame the men. That takes me back to the time when at every launch we had beautiful platforms and all the aristocracy would arrive on the day for the launch, and there was never any question of congratulation to the workforce, neither on the launching platform, or because we were never there, at the launch or dinner that followed. Always it was recrimination against the workforce.

Some managers are self-critical. Sandy Stephen ran his family firm until it was merged into Upper Clyde Shipbuilders, in 1966.

> I think one has to blame the management at that time for not taking more vigorous action. It's easy to blame the unions now, but the unions were not wholly to blame. With hindsight we should really have tackled all those demarcations vigorously, and they were capable of solution when things were good. But once times turned difficult, then it's very hard to get things right.

A Clydeside shop steward said:

> If they had been given better job security, sick pay, pensions, better working conditions, and that was possible with the vast profits they made, then in my opinion they could have won the co-operation of the workers. But they felt that gaffers wore bowler hats, and had the divine right to rule, and naturally if

the management attitude is of that nature then workers react in a not very positive manner.

The new managers who came in from outside shipbuilding in the 1960s put the blame on the old managements too. Oliver Blandford was the first managing director of the short-lived Fairfields experiment.

If you look at the areas of British industry where there is conflict, it is car making, shipbuilding, and coal, and they're all industries that fired their people every so often. If people have a long history of casual employment they are not loyal and cannot be expected to be loyal to their employer.

Graham Day is a Canadian who ran Cammell Laird for five years, and was appointed Chairman of British Shipbuilders in 1983.

British shipbuilding had not developed in plant terms, in work-practice terms on the shop floor, in non-shipbuilding management-skill terms, in strategic planning terms, in marketing expertise, the way competitive industries in Sweden, Germany and certainly Japan had.

As shipbuilding contracted it was forced to change its methods rapidly. Management was overhauled, and many of the fiercest craft divisions disappeared. The job of the plater and shipwright was merged. Welding, caulking, burning or drilling could be done by one man. Plumbers were allowed to do simple welding. But by the time most of these changes had been brought about, the fiercest recession since the thirties had struck. Only a handful of British yards remain; they make less than three per cent of the world's ships. Somehow the skill and pride of the riveters and shipwrights and the energy of the men who owned the yards did not convert easily to a modern industry where machinery and planning mattered as much as strength of will and toughness. Many craftsmen are still nostalgic about the old way of working. Pat McCrystal, a former shipwright, watched the launch of ship 534 on the Clyde as a boy.

When you built the ship frame by frame, plate by plate, literally by hand, that was shipbuilding at its best. Now you no longer live with a ship. When I started I was present at the launching of the ship. I was present sending the ship away on its trials. I lived with the ship the whole of its creation. You don't do that now.

Freddy Hopper, a former manager, started work before the First War.

It was just as the Almighty did with the fishes, you know. Just a backbone and ribs. We felt it was the only way to build a ship. We didn't take too kindly to putting them down in lumps and sticking them all together. I don't think the Almighty would have liked that. He never put people together like that.

CHAPTER 7: CHEMICALS
SCIENTIFIC METHOD

I started on the boilers. The day before opening I came to see Mr Albright. The first thing he said was 'How are your teeth?' You had to have good teeth or you wouldn't get a job.

Phosphorus plant worker

It was really like a continuous construction site. There was something being knocked down, and something new being built, everywhere. And people had to get used to this continuous change in the process and the products, of the old ones going and the new ones coming in.

Ken Webber

In 1919 a party of British chemists and engineers clambered round a shut-down chemical works in Oppau in Germany, trying to discover more about the greatest technical secret of the First World War. Trench warfare, with its extended artillery barrages, had called for high explosives in hitherto unknown quantities, and the key ingredient for making them was nitrogen. But whereas the Allies had to ship nitre rock all the way from Chile, the Germans had found a way of extracting the nitrogen from the air around them. They had thus been entirely self-sufficient in explosives. Though defeated militarily the Germans expected the old commercial rivalries to continue. They tried to sabotage the British mission in Oppau by painting over the dials, and removing sections of pipe. On the way back to Harwich the team had their notes and reports stolen from their baggage.

Although the British chemical-makers still had much to learn, the wartime experience had brought a transformation. Other industries were stunned by the new conditions of 1919, and some never recovered. But over the next forty years, by putting a new emphasis on science and research and deliberately attempting to catch up with Germany, the British chemical industry became one of the world leaders, competing on equal terms with all comers. For those who worked in it this was one of the most spectacular turnarounds, characterised not only by commercial success but by good labour relations and good wages.

Though the manufacture of chemicals was bracketed with the new motor and electrical factories as one of the 'new' industries between the wars, it was not new but had simply managed to change itself. There was an old Victorian industry whose world leadership had once been as great as the shipbuilders. They had despatched heavy chemicals, sulphuric acid, and fertilisers to all corners of the globe. The greatest export had been in the alkali products, principally soda, essential for making soap, glass and paper. In the nineteenth century, small chemical companies were clustered along the Mersey, the Clyde, and the Tyne. Their working conditions were appalling. In Widnes, one of the main centres, the air was black from burning a million tons of coal a year, and foul from the fumes that came off the retorts and vats. The town was surrounded by wastelands of alkali residue and defunct works. The industry was unsophisticated and used primitive technology. Men stirred cauldrons with wooden poles; dangerous acids were decanted haphazardly from one open container to another; measurements were rough and ready.

In the more specialised and scientifically made chemical products of higher value, such as dyes and medicines, Britain hardly competed at all. In 1914 Lancashire's enormous cotton textile trade depended on dyes imported from Germany for four-fifths of its needs. Between 1900 and 1914 competition from Germany and the United States grew. The *Chemical Trade Journal* made criticisms which had a familiar ring for the time.

A chemical company research laboratory in 1912

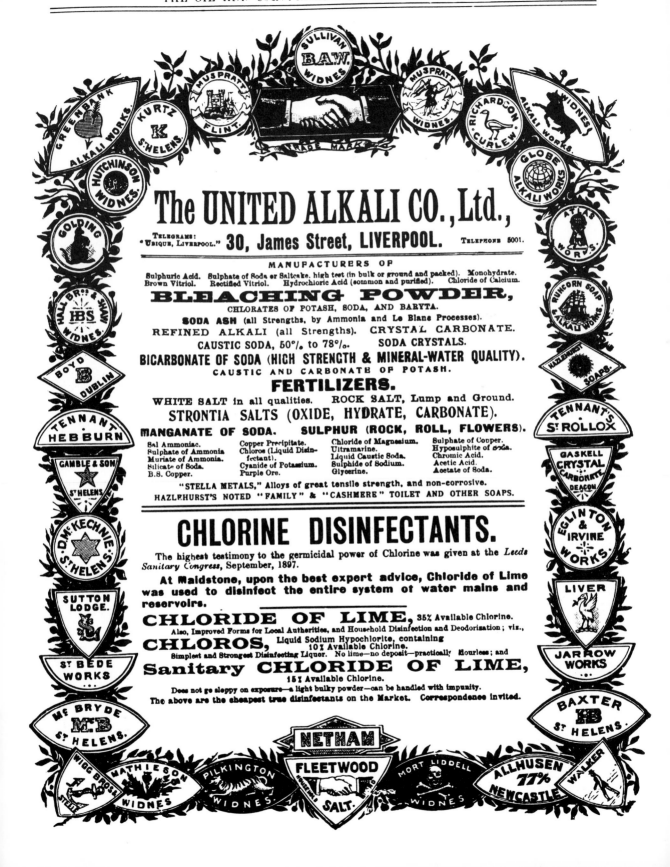

The heritage of 19th-century firms that made up the United Alkali Company. Many relied on the already superseded Le Blanc soda process

The fault with chemical manufacture in this country is the difficulty of persuading those interested to spend their money in improved plant. In days gone by, coal was cheap, labour was rough, cheap and ready, and, for the rude methods then involved, any old boilers, second-hand machinery and cheap supervision was considered quite good enough in the manufacture of chemicals. Our continental neighbours, as well as our American cousins, can now say with pride 'Nous avons changé tout çela'.[32]

There was one major exception to all such generalisations. Brunner Mond was the most successful British chemical firm. It had been set up at Northwich in Cheshire by Ludwig Mond, a German Jewish émigré with a missionary belief in the importance of applying science to the needs of industry. By introducing a new process for making soda from salt Brunner Mond took 90 per cent of the alkali trade. With a large research organisation, professional management, and an enlightened attitude to their workforce, the firm had by 1914 left the rest of the industry behind.

The outbreak of the First War dramatised the wider inadequacies of the British chemical industry. Cut off from the dyes they needed to colour cloth, the Lancashire textile mills found it hard to continue work. Even the khaki dye for army uniforms had come from Germany. There was a severe shortage of medical and photographic supplies. Most alarming of all was the absence of plant to make explosives. To meet the crisis chemists were called back from the front in France, and government took direct charge. New works were put up by the Ministry of Munitions as well as by private firms. The number of employees doubled, and 600,000 tons of high explosives were produced in four years, with output rising from a level of one ton a day to six hundred tons a day.

A mission to Germany brought back technical secrets that allowed British chemists to catch up

In the course of this titanic effort more money was poured into research, and university departments were expanded. Successful firms like Brunner Mond entered new fields, and there were mergers to make other companies more effective. An entirely new dyes industry was created, centred around the new British Dyestuffs Corporation in which the government had a sizeable stake. At the end of the war, heavy import restrictions were imposed to protect the fledgling sectors, and to develop new ones. The trip to Oppau to try to recover the secrets of the German Haber Bosch process for making nitrogen out of thin air was the continuation of the wartime drive. A government committee had said, 'Nitrogen fixation is essentially a new industry requiring for its initiation and development the actual support of the government.' Their interest was less in using the plant for manufacturing explosives, than for making vast quantities of cheap nitrogen fertilisers.

On Teesside, in the 1920s, a new complex was built to exploit the commercial possibilities of the partly-stolen nitrogen process, using

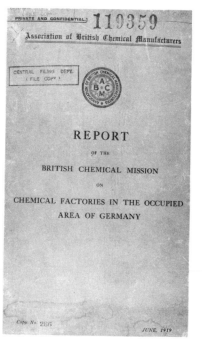

[PRIVATE AND CONFIDENTIAL] 119359

Association of British Chemical Manufacturers

CENTRAL FILING DEPT. (FILE COPY)

A.B.C.M.

REPORT

OF THE

BRITISH CHEMICAL MISSION

ON

CHEMICAL FACTORIES IN THE OCCUPIED AREA OF GERMANY

Copy No. 286

JUNE, 1919

153

some of the secrets brought back from Oppau, and was taken over by Brunner Mond. Billingham was the prestige project of the new science-based chemical industry, constructed to handle the highest pressures that had ever been worked with, 250 atmospheres, and temperatures of 5000 centigrade. But there were extraordinary contrasts between the new capital-intensive plants and the old ways which still continued. The worst excesses of the nineteenth century lingered on beside the most advanced technology and modern management. Conditions for chemical workers depended on the age of the process and the attitudes of the employers towards those who worked for them. Frank Dodd started at the Newcastle Zinc Oxide Company, typical of hundreds of small and independent works.

Low technology still continued: pouring sulphuric acid on to cadmium bars in the barrel, at a small chemical works

It was in a half-culvert. There was no light. It was a drab, dark place. It was an old lead works which they had rented, and had this furnace and we made zinc oxide. There were no facilities whatsoever. We had no protective clothing. We brought our own. No facilities for making tea other than on top of the furnace. No changing place. No lockers. It was a filthy place. We had to put all our food fairly high up or the rats would get it.

In the twilight world of the old chemical industry hours were long, and accidents from burns or spills or an escape of gas were frequent. Factory regulations were often ignored, and fines were low even when prosecutions were brought. There were no goggles or safety boots.

Billingham was built in the post-World War I recession, as the most advanced chemical plant in the country

The plant where we made TNT had about an inch of water on the floor, and was worked by an old steam engine. It must have been a hundred years old, and they didn't allow an electric motor because of the sparks. The windows were broken. They'd bought some old policemen's uniforms for us to wear. They were in a very bad condition and they all went into holes very quickly.

Dangerous conditions went with the job, and were common to even the best-regulated firms. But there were massive differences in the provisions that managers made for their men, and in the state of labour relations in different companies. Frank Dodd describes the autocratic management he first worked for on Tyneside.

We were treated as badly as they could possibly treat us. The manager's word was law and if anyone was foolish enough to argue with them he was dicing with his job. There were no labour relations. They'd have to do little to get the sack.

Compared with other industries, however, chemicals was usually free of labour disputes and strife. Over twenty unions represented the chemical workers, but the fact that there was so little piece work, because many of the processes were indivisible and done by shifts or crews of men working together as a team, removed many of the usual causes for friction. In chemicals the quality of the work mattered as much as the quantity. Towards the end of the First World War a government commission looking into industrial unrest cited the chemical industry as a model to others. They were impressed by the evidence of the works manager of the United Alkali Company, Mr Stuart, whose approach to grievances was far from typical of management of the time.

I sympathetically hear the men's side of the case, look at it from their point of view, and imagine myself for the time being one of the workmen, asking myself what would be my opinion of their contention if I were one of them. Then I place before them the case for our company, discussing the two sides of the question in a courteous and friendly spirit.[33]

The progressive firm with the longest tradition of treating its people well was also the most enterprising and financially successful company, Brunner Mond. When most industrial workers were still doing ten hours a day, in the 1890s Brunners had cut the working day to eight hours and introduced a week's paid holiday. They laid on doctors and dentists and basic welfare provisions, and ran the business on paternalistic lines, like many companies in Germany, but very few in Britain. Charles Nickson began to work for Brunners at Northwich in 1920.

They were very much ahead of their time in the treatment of labour. They paid more wages than the local rate, and more than the union rate. The men got a week's holiday, and took it when they wanted it, rather than when they were told. Also they gave them an extra week's money to spend, so there was 53 weeks' pay for a year's work. That was considered quite something in those days.

Although management was hostile to the unions, and membership was low, by the standards of pay and conditions elsewhere the workforce had little to complain about. So the Brunner management, which was itself better trained and more qualified because of a policy of recruiting the best scientific brains from the universities, received a high degree of co-operation in its expansive plans. Compared with other industries the chemical makers already had many things in their favour. Governments were far more helpful to them than to the post-war shipbuilding industry. But the British companies still suffered from one great disadvantage. Unlike their rivals in the United States and Germany they remained small, and unable to command the capital or resources of the foreign combines. In 1925 the merger process reached a further stage in Germany with the creation of IG Farben, a huge group whose capital was larger than the four largest British companies put together. The Germans were assembling similar combines in coal, steel and shipbuilding. But the divided ownership of these activities in Britain prevented similar amalgamations, however much they were urged by governments and critics. The chemical-makers were the one group who responded and were able to meet like with like.

In 1926, after a deal completed on an Atlantic liner returning from New York, the largest firm, Brunner Mond, came together with its old competitors, the United Alkali Company, the British Dyestuffs Corporation, and the Scottish-based explosives group, Nobel Industries. The new company was to be called Imperial Chemical Industries, and was a giant firm by British standards. With a sense of history Sir Alfred Mond, the first Chairman, told his senior managers that they were on trial.

> We are not merely a body of people carrying on industry in order to make dividends, we are much more: we are the object of universal envy, admiration and criticism, and the capacity of British industrialists, British commercialists and British technicians will be judged by the entire world from the success we make of this merger.

ICI controlled 40 per cent of the total British chemicals output and was closely linked with other companies who drew their own raw materials from it. Through the sheer size and success of its operations it influenced the way other chemical firms developed as well. Labour relations were based on the Brunner Mond tradition, and a system of works councils was introduced for full consultation. At a time when old industries were starved of cash and in depression, twenty million pounds were spent to continue building the complex at Billingham, designed to provide the Empire with nitrogen fertilisers. Still more

How ICI depicted their labour policy, in a company magazine that went out to their employees in 1928

THE BRIDGE

money was put into the development of a new plant that would produce oil from coal through hydrogenation. To allow this expansion, more graduate chemists were recruited. Walter D'Leny started at Billingham after Oxford.

> My first experience was being put on a shift under a foreman, and I did that for six months, and this was the general experience of all graduates who didn't know about the industry at all. They had to learn their trade. It proved invaluable later on

when we had to start the hydrogenation plant, because I was
able to tell the process workers what to do.

Peter Inglis was a metallurgist who worked on the high-pressure pipes
and pressure vessels needed for the same hydrogenation scheme.

We were all very excited about the new processes. There was a
sort of pioneer spirit. Very often on a Sunday morning you
would find at least half the research department in working.

With the slump, there was an overestimate of the demand for fertiliser, and the great oil-from-coal scheme never realised the hopes placed
in it. Based on a widespread belief that the world's oil supplies would be
running out by 1950, the plan was to use the plentiful Durham coal to
make 100,000 tons of oil a year. Ramsey MacDonald opened the new
plant in 1931, and the process was nursed by the government because of
its strategic value, but it was always highly expensive, and was closed
after the Second World War. The major developments between the wars
were not in 'heavy' chemicals but in new organic chemicals. Most of the
industry's growth was with new synthetic dyes, and fibres based on
cellulose, and the first plastics. Perspex was developed in 1935. New
drugs were discovered.

Research conducted in government laboratories, set up after the
formation of the Department of Scientific Research, and in the companies' own laboratories was fundamental to this growth. Scientists
were paid to work on a large number of experiments in the hope that a
few of them would bear fruit. ICI had over 500 scientists on the research
side alone. At Winnington Dr R. O. Gibson was experimentimg with
various gases under high pressure, when a major discovery was made.

We started an experiment on a Friday. We worked on Saturday
and didn't dismantle the apparatus till the Monday. My colleague Forsyth pointed out that the piece of metal that we had
in the reaction area looked as though it had been dipped in
paraffin wax and was able to obtain enough from the sample
for it to be analysed, and shown to be a polymer of ethylene.
That was the first sight of ethylene.

What they had found became known as polythene, when it was fully
developed several years later.

However advanced the research that was in progress during the
1930s, most chemical works remained unpleasant places to work in, or
live close to. A new phosphorus plant which opened at Widnes in 1933
brought welcome jobs. The fumes also tarnished bright metal in nearby
houses and rotted the curtains at the windows. Walter Parkinson was a
process worker.

They had a crane lift the lid off, and if the stuff hadn't been
burnt out properly there were clouds and clouds of these
fumes. It used to come in on the town if the wind was that way.

A process worker drilling out slabs of amorphous phosphorus at Albright and Wilson's factory

And they used to stop the buses. They couldn't see. That upset people quite a bit, but the council didn't take it up much because it was creating employment. Later they stopped us doing this sort of thing, so we used to do it at 3 o'clock in the morning instead.

Much chemical work remained heavy and dangerous. Tighter safety regulations helped, but they could do little to alleviate the results of long-term exposure to toxic substances. Phosphorus workers at Widnes risked the same 'Phossy jaw' that Victorian matchmakers had suffered from, so the company had a full-time dentist and supplied free toothpaste and toothbrushes. In the remote explosive factories, men and women had to get used to the effects of nitro-glycerine. Sammie Weir worked at an explosives plant on the Lanarkshire coast.

> Getting it into your system is a very painful and rotten experience. You get an NG headache, a thumping headache. I've seen them unconscious with it, lying on the bankings outside, especially. We had to take this as part of our job. We didn't like it but we had to accept it.

Walter Parkinson remembers that the carbon tetrachloride section in his firm was used by the management as a 'Devil's Island'.

> It was a very bad plant to work on. If a man in the rest of the works did anything wrong he was threatened with the sack, or going on the carbon tetrachloride plant. And he invariably took the sack. The fumes were very pungent and on top of that there was the danger of chlorine. You used a lot of chlorine in the manufacture of carbon tetrachloride and it was a deadly gas to use.

To reduce the dangers, special clothing was issued to workers in high-risk areas in most chemical works in the 1930s, though it was said that parsimonious small companies bought used gloves from ICI. Frank Dodd describes the clothes he had to wear to make sodium.

> We had clogs with rubber bottoms. We had to have spats made from heavy material to stop anything getting past the clogs and leggings. We had a big apron tied round us, and on our heads we had a hat like the Ku Klux Klan, covering us so nothing could go on the neck. And we had three pairs of gloves each.

Even with this protection sodium workers only worked with the chemical for ten minutes at a time. Yet despite the risks, the attractions included higher pay, particularly for shifts, and the prospect of continuous work. Chemicals brought new opportunities to the north-east and north-west when shipbuilding, cotton and coal were in decline. Fred Leach started in Widnes during the depression.

> For me the chemical industry was a very steady job, it was an

Packers who shovelled bleach into barrels wore protective clothing

expanding job and it was an interesting job. The people in the factory knew that they had work for them. And some of the industries, particularly in this town, they were working very sporadically. They might work two or three days and then be told: 'Well, don't come in because we have no work'. But not so with the chemical industry. They were improving all the time.

The chemical industry was growing fast, constantly expanding the range of products and the size of plants. Though also hit by the depression the industry recovered quickly, and the total number of chemical workers doubled between the wars. Chemicals benefited from the revival of British farming under protection, as well as from rearmament. Nitrogen was the basic ingredient of both fertilisers and explosives. By the late 1930s Britain was catching up with both the United States and Germany, though there was no real measure of its comparative efficiency. The chemical-makers were protected by tariffs at home, and managed to avoid the cut-throat competition in international markets that other industries succumbed to, by joining international cartels to keep up prices, and to share markets. ICI made a series of international trading agreements, first with DuPont in the United States, then with IG Farben in Germany, to divide the world market between them. Britain stayed out of Europe and the United States, but had the British Empire, and much of South America and Asia, to itself.

There was no clearer recognition of the changed position of the industry than the fact that, when the Second World War broke out, Britain was no longer dependent on imported supplies as she had been in 1914. Government had involved the chemical firms closely in the rearmament programme. Seven new explosives factories were built in the three years before 1939, and strategic raw materials were accumulated. At the Widnes phosphorus plant of Albright and Wilson, Walter

Parkinson watched the supplies of phosphate rock that were being stockpiled.

> They acquired this big piece of wasteland between the canal bank and the main works, with a railway siding beside it. They started bringing in the phosphate rock, which was very small, only pebble-sized. And people said, 'What's all this for? Why is it coming regular?' And then it dawned there was something doing.

When war was declared troops moved in to guard the factory, which made phosphorus for shells and firebombs.

Almost every part of the chemical industry was mobilised to make everyday products that were now needed for the war effort, as well as explosives and mustard gas. The First War had been called 'the engineer's war'. The Second World War was 'the scientist's war', and the application of pure science to practical problems accelerated as never before. Research spending more than doubled in five years, and major breakthroughs came in new drugs, from anti-malarials to penicillin, and new agricultural chemicals including DDT and weedkillers. Polythene came into its own, as a lightweight insulation material that allowed radar equipment to be carried in aircraft. As the largest employer of scientific manpower in the country ICI played a part in developing the atom bomb, codenamed the 'Tube Alloys' project. Enoch Hatton was involved as a production worker.

> When I was working with Tube Alloys I was told that it was a very important project, and that we had to do the job which was very secret, and not to tell anybody about it. I was not aware what the implication was.

ICI even lent their labour director to government, to advise on how industrial relations in other parts of war production could be improved. For the long term, the most important wartime development was the realisation that chemicals could be based on oil. Petrochemicals were advancing more quickly in the United States, but in 1942 the Shell laboratories made a synthetic detergent which was the first oil-based chemical in Europe.

The switch from coal and coal tar to oil as the basic raw material for chemicals was to bring a transformation in the scope of the industry, and in the lives of those who worked in it. But for several years after 1945 Britain still lagged behind, and it seemed as though the progress of the pre-war years might be thrown away. In the United States, with its own oilfields and refineries, oil and gas were being piped directly into the plants. They provided the feedstock to produce the chemicals needed in large quantities for the plastics, artificial fibres, and detergents that were creating a huge new demand for themselves. In Britain, as late as 1950, only six per cent of production was based on oil, and the chemical works still relied on batteries of coke ovens, trainloads of coal, woodpulp from Scandinavia, or the fermentation of molasses for their feedstock. In a familiar story, post-war demand was so great that most efforts went into meeting traditional markets in old ways, and there was little time to knock down the plants of the 1930s and reconstruct. This affected productivity.

A mission sent to the United States found that the sales value per employee of many American heavy chemical factories was at least three times that of the British. This had little to do with overmanning, or ways of working, in an industry that still enjoyed good labour relations. 'There is no evidence that the higher economic productivity of the American industry is due to any greater diligence on the part of the hourly-paid workers.' It was because the industry had not yet re-equipped itself on a sufficient scale. The same mission found that capital investment per man was two to three times as high in America as in Britain. Peter King of ICI remembers the immediate post-war years.

> Partly, it was resting on the laurels of success during the war. A hell of a lot had gone on, a hell of a lot had gone well, and I suspect there was a sense of saying, 'Now you've won, when do we celebrate?' But of course it wasn't a time for celebrating. It was a time for working even harder.

Britain was saved from being left behind by the entry of new firms which broadened the base of the industry. When the traditional chemical companies were slow in moving from their old raw materials, the oil companies invaded their territory and gingered them up. In the 1950s and 1960s chemicals became the most dynamic part of the British economy, with rising productivity and rising production that out-stripped the rest of industry. Harold Hodge was at Esso which, like Shell and BP, came into petrochemicals on their own.

> We invariably underestimated the market. Fortunately it was at a stage that, even if we went wrong, it didn't matter too much. That was just a justification for another even bigger plant. Plants were going in one after the other and each one was two or three times the size of the previous one.

In the ten years from 1950 the proportion of chemicals produced from oil rose from six per cent to 50 per cent and investment was running at £150 million each year. At Wilton, on the southern side of the Tees from Billingham, ICI set up a new plant to 'crack' oil into ethylene and propylene and produce a range of organic chemicals. One of the products they could now make cheaply and in large quantities was poly-thene, which they had discovered themselves, but which the Americans had put into mass production first. In the same period ten major new petrochemical plants were built, some of the biggest going up directly alongside new oil refineries at Fawley, near Southampton, and at Grangemouth in Scotland.

These rapid changes affected the workforce more than anyone else.

Lord McGowan played a central part in the formation of ICI in 1926, and dominated the company until his retirement as chairman in 1950

Launch of 'Terylene', 1952

Works were in a state of turmoil, with construction work going on beside plant that was already in production.

> There was something being knocked down, and something being built, everywhere. And people had to get used to this continuous change both in the processes and the products, of the old ones going and the new ones coming in.

The new work involved more skill and judgement, but less manual labour. Old chemical works had made products in batches rather than continuously. Even when there were continuous processes, the heavy valves and taps had to be opened or closed by hand, and they were sometimes so heavy that it took two men to turn them. Instruments were scattered round the plant, and were sometimes crude.

> Some of the older men could tell of the days when they had a thermometer stuck up on the top of a vessel about seventy feet high, and they had a telescope to read the temperature, and that's how they controlled things. A lot of it was done by the experience of the blokes. They could put their hands on the mains and say, 'Well, that temperature's OK.'

In the 1950s and 1960s raw materials came to be handled mechanically, and the operation of the plants was brought into central control-rooms. A little later mechanisation became automation, and computers were introduced. Douglas Marlow worked on a new paraquat plant in 1966.

> The first time we went on paraquat we were a bit scared, because the plant was massive. You looked round in amazement. We really thought we had bitten off more than we could chew. But it came surprisingly easy, because every man had his section, so each man never had so much to look after really. It was very exciting. I really enjoyed going on the paraquat.

In the way in which its workers went willingly and co-operatively into new plant and processes, the chemical industry was reaping the rewards of its concern for them in the past. On an industry-wide scale there had been a Joint Industrial Council of both employers and unions since 1920. At factory level, most works, not just ICI, had some sort of consultation procedure, at which management, supervisors and representatives of the workforce sat down together. ICI's own Works Councils, originally designed to short-circuit the unions, were adapted to suit a less paternalistic age. Trade Union membership had grown in the industry since the 1930s but was still less than 50 per cent in 1960. There were few strikes, and those that did occur were small and localised. High wage levels helped considerably, and with their high profits the chemical firms could afford to be generous. Yet other industries, like the motor industry, managed to pay high wages and have continual conflict as well. The success of the chemical-makers was due partly to attitudes, and to particular features of the job itself. There was no production line to impose its own pace, and few repetitive tasks to breed alienation and frustration. Work in the new chemical plants might be more lonely and isolated, but there was a certain variety, and scope for people to exercise their own judgement. With some processes the common danger, and the need to combine technical skill with scientific knowledge, threw managers and workers together and provided a bond. Ken Webber was manager of a carbide plant at Runcorn.

> We had a very close relationship with the workforce on a sort of day-to-day almost minute-to-minute basis, because it was a dangerous process, and if you had fires or spillages or explosions, the managers or supervisors had to be in the thick of it helping lead the team. And there was a great mutual respect. They did work together well and if they hadn't the whole thing would have gone completely awry.

Automated control-room of a new agricultural chemical plant, 1983

Because the workforce grew with the industry, and learnt on the job with processes which were changing constantly, custom and practice were never a particular problem. The industry did not employ thousands of craftsmen imbued with a traditional way of working and the preconceptions that went with them. Instead of jobs becoming less and less skilful and demanding, the process known as 'de-skilling', chemicals could sometimes make claims to 'up-skilling'. Arthur Barker was a process worker.

> The process worker became a very skilled man. Instead of being a heavy, lumpy, dumpy man, he had to become a bloke who knew instruments, and how to use instruments, because the machines were made that way. Whereas years ago you only needed someone with a bit of muscle.

Even in those parts where the industry did use skilled men belonging to the main craft unions, it managed to do so with a greater flexibility and co-operation than many others. In 1965 ICI negotiated an agreement by which craftsmen would do any reasonable job within their scope. Sir Michael Clapham was a Deputy Chairman of ICI.

> If you were putting an electric socket in the wall you wouldn't have to send for a carpenter to cut the hole out, and then a bricklayer to knock a bit of brick away at the back, and then a painter to paint around it. You didn't expect an electrician to be a plumber, or a plumber to be an electrician, but you expected them just to carry through with the work as they would in their own home.

Though the growth rate continued to be spectacular, and the profits were high, the chemical-makers had to make readjustments in the 1960s. Plants had become so huge, and research costs so high, that a large scale of operations mattered more than ever. Firms amalgamated and reorganised. Even ICI contemplated a further merger and in 1962

tried unsuccessfully to take over Courtaulds for its artificial fibres business. More attention was paid to marketing and selling, in an industry which had placed such a strong emphasis on research and production. But the greatest opportunities seemed to lie in expansion overseas. The chemical industry had no tradition of competitive selling abroad. The cartels between the wars had simply divided the world up into spheres of influence, and confined ICI's activities to the home market and the Commonwealth. This had ensured survival in the 1930s, but was now a liability. Sir Michael Clapham took part in the decisions to take ICI overseas.

> A lot of people were thinking the same way in the 1950s, that a company which traditionally spent a third as much on research as it did on all its capital expenditure had got to make use of the inventions that came out of that research all over the world. It was quite shocking that, with some of our very great inventions like polythene, we hadn't the ability to exploit them in Europe or America. We simply hadn't got any organisation who could take it on, and so it was licensed to people who then became our biggest competitors. We had got to be multinational, or we would never be in the big league.

The policy involved both selling more abroad and setting up whole plants overseas. In eight years, ICI increased its sales to Europe by 500 per cent. Soon one-third of its assets were overseas. In the United States, British-owned factories captured a quarter of the American market for polyester. British chemical workers feared this would lead to redundancies at home, but in the expanding climate of the 1960s their fears were misplaced or at least premature. While firms set up abroad, home production continued to expand and working conditions to improve. But as international competition grew keener, so did awareness of the need for efficiency. Productivity in chemicals was high by British standards, but lower than in America, Germany or Japan.

The growth of chemicals continued into the 1970s. Output per worker was almost twice as high as the rest of British manufacturing, capital per worker three times as high. Suddenly the boom collapsed. In 1974 oil became an expensive raw material, and for an industry so dependent on cheap oil the effect was dramatic. Growth slowed down to two per cent a year where it had averaged seven per cent. The petrochemical industry was particularly hard-hit, though its huge size and multinational nature allowed it to survive even in the less favourable climate, and it continued to grow at a rate faster than the industrial economy as a whole. Managers found it hard to believe the market could change so rapidly.

> By 1973 virtually the whole of the chemical industry throughout the world was dependent on oil to make its products. It had become totally enslaved to oil. It was oil, oil, oil, and when the

price went up fourfold that was very nasty indeed. I don't think we could really believe it. 'They've got it wrong.' 'It'll come down again.' 'It can't be true.' Then the realisation of what it would do to costs and prices. That's when the market turned sour.

There were other problems besides oil. The demand for synthetic fibres was falling away. 'Orlon' and nylon were no longer fashionable. Technology exported abroad to areas with lower wage costs was creating a new generation of foreign competitors. The chemical firms responded to the challenge by cutting the labour force and moving operations overseas to lower cost areas. Where ICI had employed 131,000 in 1951, they employed only 84,000 in 1980. For the first time there was a direct relationship between the decline in employment and the emigration of the industry. A major victim of this trend was the Wilton polythene plant, one of the largest centres of ICI petrochemical production. Rather than try to cut labour costs further at the British site, ICI abandoned Britain altogether and relied on polythene made in Holland for British markets.

Though the quantity of plastics produced from petrochemicals has declined, fertilisers and specialised crop and pest-control chemicals

Wilton, the major new petrochemical works opened by ICI in 1954. It housed plants and processes that changed constantly

have continued to prosper. The laboratory research of the last twenty years is now being used to realise the commercial prospects for the next twenty. The rapid growth and striking commercial success of chemicals has been based from the beginning on an ability and willingness to work at the frontiers of scientific knowledge, and utilise that knowledge on a massive commercial scale. The life of a new product could be as little as two years, and while one discovery was being exploited the profits it generated were being used to uncover the next one. The industry calls it the 'roll-on' effect. John Harvey-Jones became Chairman of ICI in 1982.

> If any industry is to continue to be successful, it has to renew itself and change the whole time. A very good example of the life-cycle is indeed the petrochemical business. There wasn't so much as an ethylene cracker at all in the United Kingdom before the war. The first one was built by ICI around the early 1950s. Since then we've built six and at the present moment we are only operating one, so the other five have all been built and have all been shut down. Those aren't products that are going to go away, but their explosive growth has gone and will be replaced by other products with an equally explosive growth. We've seen now the whole life-cycle of a business grow up, flare up almost like a rocket, growing at an enormous rate and then stabilise. And the period of that has been from 1950 until today, so that's a thirty-year cycle.

In the 1980s chemists were turning to biochemistry for new pharmaceuticals, to stronger engineering plastics for use in cars and even in engines, and to new chemicals for the electronics industry. Though not immune from the effects of slumps or managerial mistakes, chemicals has been since the 1920s one of the most progressive British industries, increasingly science-based, organised in larger units where economies of scale are required, with good labour relations. There were other industries, like coal, whose whole survival rested on the demand for a single product. Without the freedom to change, they became beleaguered. But the only way chemicals has survived and dealt with foreign competition is by making rapid switches from one product to another. What they make today, and the processes they use, would be unrecognisable to the chemical workers and chemists of the 1920s. The industry thrived on being ahead. This is what originally attracted Walter D'Leny to work in it.

> It had very much the glamour to the young man in the 1920s and 1930s that some of the new electronic industries have today. And there were a lot of good brains coming into the chemical industry at that time. Managements were looking forward. They could see that they had good commercial possibilities. It was a new industry. It wasn't tied to out-of-date practices in any way and so everything worked in its favour.

CHAPTER 8: COAL
A SPECIAL CASE

. . . There is blood on the coal, there will always be blood on the coal, but we feel that blood should be shed for the mass who are our kin, not for the enrichment of a few who have battened on our pain in the past.[34]

Bert Coombes, 1944

A point has now been reached where the miners are in a mood of sullen resentment and anger in relation to their industry – a mood so deep that no matter what proposals are made in the present emergency in regards to wages and working conditions, their confidence will never be restored until it has been taken over by the State . . .

Will Lawther, Miners' President 1944

To nationalise this particular industry of all industries would be a policy of despair; another way must be found which will still enable the best elements of private enterprise to remain alive and serve this country in the future as they have served it in the past . . .

Robert Foot, Colliery Owners Chairman 1945

In 1914 there were over a million coal miners in Britain, more than in any other activity except farming. The number was still rising, because coal dominated the economy. Coal had allowed the country's massive industrial advance to occur and had determined the areas of Victorian Britain in which it took place. The coal that was brought up from 3000 pits fuelled not only steel, engineering and textiles but provided the raw material for the new electrical and chemical concerns. Coal was needed for the railways and the gasworks, and was one of Britain's greatest exports, as the coal wagons moved endlessly to the ports of north-east England and south Wales.

Coal had other claims to being special apart from its size. At a time when factory conditions above ground were improving, miners still worked in circumstances that were notoriously difficult, dangerous, and unhealthy. Dick Brown began work in one of the oldest pits in south Wales, at the age of fourteen.

> I started work on a Monday night in August. A friend of mine living down the street took me to work. I was introduced to the mate or butty I was to work with. The first time I'd ever seen him. Whilst we'd been indoctrinated into accepting mining as our way of life, frankly I cried my eyes out when I went home that first morning after working a night. I was frightened to death by the stench, the cockroaches, the mice and the general atmosphere that prevailed in the pit. It was a lot worse than we were led to expect.

Many of the mining conditions were unavoidable, however the job was organised. But the belief that the profit motive made them worse than they needed to be, and the harsh and often narrow-minded attitudes of the coal-owners, had produced a highly political workforce. There was a long history of confrontation between the miners and employers, and coal saw more days lost through strikes and stoppages than any other industry. Because coal supplies were so critical to daily life, government had been increasingly drawn in to settle disputes that the miners and owners could not agree between themselves. In this way miners had gained both a minimum wage and an eight-hour day before the First World War. Just as the pits were recording their greatest-ever output, extracting 278 million tons of coal in 1913, the coalfields had become the principal battleground for industrial and class warfare.

During the First World War the government had to take direct control of the mines to stop labour disputes threatening the coal needed for the war effort. But as soon as the war was over the old struggles were resumed. In 1919 a national coal strike was called again, after a wage claim had been rejected. To stave it off, the government appointed a Royal Commission to look into the coal industry's problems and see what might be done. Though the Commission was split, its Chairman, Lord Justice Sankey, recommended that the only way the coalfields could be made to run smoothly was by taking the mines into full public

A low, wet seam in a south Wales coal mine that has since been closed

169

ownership, as the miners were demanding. Nationalisation was necessary on the grounds that

> The relationship between the masters and workers of the coal-fields in the United Kingdom is, unfortunately, of such a character that it seems impossible to better it under the present system of ownership.[35]

Lloyd George's government found the call for nationalisation a severe embarrassment. Not surprisingly, the coal owners were bitterly opposed. Only the miners, using Labour's new parliamentary strength to which they contributed so much, were determined that the mines should belong to the people. Though other parts of Sankey's report were implemented, the call for nationalisation was rejected. But twenty-seven years later, after a period of depression and decline, coal became the first industry to be taken into public ownership by the new Labour Government of 1945. The National Coal Board inherited ill-equipped mines, bad working conditions, and a record of poor industrial relations. But at last it could be seen whether the problems of the mines were principally human and political, as so many believed. Though little could be done to reverse the long-term decline in the use of coal, it was under nationalisation that a modern mining industry was finally created.

The industry that Sankey examined in 1919 was scattered from the lowlands of Scotland, through Northumberland and Durham, Yorkshire and Lancashire, the Midlands and south Wales, and no two coalfields were alike. In some areas coal was easy to extract, and found in seams seven or eight feet high, close to the surface. In others the coal was deep in the earth in faulted and inaccessible seams. Some mines produced coal that was good for coke, so that steelworks had been established among the collieries. Others produced high-quality household and steam coal. Some concentrated on the export trade, because they were so close to the sea. In south Wales over half the coal had been sent abroad. Each coalfield was self-contained, its contacts with other areas almost non-existent. Among the owners these differences encouraged the highly competitive, small-scale nature of the industry. There were few large coal firms: in the 1920s there were still 1400 different coal companies.

The miners themselves lived in communities that were as dispersed as the collieries. Around each pit was a mining village entirely bound up in the fortunes of the coal that it produced. The diversity meant that no two coalfields had quite the same method of working, or the same pattern of hours and pay. So long as demand had been high it did not matter that more miners were needed each year to produce the same quantity of coal, and that productivity was falling. In the early 1880s output per worker in coal had stood at over 300 tons a year. By 1913 it had fallen to 250 tons, and output per man continued to fall in the early 1920s. The overall picture was of an industry which, like cotton, was

Roof work at the Clay Cross Colliery, Derbyshire. Roadways were often in poor repair, narrow and unsuited to conveyor-haulage methods

standing still, fixed in time. The Victorian lay-out and engineering of mines first built forty or fifty years before still survived, along with the attitudes, and insecurity, and style of management that went with them.

Machinery to cut the coal at the face, and underground conveyor systems, already existed, but they were being brought into use much faster abroad than in Britain. When Gordon Lunnon began, the coal was still cut and moved as it always had been, by human muscle.

> It was all hand got. Pick and shovel, sledge and wedge. Everything was by hand, there were no machines at all. A man and a boy could fill about five or six tons of coal in a shift and that was it. You weren't allowed to use a shovel on the coal, it was by hand, and no one wore gloves. You would be cutting your hands to pieces. It was graft. We used to go home too tired to eat our food.

Working conditions varied widely. Some mines were very hot, and miners stripped off to work. There were regular dangers from gas or flooding. Seams could be as narrow and low as 18 inches, where it was necessary to work lying down, often with water on the floor. With the seam a bit higher, they could crouch, as Stanley Millard remembers.

> Where I was working was a low seam, two feet eight inches. I used to work on my knees all the time and tuck my knees underneath me and sit on the back of my heels. Then with your head bent forward, you'd be picking underneath the bottom of the coal, so you could free the coal for it to drop. You'd be working all day to fill two or three trams.

In south Wales miners worked in pairs at the coal-face, operating the 'butty' system. Each collier was assigned a young boy, whom he taught

171

the job. He helped move the supports and materials, and took the coal from the face to fill the tubs. In a thin seam this was particularly difficult.

> The job of the boy would be running along with a curling box, sliding it along the floor, and he would be horizontal with the weight of his body on the handles of the box. It was very heavy work.

Men bought and maintained their own tools and work clothes, and in pits where there was no gas problem they bought their own candles. Bill Sparham started when he was fourteen, in 1922.

> We worked with candles in a knob of clay. You just tucked it on the wall, on the side of the wall to shine as a light, and we used to buy these candles in a bunch of twelve, 6d for twelve.

Miners had to be skilled not just at cutting coal, but at setting and cutting the wooden pit-props which held up the roof. The danger of rock falls was always present. They trained themselves to listen out for the sound of creaking timber, or falling dust, that indicated something was wrong. John Rees managed to survive one fall.

> I kept shovelling, and the next thing I knew I was in the crouching position. Something had virtually forced me to the

The minimum age for working underground was raised to 14 in 1911. When this group was photographed at the turn of the century, many of the pit lads were 12-year-olds

The underground office of the colliery overmen at a Durham pit, 1920s. Each was responsible for a part of the mine

floor and I was covered all in black, in darkness. Naturally I imagined the worst. I thought the whole lot had come in on top of me but it was just about a ton of coal. It had completely buried me, and by struggling to get through I had all abrasions on my arms and on my neck. But during that time the men had seen what had happened and they jumped down and scooped the coal off me, and they started pulling me out by the head and the arm, but I was caught by the pair of timbers across my legs. It only took about three minutes but to me it seemed like an eternity.

Accidents were a part of normal expectations. In the 1920s thirty-two miners were injured every hour, 500 each day. Wounds filled with coal dust to leave blue scars for life, and miners had little chance of ending their working careers in full health. If serious injury or the loss of a finger or thumb was avoided, there was the prospect of silicosis or pneumoconiosis from coal dust. Though no single accident matched the disaster at Senghenydd in south Wales in 1913, when 439 miners were killed, the fatality rate in the mines rose over the inter-war years because the deeper pits and longer tunnels were old and poorly maintained.

Adding to the tensions of mining work were the complicated piece-work agreements by which miners were paid, which provided a cause of

Cwmcas Colliery, Glyncorrwg.

PRICE LIST,

August 9th, 1900.

		s.	d.
1. Cutting Coal ... ... per ton ...		1	8
1a. Allowance as per arrangement to cover 10 % on Coal and Dead Work ... ... per ton ...		0	2½
2. Gobbing Holing ... ... extra per ton ...		0	2
3. Headings—(Narrow)—2 shifts ... ... per yard ...		7	0
4. Do. (Wide)—1 shift ... ... per yard ...		5	0
5. Do. (Narrow)—1 shift ... ... per yard ...		6	0
6. Do. (Wide)—2 shifts ... ... per yard ...		6	0
7. Airways—First 10 yards ... per yard ...		1	8
And for each succeeding 10 yards ... extra per yard ...		0	6
8. Pillars Retained (11 yards from stall rib) ... per yard ...		1	0
9. Cutting Puckings in Headings ... ... per yard ...		2	0
10. Do. Stalls ... ... per yard ...		1	4½
10a Cutting New Roads in Pillars ... ... per yard ...		1	4½
11. Extra Payment for Traming and unloading rubbish double per tram ...		0	3
12. Turning Stalls—(not exceeding 8 yards wide) ... each ...		10	0
13. Discharging or Filling Rubbish ... ... per tram ...		0	3
14. Double Timber in Stalls and Headings ... per pair ...		2	0
15. Posts—Outside line of Gob ... ... each ...		0	7
16. Cogs—(Wooden) 4 ft. ... ... each ...		1	8
17. Do. do. 6½ ft. ... ... each ...		2	6
18. Converting Narrow into Wide Headings ... per yard ...		1	6
19 Rubbish coming down on top of Coal per inch per ton extra ...		0	0¼
19a Clod per inch per ton when over 12 inches, same as at Blaengwynfi ...		0	0¼
20. Tumbling places ... ... each ...		3	0
21. Ripping Top for Double Timber ... ... Allowance ...			
22. Cutting Extra Bottom for Timber ... ... Allowance ...			
23. Re-opening Stalls ... ... per yard ...		1	6
23a Width of Stall Roads—4ft. 6in.			
24. Drawing Posts		0	1
25. Double Shifts—(if required) in Stalls... extra per ton ...		0	2
26. Hauliers ... ... per day ...		4	6
27. Six Turns shall be paid for Five Night Turns worked ...			
28. Headings to deep [or Dip] ... extra per yard ...		1	0
29. All Coal under 2ft. 10inches thick ... extra per ton per inch ..		0	1

Piece work was the biggest single cause of the disputes that were common in the coal industry

antagonism in themselves. Wages were made up from an intricate system of prices for different jobs. Prices varied from coalfield to coalfield, and often between different faces within the same pit. A manager describes the system that prevailed.

A price list was a list of figures and costs which itemised everything which a miner did, for which he should be paid. So much for erecting timber to support the roof, so much for making a pack behind the face, so much for every ton mined or so much per cubic yard, extra payments for water, extra payments for dirt. My Thursdays and Fridays were always taken up with long, long arguments and debates with the Lodge committee of the union.

The level of aggravation varied across the country. On the wide regular seams of Nottinghamshire or south Yorkshire it was possible to make predictable and uninterrupted progress for years with little argument. But in south Wales or Durham, where miners were constantly meeting geological faults, or flooding, disputes over piecework rates were constant.

In compensation for the conditions they worked under, the miners expected high wages, and so long as the coal boom continued they were able to earn them. At the time that the Sankey Report was published it was expected that pre-war output would be exceeded, and that the export trade would be as great as ever. But the trade downturn that followed the First World War, and the changed markets, were soon to have as devastating an effect on the coal trade as on the other staple industries. With the slump at home, particularly in steel, less coal was bought by industrial users. With world trade down, less coal was needed for shipping. Large tonnages had been sent to the bunkering ports around the world, on which British merchant ships depended. Now there were fewer ships, and more were converting to burning oil rather than coal. Foreign customers began to buy cheaper coal from newer mines in Germany or Poland, with lower costs. In the unprecedented situation of falling demand, the effect of outdated pits and low productivity began to tell. British coal became more expensive and less competitive, and the whole industry was plunged into a deepening crisis throughout the 1920s.

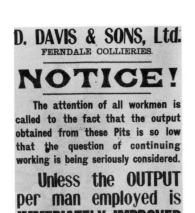

D. DAVIS & SONS, Ltd.
FERNDALE COLLIERIES.

NOTICE!

The attention of all workmen is called to the fact that the output obtained from these Pits is so low that the question of continuing working is being seriously considered.

Unless the OUTPUT per man employed is IMMEDIATELY IMPROVED the Pits must stop.

F. LLEWELLIN JACOB,
GENERAL MANAGER.
1st November, 1921.

The mine-owners did not react by trying to modernise the mines, though in most of Europe output per man was considerably higher. Because labour costs were so much greater in Britain, they concluded that the only way of restoring competitiveness was to cut back on the pay and conditions of their men. It was this collapse in demand, and the owners' response to it, that made labour relations on the coalfields even worse than they had been before. Between 1919 and 1926 over a hundred million working days were lost through strikes. A long stoppage came in 1921 when the government ended the wartime controls which had kept up both prices and earnings, and the owners immediately lowered wage rates. When world coal prices slumped further in 1925, the owners responded in the same way, announcing that miners would have to be paid less.

To avert yet another national strike the government granted a temporary subsidy to prop up wages and appointed yet another Royal Commission, the second in six years, chaired by Sir Herbert Samuel. In their evidence each side blamed the other for the bitterness, and the downward spiral of profits and wages. The miners' leaders complained about conditions in the pit villages and the accident level, and said the mines were inefficiently run. The coal-owners alleged that low wages were largely the miners' own fault, for insisting on working hours so short that economical operation was impossible. They accused the miners of not working hard enough, and of non-cooperation.

Queuing to collect pay from a colliery office, south Wales, after the 1926 strike had ended. Wages were now lower

The Samuel Report did not come out for nationalisation, like its predecessor, but urged modernisation of the pits, to be achieved through amalgamations. But in the short term the Treasury subsidy was to be withdrawn. Faced with the loss of the subsidy, which had meant the taxpayer was paying 2/– in every 10/– that a miner earned on a shift, the owners went ahead with wage cuts, though they knew the effect this would have. The miners refused to accept the cuts and involved the whole trade union movement in defence of their conditions and pay. The action that ensued had a political and historical significance far beyond the coalfields. Though the General Strike collapsed after nine days, the miners carried on. The owners brought in blackleg labour and refused to make concessions. Through the summer the miners and their families turned to the soup kitchens. The industry's future was damaged further, as traditional export markets were taken over by other countries. The miners had no bargaining position, and increasingly less public sympathy. After seven months they were forced back by sheer desperation, coalfield by coalfield. Union power was broken with deliberate victimisation, as Dick Martin saw in Nottinghamshire.

> When we went back to the pit there was the manager standing there. 'Come on you, come on you.' And a gang of lads they would take. They knew everything. To those that had been militant, 'You're not to come, get off, nothing for you. Send for you when we want you.' This is how it happened. I knew families that never did get back after the '26 strike.

The miners returned entirely on the owners' terms, as the minimum wage was cut and hours were lengthened, and it would be

South Wales hunger marchers on their way to the TUC, 1931

nearly ten years before they were strong enough to put in another pay claim. But though the miners' sacrifice meant that the labour costs on each ton of coal had been almost halved in five years, even this failed to restore any lasting advantage to British coal abroad, and demand was still low at home. When the full depression in world trade began to hit an already weakened industry from 1929, the distress was compounded still further. By 1932 over 400,000 were out of work, representing over 40 per cent of the whole industry. Because the newer coalfields suffered less badly, thanks to cheaper production, the concentration of unemployment in the older, export-based areas was far higher. Whole communities in south Wales, Durham and Scotland were forced to fall back on charity, and the humiliating indignities of the Relieving Officer system. Villages closed in on themselves, families in work helping those unemployed. Younger men left for the new factories in the south-east and the Midlands.

The remedy of low wages having demonstrably failed, increasing pressure was put on the mine-owners to do more to change their methods and machinery. The collieries had met hard times by concentrating on the easiest or most accessible seams, and spending as little as possible on roadways or maintenance. Mining practice was already behind other countries after the First War, and was being overtaken further. By 1929 only a quarter of the coal in Britain was cut by machines at the face, but in France it was 70 per cent, in Germany 90 per cent. The way to modernise was thought to lie through 'rationalisation', the cure that was advocated for other troubled industries. A way had to be found to close old inefficient mines, and create larger companies with the financial strength to rebuild the shafts and roadways, and buy new

177

machinery. Sankey and Samuel had preached this, but the owners had not come up with any ideas on how it might be done. In 1930 the Labour Government tried legislation. The Coal Mines Act introduced a plan for reorganisation, in return for government help to keep up prices. The effect was not what the government wanted. The arrangements to keep coal prices artificially high worked far better than the parallel plan for amalgamations and closures. The new quota scheme had the effect of keeping all the small and inefficient mines in operation as well as the successful ones, by sharing out the available work equally. From the union point of view, this was a humane policy, but it put off problems for the future. Coal managed to insulate itself from the true logic of the market, but in its place there was no planning, and little new capital.

Nevertheless, some progress was made in the better mines during the 1930s. Mechanisation was now proceeding more quickly, but patchily, and with different degrees of sophistication. Coal cutters and mechanical picks were now widespread. Used with the conventional system of mining they allowed men to produce coal faster at the face.

> They introduced the automatic pick, driven by a blast of air, and that helped a lot. It was better than using the mandril because it had more driving power behind it and could get more out easier.

In most mines, mechanically-cut coal was still removed from the coal face by hand. The next degree of mechanisation came with the provision of short conveyors to take coal to the trams or tubs. Though the new machines reduced labour and helped profits, the miners did not always see the benefits in their own wages.

Automatic coal-cutter at a Durham colliery, 1934. Early machinery was noisy and increased dust levels

> They put conveyors on the faces. Tin shoots on little wheels and a little engine on top. And you threw the coal on that, and this conveyor would be tipping into the trams. They cut prices down, thinking we were having it easier instead of when we used to carry it out in the curling boxes.

A further stage in modernisation would begin during the Second World War with much larger power-loading machines that both cut and conveyed coal in one automated process.

By 1938 the proportion of coal cut by machine had doubled to 60 per cent. The figure for Germany was 97 per cent. Mechanisation brought a slow increase in productivity, but miners disliked it at first, because one of the senses vital to safety, the sense of hearing, was affected. Bill Gibson experienced the change.

> I was in my twenties. In the old style of working we were trained as young lads to listen to every creak and groan and every little dribble of coal that always indicated there was danger. But once the conveyors came in with all their row, that was gone by the board. You just hoped for the best.

From now on miners had to shout to make themselves heard above the racket underground. But the first machines also brought entirely new dangers of their own. Still at a primitive design stage, they could cause accidents to men not used to operating them, and made the existing hazard from dust even worse. Charles Webber remembers the first coal cutter he worked with.

> It was something like a chain saw, which would cut the coal underneath. It had a four-foot-six blade which used to go underneath the coal and cut about nine inches. Miners were working then in dust, nothing but dust. We were eating dust. And that was the cause of a lot of people having pneumoconiosis.

All these improvements at the coal-face itself were of little use unless there was a similar renewal of the way in which coal was brought up to the surface. Improving the haulage systems was more difficult, because the roadways in the older mines were narrow and tortuous, with long and roundabout routes from the bottom of the shaft to the coal-face. This was often due to the bizarre illogicality of the mineral rights laws. Engineers developing mines had to observe underground boundaries that followed streams and hedges dividing property on the surface. One coal mine might have three or four landowners with the mineral rights to the coal beneath, entitled to a royalty.

> Someone might own a few acres of ground on the surface and it might cost you a penny a ton for all the coal taken from under that property, however deep it might have been. So very often we bent our lay-outs, our roadways, to avoid expensive

properties. That was no good at all from a mining engineering or safety point of view.

Because of these twisting routes, and the small size of the tunnels themselves, most British pits were unsuitable for the new underground railways or long-distance conveyor-belt systems being put into European mines. In Britain most coal was still brought to the shaft by pit ponies hauling tubs, and there were still 70,000 ponies in the 1930s. This was slow and labour-intensive. In Britain one haulage worker was needed for every five tons of coal mined; in Holland one was needed for every 25 tons.

The different speeds at which haulage was improved and machines were introduced reflected the very different experiences of the various coalfields between the wars. In parts of Scotland, Yorkshire, Lancashire and the Midlands, where the coal was better, many companies made reasonable profits, and there were progressive managers who saw the benefits of amalgamations, and modernised their pits. In south Wales and Durham conditions were more difficult, and companies spent less money. This affected attitudes among the miners themselves, and among the managers. In the late thirties Sir William Reid, then a young mining engineer in Scotland, went down to Cardiff to read a paper on the new pit that his company was developing at Comrie.

> I was treated so badly at that meeting I was shocked. They didn't believe a word I said. They didn't believe that 3½-ton mine cars could ever go underground. They didn't believe that diesel locomotives could be used safely and usefully in a colliery in this country.
>
> It let me see that south Wales' technical thinking was so far behind that they couldn't visualise moving forward as we were doing in the natural course of events.

There were the same differences in attitudes to labour relations between south Wales and Durham and the more prosperous areas. In south Wales the mutual distrust between miners and managers was complete, and both sides were dug into a bitter and enduring warfare. Owners were seldom seen, and managers lived apart. In Yorkshire, Nottinghamshire and Lancashire a more caring style of management was common, though by no means the rule. Some ran cricket and football teams and took a paternalistic interest in village affairs. Keir Nixon remembers one pre-war manager in Ollerton, Nottinghamshire.

> Monty Wright was the man I worked under chiefly at the Butley Colliery Company. He was a gentleman to my way of thinking. We saw him down the pit practically three times a week. He knew absolutely everybody in the pit by their Christian name or surname. He was a Catholic, and a lot of the miners changed over to Catholicism to further their own ends.

Opening ceremony for the Grassmoor Colliery pithead baths, Derbyshire, 1929. Costs were shared between the owners and the Miners' Welfare funds

Nottinghamshire had seen the organisation of the 'non-political' Spencer Union, which broke away from the Federation of Mineworkers and co-operated closely with the employers. The Spencer Union became notorious in other parts of the country when it sent labour into south Wales to break strikes, a tactic only defeated by a wave of underground sit-ins in Welsh pits in 1934. The Nottinghamshire miners believed they could communicate with management on equal terms, according to Dick Martin.

> We had union men that weren't militant. It was easy for a man to go into the gaffer's office and thump his table as a union man, but I always found most of our union men at that time would try and make a pal of gaffers. So if you wanted something from the manager you could go and say, 'Well, couldn't we do anything for so-and-so because he's not a bad bloke, y'know', and they got more out of the gaffer like that, and more so in this area. That's why we got better paid money than Wales and north-east. Where we were getting 10/4d they were only getting about 6/4d.

The situation in south Wales was quite different. The owners regarded the area Miners' Federation as a politically-motivated body. They felt that the union distorted the economic truth with their frequent references to profits in a period of sustained losses. The consensus among the miners was that the owners were oppressive, and chiselled over piece rates. Powell Duffryn, the leading Welsh company which took over many failing pits, was nicknamed 'Poverty and Dole'. The

Chairman of the South Wales Coal Owners Association was an intransigent boss of the old school, whom the miners compared with the Sphinx of Egypt. Foster Lewis watched him across the negotiating table during one meeting.

> He sat at one end. The Miners' President sat at the other. Having heard the case stated, Mr Evan Williams did not say 'Yes' or 'No', or anything. He merely shook his head. So the President tried another tack to support his argument, and then he had the same response. He just shook his head. So not a word was spoken by the coal-owners' representative.

For the miners there were some welfare improvements, grudgingly granted, including paid holidays from 1938. But even when wages began to creep up again, levels were below other jobs. The only real advance for coal mining as a whole was the state takeover of mineral rights, which was also put through in 1938. Otherwise an industry that had enlightened companies within it, capable of treating their men well and making profits, was weighed down by the hundreds of worn-out businesses, paying low wages to a workforce that was getting older as younger men left for the better-paid jobs elsewhere. The old, bad, coal industry was the one the public heard about, and the one that provided the case for state ownership.

The Second World War turned the crisis in the coalfields on its head, but did not take it away. There had been too many coal miners and too much coal; now there was a desperate shortage of both. But though government took control of the mines again, and 'Bevin Boys' were drafted to serve in the pits, the battle for production on the coalfields was unhappier and less successful than that of any war industry, and coal output dropped during the war years. In 1945 Harold Wilson, then a civil servant in the Ministry of Fuel and Power, gave his verdict.

> Almost the only black spot on the Home Front during the war has been the coal industry. From the beginning of 1941 onwards the country has constantly been in danger of having insufficient coal for military operations and home requirements, and the government and the people have been confronted with one coal crisis after another.[36]

The continuing difficulties arose principally from the shortage of men. Every miner was asked to put in a six-day week, following a printed letter from the Deputy Prime Minister, Clement Attlee. But they had to work with equipment that was breaking down through lack of proper maintenance and a shortage of pit-props and other materials. Days lost through absenteeism also rose, doubling during the war. The miners came under a torrent of abuse from the newspapers and the general public for not doing their bit. Absenteeism was a result of increased illness and exhaustion after the loss of a rest day as much as anything else. In so far as it was deliberate it also reflected the frustration that many felt

Above: *Wartime demand put new pressure on both owners and miners*

Below: *Labour disputes continued on the coalfields during World War II*

at being trapped in the mines by the Essential Works Order, unable to join the forces, or move to other munitions jobs with better pay.

As labour disputes over piece rates continued, the managers blamed the falling output on miners' bad habits. To get both sides to talk to one another the government insisted that pit committees be established in every mine. Many managers wanted them to discuss disciplinary matters and absenteeism only. The unions wanted to talk about improvements that could be made to increase output and earnings, by making sure there were enough tubs, or dealing with roof or water problems on particular seams.

> Quite a number of the managers resented the interference in the running of affairs. They found it an encroachment into their authority and their right to manage as they saw fit. Any sensible argument or discussion resulted in a very negative answer.

In all the criticism of the industry there were always two strands, the psychological and the technical. During the war an increasing number came to believe that the psychological problems overrode all others, and that the miners would only work with goodwill and the rifts be healed under state ownership; technical change could then follow. In 1943 the Minister of Fuel and Power, Gwilym Lloyd George, urged a complete state takeover, but Churchill rejected this. Nevertheless the mines came increasingly under the government's wing. A conciliation scheme brought all sides together to discuss pay and conditions on a national level, and miners were given a substantial increase in minimum wages. A wartime National Coal Board was set up under the Ministry to run the mines '. . . on the basis of National Service', and to be responsible for labour relations, production and re-equipment. More conveyors were installed, and American mining machinery was shipped in, including the first automatic cutter-conveyors.

Towards the end of the war the Ministry asked a group of engineers to report on the technical state of the industry overall; and the best organisation for improving it. When published, Sir Charles Reid's report was a catalogue of everything that had been wrong with the pre-war industry, and an indictment of the coal-owners for their failure to re-equip, train their men, and market the coal to meet customers' needs.

> The employers as a body have been prepared neither to accept the principle of the survival of the fittest, nor fully to abandon their traditional individualism. In relation to their own undertakings the short view has too often prevailed.[37]

The Committee said that the problem of co-operation was the most difficult the industry had to face, and that attitudes were coloured by 'past history, future hopes, and the degree of trust placed in the honesty of purpose of the other party'. They dodged the question of ownership, but talked of the need for a major reorganisation, with a powerful authority capable of enforcing mergers and planning production across the country. Since the private owners had shown themselves incapable of doing this before the war, nationalisation seemed the only answer. The colliery companies made a last-ditch attempt to produce their own scheme for change under private enterprise. In an emollient report written by a former Director-General of the BBC, they promised that they would henceforth run the mines in a new spirit, 'in a sense of Trusteeship for the Nation'.

From the moment of the Labour victory in 1945 it was obvious that nationalisation, which had been party policy for years and had been recommended by Sankey in 1919, was going to happen. The colliery owners accepted their lot, and tried to negotiate the best possible terms. Compensation was generous, and over £164 million was paid out to private shareholders and family trusts, who were then free to invest in less troublesome and newer businesses. At the start of a new era the miners had also reorganised, with the National Union of Mineworkers replacing the separate coalfield unions. Miners expected that national-isation, for which they had fought for so long, would bring a degree of real control by the workers themselves, and were disappointed with the Coal Board's constitution.

On 1 January 1947 coal became the first British industry to be taken under state control, and the NCB flag was hoisted at all pits. Dick Brown was at a colliery in south Wales on Vesting Day.

> We all assembled, the day shift that was due to go down at seven o'clock. The manager came to a point in the colliery and he said, 'This is your colliery'. That was the beginning and end of it all, because nothing was further from the truth. We still had to work for our living. The manager was the same manager, he would still make the agreements, good or bad.

Sir Humphrey Browne had previously been with Manchester Collieries and was now the production director of the north-west Division of the NCB.

> Vesting Day was rather painful because there were ceremonies everywhere saying how glorious nationalisation was. And the trade union leaders were really having a field day. I sort of stood there and smiled.

The new National Coal Board, having absorbed over 800 colliery companies and 1500 pits, was an enormous enterprise. Three-quarters of a million men came under its command, and admirals and generals were recruited to provide the sort of firm leadership the government felt necessary. Thus many of its highest officials lacked experience of in-dustry, or of coal, or of miners, and the Board was criticised for its large headquarters staff and bureaucracy. Nevertheless it set out firmly to tackle a daunting task. The shortage of coal continued on from wartime and grew worse than ever in the winter crisis of 1947. Higher coal pro-

Vesting Day, 1 January 1947

duction was seen as the key to Britain's whole industrial recovery, and though the Board could not transform working conditions and equipment overnight, it had full government backing and much public money to spend.

The miners saw the new atmosphere themselves. Accustomed to penny-pinching, Dick Martin was still working the conventional system of mining in Nottinghamshire.

> There was plenty of everything. When you used to go to the gaffer for six road nails to mend the rail up to your stall, you could have a sackful. You had plenty of pit-props, plenty of everything. You got plenty of gaffers, deputies. Assistant to this, assistant to that.

As the old financial constraints were removed with the new priorities, managers were judged not by their ability to make a mine pay for itself, as in the past, but by their ability to turn out as much coal as possible. Walter Fox was a mine manager, also in the Midlands.

> It didn't matter what it cost in overtime or machinery, as long as they could turn out the tonnage. That's what mattered. That's what they got promotion on. I was in charge of one development and I wanted a conveyor. It was an American type, and it was £38,000. 'Don't matter, you can have it.'

Managers used to working in small colliery groups found themselves in charge of whole areas, with new opportunities.

To provide a basis for rational development, the first national plan for the coal industry was rushed through. When 'A Plan for Coal' was completed in 1950 it assumed that demand would go on rising, to reach 250 million tons in 1960. This target was to be reached by modernising the old mines, and opening new ones in the profitable coalfields of the Midlands and Yorkshire. Some mines were judged to be beyond their useful life, and 130 were closed within ten years.

More would have closed but for the relentless demand, which made it necessary to keep even the most inefficient mines going as long as there was coal to be had. An intensive programme of mechanisation was implemented. British mining engineers went to look at techniques in the occupied German coalfields, and British machinery companies expanded to produce the thousands of coal cutters and conveyors that were ordered. Roadways were straightened and widened. This made it easier to install new haulage systems, and the pit ponies could be gradually retired. There was more electrification of winding gear. Timber pit-props were replaced by steel supports and arches, and better ways of holding the roof up and stopping falls. This improved safety as well as productivity. Within ten years the number of deaths from accidents halved. By the early 1950s, £60 million a year was being spent. For Philip Weekes, then a manager in south Wales, they were exhilarating times.

> It was a bonanza period for a young mining engineer. We suddenly had enough capital to do the things which we needed to do and should have been done many years before. We mechanised everything we could lay our hands on, and we had very full co-operation from the union.

Given the industry's past record, co-operation between the NCB and the union was essential. Unlike workers in other old industries the miners seldom objected to new machinery as a threat to their jobs. It took some of the sweat out of their work, and even those with the bitterest memories of the thirties were impressed by the seemingly unending call for coal and the severe shortage of labour. But it remained an ageing workforce: nearly half were over forty in 1947. Absenteeism was still high. At a time of full employment, there were no longer wartime restrictions to compel men to stay in the mines rather than leave for cleaner jobs elsewhere. So the NCB put a high priority on improving conditions to make the existing miners more satisfied, and the jobs less off-putting to school leavers whose miner fathers often advised against the pits.

The Coal Board's recruiting advertisements proclaimed: 'Pride and Prosperity have returned to the mines . . . the National Industry with an assured future', and 'Coalmining gives you a job for good'. Some of the improvements were elementary and long overdue. At European mines pithead baths had been standard fifty years before. In Britain only half the mines had them on nationalisation, but the Coal Board

Looking for work with a future to it?

Coalmining gives you a job for _good_

dealt with this quickly. William Young remembers the impact that baths made.

> The first day the men bathed there was about three hundred men under the showers all at once. They were singing and shouting. They used to issue us with carbolic soap. And the smell was great. And when I went home nice and clean, the wife didn't know where she was. Because before that I used to have a bath in front of the fire in the old tin bath.

With fewer injuries from roof collapses and explosions, a major campaign was mounted to deal with the other great hazard, the coal dust which caused lung disease. The new coal-cutting machinery only increased the dust levels at first, but ways were found of suppressing it by spraying water on the cutters.

The NCB worked far more closely with the unions than under private ownership. The system of pit committees was retained and extended, but there were still complaints about militant agitation. Even the communist General Secretary of the NUM, Arthur Horner, was persuaded to take part in a Coal Board film urging miners to abide by their agreements.

> Let us have any concrete complaints so that they may be properly examined, and let us cease this general attack upon management as a class as well as upon people in responsible positions.[38]

The number of days lost through strikes dropped. But in the first twenty years of nationalisation, coal continued to have half the disputes in the whole of British industry, and the Byzantine system of piece work, with its price lists and allowances for different work and conditions, was still the cause of most of them.

With almost all the coal going to the home market the government wanted to keep the selling price low, to help the rest of industry. The notion of coal as a 'service' for the nation was still widespread, though the Board managed to make a profit in six out of its first ten years. Since the income from coal sales was not enough to pay for all the capital expenditure, the Board borrowed heavily from the government. Philip Weekes described the years in which the nationalised industry was often criticised for not spending enough.

> Demand far exceeded supply. We were exhorted to expand, invest more, produce more. I must admit I didn't care very much what the quality was, as long as it was black and there was enough of it and we got it into the wagons and got away with it.

The great coal juggernaut was still rolling onwards, powered by spending schemes that would take eight or ten years to complete, when it was realised that things were going seriously wrong. James Hislop was a manager in Scotland, and saw the coal stocks begin to accumulate out-side his office.

> In 1957 we had a heck of a job selling coal. I had a mine with a big stocking area, and I was bringing coal into that stocking area from other mines, and got rather alarmed about the whole thing.

The same was happening on all the coalfields, where the growing stockpiles were known as 'the Mountains of Mourne'. What the NCB had failed to anticipate was the speed at which other fuels would become competitive. Oil had once been twice the cost of coal, now it was cheap and plentiful. One by one the traditional customers for whose benefit the coal industry had been expanded began to desert it. Mills and factories were converting to oil if they still needed to raise steam, otherwise to electricity. The electricity boards were themselves convert-ing to oil, and began an extravagant nuclear-power programme. British Railways, who had taken eleven million tons of coal a year, replaced steam locomotives with diesels. A Clean Air Act stopped regular coal from being burnt in city grates. Even the headquarters of the NUM were found to have converted to oil-fired heating, though this was speedily altered back. With a fall in demand more rapid than in the depression of the 1930s, coal output fell from 223 million tons in 1957 to 190 million tons in 1961, and 173 million tons in 1966. In the space of a few years the industry became completely demoralised again.

> From being exhorted by governments and newspapers to pro-duce as much coal as we could irrespective of cost, we were suddenly told that they didn't want our coal. That produced considerable resentment, not only with the unions but management too.

At first, measures were taken to protect coal. Imports were stopped, a duty was placed on fuel oil, and the electricity industry was told to use more coal. Nevertheless the new Chairman of the NCB, Lord Robens, had to preside over a massive contraction. In 1957 there were still over 700,000 miners; by 1970 there were fewer than 300,000.

Although the turnabout could be taken as an indictment of the Coal Board's forecasting, many others had failed to foresee oil's rise. Yet faced with the unavoidable fact of falling demand, nothing showed the difference between private and public ownership better than the way it was handled in the 1960s, as compared with the 1930s. It was a tragic irony that the improved relations that the Coal Board had built up with its workers in the first ten years, then allowed it to dispense with them more easily in the second ten years. Central planning to increase pro-duction was converted into a scheme to reduce production and conduct an orderly retreat. A concentration on the newest and most profitable areas, where a ton of coal could cost half as much to produce, meant that most job losses and closures were in south Wales, Scotland, and the

Lord Robens, Chairman of the NCB, 1961–71

north-east. Sir William Reid was Chairman of the Durham Division of the Coal Board.

> We discussed with the miners' union how far we should go and what collieries we should close, and sometimes changed our programme to help the union. We carried out the closure of over 80 collieries in the sixties in Durham without a single strike or go-slow, by properly explaining to the men what we were doing, and by using vacancies in neighbouring collieries.

By combining early retirements, transfers to other collieries and even other coalfields, the reductions went smoothly to start with. The level of unemployment was low, and there were other jobs to move to. But as pit closures reached a rate of one a week, the National Union of Mineworkers began to protest more strongly. They felt betrayed when the Labour Party, which had talked of saving the mines while in opposition, came to power and continued the run-down. Westminster and Whitehall, confident that oil would remain cheap for the foreseeable future, now regarded coal as they saw cotton, as part of a bygone age, to be abandoned as fast as was socially possible. In 1967 a White Paper on energy anticipated a rapid fall of output to 120 million tons in 1975. Lord Robens' efforts to keep spirits up were severely tested.

> In private, in the department and elsewhere, I vigorously opposed the total outlook of that White Paper because it was in fact designed to shut down the coal industry at a far greater rate. Recognising that I was up against the problem of apathy on the part of the department, a lack of a real energy policy, I struggled hard to maintain what we could maintain. But when a Labour minister agreed to put a nuclear-power station in the middle of the Durham coalfield, I said to myself: 'What hope is there? No help from government, that is for sure.'

Miners accepted the closures with a mixture of resignation and incomprehension. For those who stayed there could be higher wages when they moved to new pits. But there were also longer travel times, and a different working atmosphere in larger collieries no longer linked with one community alone. Many miners were shocked by the finality of the closures. Once shut, a pit could not be reopened. Water seeped in, strata converged, and tunnels collapsed.

> We couldn't reconcile ourselves to why it was being done. Naturally you are going to get pits closing that are running out of reserves, but that could not be the case as far as the Rhondda was concerned. They closed the majority of the pits in the Rhondda despite the fact there was a great deal of coal left over. It was butchery.

In 1957 there had been 833 pits open; by 1970 only 293 were left.

In the mines that were still working, productivity was higher than ever before. The number of labour disputes had been drastically cut by the removal of piecework, which was the NCB's major initiative in labour relations in the 1960s. The changeover to paying a standard wage whatever the work done, instead of payment by results, divided management and miners themselves. Just as in the motor industry and shipbuilding, which made the same switch, a trade-off had to be made between the removal of constant disputes and arguments and the simultaneous removal of incentives which might make the work faster when it was not interrupted. Will Paynter was leader of the south Wales miners, and fought hardest for an end to piecework.

> I don't think you'll ever get a time in the coal-mining industry, while piecework prevails, when you won't have strikes, and they arise out of this problem of abnormalities, of conditions that you face in coal mining that you cannot anticipate and fix a price for.

The National Power Loading Agreement of 1965 brought standard rates of pay to the whole industry for the first time, and reduced the differences between the wages of those who had always been paid by the day working on the surface or at maintenance jobs, and those who worked on the coal-face and had always earned the most. At a stroke the government removed the whole nineteenth-century system of measurement and allowances, which had caused so much trouble in the difficult mining areas, but had also helped high production through the bonus systems in the better ones.

> I was an overman and I'd got about 80 people working for me, all fine men. With the advent of the Power Loading Agreement, to a man they all forsook the jobs they were in and accepted other jobs, because they could get as much money working half as hard as they were doing. They said, 'This is it, I'm not flogging myself for this price'. It evened up the bottom with the top, so the bloke who really went to town was no better off than the bloke who didn't care less.

Dick Martin was one of the face workers who did not like the scheme.

> We were all on good money, on contract. When the Power Loading Agreement came in money was in the tin so what had you got to do? You wouldn't go and do six foot if you got as much for doing four foot and that was stupid to me. A lot of the old colliers said they've knocked the incentive out of pit work.

Later a bonus scheme was reintroduced when Joe Gormley, the leader of the Lancashire miners who had always opposed straight daywork, became President of the NUM. Yet despite the fears some had about the scheme, the closure of old pits and the introduction of machinery was now going so fast that productivity rose more rapidly in the 1960s than it had for a century. In ten years output per man rose by 50 per cent.

By the end of the 1960s very little coal was undercut, and loaded onto conveyors. Instead the much faster 'longwall' mining system was in operation in nine out of ten pits. On faces up to 200 yards long machines traversed up and down, shearing coal away and simultaneously loading it onto the conveyor. Rather than have to stop and erect pit-props before the machines or conveyors could be moved forward, self-advancing roof supports meant work could be almost continuous over two or three shifts.

In the course of these changes the old skills of the hewer, working with nothing but his own tools and his knowledge of the best way of bringing down coal, disappeared. Coal-mining was still dirty and oppressive work, but it was now done in teams in which machine operators and fitters, engineers and electricians worked together. Some parts of the work were more tedious. Dick McGee, at Thoresby Colliery near Mansfield, was on a haulage job that was now automated.

> I was put on a button job, and all that was required of me was to sit there and just watch how one belt ran into my belt. If this belt on my right stopped, you had to stop yours. If this belt on the right started, you had to start yours. It was an easy type of job compared to some jobs I've done.

Though mining now had more in common with other industrial jobs, pay levels had fallen in relation to them. In the early 1950s, miners' wages were a quarter more than the average industrial wage; by 1970 they were lower. It took two national strikes to readjust this, in 1972 and 1974, when the miners showed the government and the country that their industrial muscle was still not to be underestimated.

Mining was still dogged by the traditional difficulty of dealing with the ups and downs of coal demand, the so-called 'switchback' effect. The decline of the 1960s was not the end of the story, as it was for cotton. Just when the mines had been reduced in the early 1970s, the OPEC oil crisis changed all the calculations once more, and coal was suddenly 50 per cent cheaper than oil again. The Miners' Union was shown to have had more prescience than anyone else, with its warnings against closures. The Coal Board hurriedly planned to start raising production, by opening new mines and coalfields. A super-mine at Selby would produce ten million tons alone. Then the switchback headed downwards once more, as the recession of the late 1970s reduced demand, and foreign competition became a threat. The steel and electricity industries had to be dissuaded from buying cheap supplies from the United States or Australia, where coal could be sliced from the earth's surface in open-cast mines at a quarter of the cost of European deep-mined coal.

In eighty years, mining has lost some of its old claims to being special, and gained new ones. It is no longer the size that it once was, nor as torn by conflict, nor are the everyday working conditions as bad as they were. But the economics of coal mining have become increasingly extraordinary. Because of the post-war concentration on production

at all costs, and the years when coal prices were kept artificially low to help other industries, and the brief that the industry should be run as a 'service', miners and managers have been confused about the industry's role. Did the industry provide the best service by harbouring the country's fuel reserves, or by maintaining jobs in areas where they were sorely needed, or by trying to run at a commercial profit?

In a pit on the new Selby coalfield, a giant cutter shears coal continuously, under a self-advancing steel roof, and loads it on to conveyors. The NCB want to concentrate the industry in similar mines

Successive governments gave different answers. But none could avoid the increasing cost to the taxpayer of maintaining the coal industry. Losses rose through the 1970s. In 1982–3 the Coal Board lost a record £485 million. Most attention focused on the great variations between the costs of mining in one part of the country as against another. The surviving pits in the old coalfields were responsible for only a small fraction of the NCB's total output, but contributed three-quarters of the loss. Each ton of coal mined in south Wales in 1983 was at a loss of £16. Some who work in the modern pits in good areas see the long subsidy to loss-making pits as holding them back. One manager said:

> I think a real assessment has got to be made as to whether the Welsh mines can be made profitable, whether by investment they can be made to pay. You can't keep feeding a hundred million a year out of the profitable mines, otherwise you will get to a stage where nothing pays and we shan't be competitive.

A retired south Wales manager, who had served under both the private owners and the NCB, followed a different brief.

> To have an accountant's point of view with regards to an industry is entirely different to having the point of view of an engineer that's engaged in the industry. Two different things entirely. The accountant lives only for today, and if the balance sheet is no good for today all he's concerned with is winding it up.

In the 1980s the Coal Board became increasingly commercial, in its attitude, and in the instructions it was given by the politicians. A new chairman was brought across from the steel industry, where he had presided over a halving of the workforce. Coal Board chiefs talked with a new candour about the need to abandon 'Victorian holes in the ground'. Lord Ezra was Chairman of the Coal Board until 1982.

> What we've got to do is ensure that we accelerate the rate of replacement. There are a number of mines which for purely geological reasons – it's nothing to do with lack of effort – are unlikely to be able to produce coal which can be competitive on any basis, and which have a limited life anyway. And so it is a question of reaching agreement to replace those mines with new mines with new equipment and high productivity which will stand up to any form of energy competition including imported coal.

Because of the transfers many miners have spent time in both types of pit during their working lives. Ernest Hall began working in the wet and narrow seams of the Craghead Pit in Durham, which produced about 7000 tons of coal a week. In 1969 Craghead was closed.

> They realised what they were doing. They said, 'We're closing the pit'. That's all they were bothered about, because they weren't making a profit. They didn't realise what else they were doing. It was smashing the whole community up. People that was going to have to move away from their parents. People that had got children, maybe fourteen, ready to leave school, and some with babies, having to come to Nottingham or Yorkshire.
>
> They only understand one thing, that it's not paying.

Craghead closed at a time when there were still jobs to be had in other coalfields for those who wanted to move. Ernest Hall is now a chargehand at Kellingley in Yorkshire, one of the biggest pits in Europe, where 2000 miners produce 60,000 tons of coal a week from wide and regular seams, with the most modern machinery. He is satisfied with his pay, and proud of the new pit, but like many miners he does not accept the Coal Board or the Treasury's arithmetic or concept of profit, as applied to the industry he has spent his life in. He says he would strike to prevent a new round of closures.

> It's up to the ones like us at Kellingley, or other good pits that's making a profit, to stand up and stick up for those men and say, 'Right, we'll back you up, you're not closing that pit'. If there's coal there and they can get the coal why should they close it?
>
> They'll always need coal. Always. Is your oil going to last? Is your North Sea gas going to last? It'll come back, don't worry about that. They say it's dying off, coal, but it will never die off.

CHAPTER 9: FARMING
WORKING THE LAND

Agriculturists must make up their minds to face their difficulties without Government interference and without expecting the Government to subsidise them.

Cabinet Committee on the Agricultural Situation, 1922

We are anxious to help you, and if you will organise your industry to provide an adequate supply of good-quality produce, we will help and encourage your schemes and protect you against foreign imports.

National Government, 1931

The countryside means different things to different people. The majority who live in cities and towns share a vision of an unchanging and timeless rural Britain, with its hedgerows and villages, where old values still survive. To farmers and farm labourers, working the land is a business and a job, and when agriculture is judged as a productive industry like any other, then its recent history has been very different from the general experience of Britain at work since 1900. Farming, a part of national life in which so much emotional capital is invested and in which tradition is supposedly held most dear, has seen greater and faster changes than almost any other sector.

In contrast to many town-based industries, farming started with a great decline at the end of the nineteenth century. It then made a remarkable recovery to the point where British farmers now pride themselves on their efficiency and productivity in comparison with the rest of the world. Still farming wheat in Norfolk, at the age of eighty-two, Cyril Muskett took part in the turnaround. He can remember the ruin that faced his family just after the First World War:

> Farmers were in a very poor way. I remember when we first bought this farm that valuation deteriorated by £1000 in one year. Horses we paid £147 for, one year later they were valued at £47, and we had ten horses. Well, that was a great deal of money. I remember my father coming home. 'Look here', he said, 'I can't get any money from the bank, I have used my money, I have used your money, I might as well shoot myself.'

The problems that faced cereal growers in East Anglia were not new, but were returning after the interruption of the First World War. British farming had been in overall decline since the 1870s. The free trade that benefited most industries by allowing the free export of their products all over the world made it possible for countries with a better climate and more space to grow cheap food and send it to Britain. Farmers could not compete with the price of grain from the virgin prairies of North America. When they switched to producing meat, they were hit by the development of refrigerated shipping. Beef from Argentina, and mutton from Australia and New Zealand, undercut the home prices, as did bacon from a more efficient Denmark. Governments did nothing because cheap food was politically popular, and agriculture was sacrificed to the needs of the cities. Millions of acres fell out of cultivation; less was ploughed up to grow wheat and more was given over to pasture. In thirty years after 1870 wheat production was halved. Farmers' and landowners' income dropped, and farming standards fell as less was spent on upkeep. Farmworkers' wages fell behind, and they flocked to the towns. In the years before the First World War 'the Land Question' had already been recognised as a social as well as an economic problem. Reformers saw the poverty and poor housing in the villages. Farmers talked of themselves as the Cinderella industry. By 1914 the country grew only one third of its own food.

Harvesting in Herefordshire

At a surprisingly late stage in the First World War, the full danger of the reliance on imported food was realised. German submarines torpedoed hundreds of ships carrying food, and at one point the country had only six weeks' supply of wheat left. The emergency brought a total switch in the policy towards farming. Government intervened directly, to get more land growing grain, and bring in women volunteers to help. With the Corn Production Act of 1917 farmers were guaranteed high prices and stable markets, and farm wages were to be maintained at a fixed level. An additional three million acres were brought under the plough in two years. As in other industries, the organisation of the enemy was studied carefully, to try to explain the great advances in German farming during the period of British decline. Figures were produced by the Board of Agriculture to compare average production in Britain with Germany, where soil and climate were said to be inferior. They showed that:

The formation of the Women's Land Army was part of the campaign to plough more grassland in World War I

> On each hundred acres of land –
> 1. The British farmer feeds from 45 to 50 persons, the German farmer feeds from 70 to 75.
> 2. The British farmer grows 15 tons of corn, the German farmer grows 33 tons.[39]

The German success was attributed to the high tariffs which had protected her farmers, and also to better education, more scientific farming, and the heavy use of fertilisers. At the time, British politicians seemed to take the point. The Prime Minister, Lloyd George, promised that help for farmers would be continued after the war, and that the strategic lessons would not be forgotten. But the promise was not kept. Three years after the War, world food prices were tumbling, and the British government's policy of subsidising farmers by price guarantees laid a heavy expense on the Treasury. In 1921 the government decided it could no longer afford to help, and withdrew support. Britain was once again an open door for cheap food from abroad. One farmer recalls:

> Now what happened after the First War when Lloyd George's Corn Production Act was repealed was that the whole thing collapsed, and people went bankrupt and farmers headed the list of bankruptcies, and cattle that had cost a price at the time of purchase, when they came to sell them, they were selling them for half what they had given for them.

Recognising that farmers' incomes would fall, the government took away the guaranteed wage for farm labourers at the same time. Len Sharman was working in Suffolk.

> Farmworkers' wages were about fifty shillings a week. In two cuts they were down to twenty-five shillings. And that's when things started going wrong. That's when times really began to get hard.

West country farmers at Exeter market, in the 1920s. Livestock prices were dropping, and they faced growing hardship

As the price of corn fell from eighty shillings a quarter in 1920 to forty-seven shillings in 1922, farmers complained of the great betrayal. Ministers were sent out to try to placate them, and explain that the troubles they were suffering from were common to most industries, and that they should adapt themselves to the economic position. Cyril Muskett went to listen.

> Stanley Baldwin he came along and he called a meeting. In the end he finished up by saying that he had listened to our complaints, and the farmers were a jolly nice bunch of people, but he could only say that they would have to find their own salvation. And that put paid to us.

Not all farmers suffered the same way. Then, as now, farming was a varied business with great differences according to the region of the country, soil and climate. The fortunes of the cereal grower in East Anglia, or the beef farmer, were not the same as those of the milk producer close to London, or the fruit grower or market gardener. Most farmers did not specialise in cereal crops or livestock, but kept a mix. Yet taken overall the 1920s were bleak years for both farmers and farmworkers. On the smaller family farms in the west and the Midlands, farmers began a hand-to-mouth existence. By spending as little cash as possible, and raising a few cows and chickens and growing the corn to feed them, they could be self-sufficient. But in the major grain-producing areas, with bigger farms and with more hired men, the situation was much worse. Many sold up, or went bankrupt. Others laid off men, and reduced wages. The advance in methods and machinery and yields was held back still further, and working conditions and wages remained strikingly poorer than conditions in the cities.

Rural life was still harsh, with low pay, long hours, and little security. Arthur Amis began as a cowman in East Anglia in 1922.

> I started full-time work when I was fourteen but I could milk
> cows earlier than that. I lived three-and-a-half miles from work
> and I had to be at the work at half-past-five, so I had to leave
> home about quarter-to-five in the morning. I used to finish
> about half-past-five at night and get home just after six, and of
> course I was ready to tumble into bed. We lived in a cottage, a
> family of 11. We had two bedrooms and a little side room and
> we managed in there. The boys in the family slept on mat-
> tresses on the floor. We didn't have beds. The food was bread
> and cheese or bread and jam, you didn't have butter on your
> bread. You had jam which was home-made because there were
> blackberries we used to gather and that type of thing, and har-
> vest time was the best time of the year because we had plenty
> of rabbits. This was how we managed.

People in the towns seldom appreciated the full realities of life in the
villages. Even Seebohm Rowntree, the champion of the urban poor, had
painted a deceptively rosy contrast with the industrial slums which he
had studied before the First World War.

> The agricultural labourer is an actor in the great drama of seed-
> time and harvest; he sees the fruit of his labours gathered into
> the barns at harvest-time; he is close to the creative forces of
> nature.[40]

In practice rural life was deprived. There were few opportunities,
schools were scattered, housing was poor, and families ill-fed. A school
medical inspector in Devon in 1923 reported that:

> Many of the children in country schools are pale-faced,
> anaemic-looking, with eyes lacking lustre, undersized, under-
> fed and sad-faced.[41]

At the root of the problem were low pay and long hours of work.
The starting wage for young labourers was 5/- to 10/- for a seven-day
week. Wages for the older men rose during the war when labour was
scarce but then fell back. For those out of work there was no dole.

> No, there was no dole. We never got the dole till 1936. It was
> like holidays. We never had a Saturday afternoon off until
> 1926, and one old farmer says, 'Well, if they're going to have
> the half-day, they must have it on Monday mornings.' Well,
> we went from half a day. We got four days a year. You'd have
> half-a-day Christmas day, half a day Good Friday. Boxing Day
> was unheard of, you'd got to go to work.

Most workers accepted these conditions because there was little alternative. It was a captive workforce, living in small communities, where
the workers still had to salute the squire and the parson. Isolated from
one another, the farmworkers were in a weak position to organise or

Striking farmworkers in Norfolk, 1923

negotiate pay. The National Union of Agricultural Workers, founded in 1872, had a low membership. The Union's General Secretary cycled over 1000 miles a year, riding from village to village to recruit support. There was a rare strike in Norfolk in 1923, after local farmers tried to cut wages by a further 5/- to £1 a week. About 10,000 men walked out and the strike lasted six weeks. At the 'Battle' of Holly Heath Farm, 300 labourers converged on a farm where the pickets had been shot at, extracted two pounds for their strike fund from the farmer, and left singing the Red Flag and 'Onward Christian Soldiers'. Frightened of the unrest, the government put pressure on the farmers to restore the wage to 25/-. One farmer explained what happened when the strike ended.

> Three of the men came back, and the governor was at the stables waiting for them. And we had been up and fed the horses, and asked them what they had come back for. Of course two of them began to apologise and this and that, and one of them we wanted to get rid of – we told him he'd better keep at home and he said: 'What will my wife say?' 'Well, you should have thought about your wife before you came out on strike.'

Once the 'troublemakers' had been sacked peace was restored, though in many places conditions continued to worsen. The men knew that working side by side with the farmer, day-in, day-out, made it difficult to protest.

> You can't work with a man ten months in the year, and come harvest time say, 'Well, I'm going to strike', can you? I mean, there's that brand of loyalty, you see. You all hang together.

199

Eviction from a farm cottage in the 1920s. Farmworkers lost their homes if they lost their jobs

It is difficult for farmworkers to strike because they are so isolated. You get one man working here and another working there. You have to remember, you were known by your Christian names on the farm and you would sometimes call the boss by his Christian name and there was that friendly atmosphere. I think this is one of the problems of farmworkers going on strike.

One of the factors that encouraged loyalty and deference to the farmer was the 'tied cottage'. Most agricultural workers were given a cottage with the job. The moment a man was sacked, he and his family could be evicted without notice, with only the Victorian Poor Law, still in operation until the 1930s, to fall back on.

My brother got wrong with the boss and he gave a week's notice and the boss, he goes to my father and he says, well, your boy's given me a week's notice and now you can take a month's notice and go. And my father says, well, what about our bargain. Oh, he said, bugger that, bugger that . . . There was no work to be had. He hadn't got any money, there was no dole, nothing like that, and he called on the Parish. They gave him four days' work a week on the roads. They didn't give him any money. They gave him a voucher for 16/- to buy groceries at the village shop. He'd got a wife and four children. In the meantime, he'd got another house but still a tied cottage. Once you're in a tied cottage, you're trapped.

For those without work there was no alternative but to join the army of casual labourers who went from farm to farm at harvest and threshing time, or to move to the cities where wages were two or three times higher, if jobs could be found. Many of the younger men left by choice, for the new factories of the Midlands and the south-east. In 1919 there were a million farmworkers, by 1930 only 590,000 remained. Politicians were inconsistent about what should be done. They talked of making

Extra men were needed when the harvest was threshed. Steam engines travelled from farm to farm

farming pay by reducing costs, but they also saw farmwork as a way of providing jobs for the unemployed. Noting the fact that in Germany four times the proportion of the population was still on the land, and in France seven times, former Prime Minister Lloyd George argued:

> If we had the same percentage on the soil as the next lowest country, we should have in a few years absorbed all the chronic unemployment which is one of the most terrible of our economic problems, and this minimum of a million would have been employed in this healthiest of occupations.[42]

But, for the country workers who remained, the occupation was laborious rather than healthy. Hand-milking took hours at a time. Ploughing meant walking behind the team in all weathers, with an old sack to keep off the rain. Some farmers who had worked with tractors in the First World War reverted to horses. Before the harvest could begin, fields had to be opened up by hand.

> I can still recall cutting round the corn in those days with the sickle and scythe so that the horses could go round first time without trampling the corn. Usually men cut the corn, and women came behind and tied up the bundles.

> You had these lines of stooks like the aisles of a church, dead straight. There was a great emphasis on skill, everything had to be straight. And when it had stood in the field for maybe ·a week, maybe two weeks, you could haul that to the stack. The horse and wagon would draw up between the rows of stooks, which were loaded on the wagons.

At the end of the year, when the summer grain harvest was separated from the straw, steam engines were still used for threshing. About fourteen men were needed to run the engine, throw the sheaves from the stack onto the threshing drum, and clear away the dust. Len Sharman remembers the grain sacks.

> The sacks weighed 2¼ cwt, and these had to be humped onto wagons, and many a man suffered from rupture for sure, for lifting 2¼ cwt onto a wagon which stood four feet from the ground.

> That's a very hard, dirty job. I'm not very big, I'm not all that strong, and that's terrible hard work. They used to say that if you carried a hundred sacks a day you'd done a good day's work. I carried a hundred and thirty-five and I can tell you I went home jolly tired that night.

In the late 1920s most grain was threshed at a loss. After the great crash of 1929 world food prices slumped still further. Other countries were suffering as badly, but they were able to use Britain as a dumping ground for their food surpluses at rock bottom prices. The journalist Philip Gibbs described a visit to East Anglia at harvest time.

As prices slumped, farmers campaigned for protection and an end to foreign food imports under Free Trade

> It was a tragic situation. Here are some of the finest and largest farms in England, into which these men have put all their fortune and labour of mind and body. Those far-stretching harvests of wheat and oats should have been a source of wealth to themselves and the nation. But on every acre of wheat they would lose five pounds at least. They were losing on almost every other crop . . . There had been a frightful slump in the price of potatoes. It did not pay to rail their cabbages. They dropped four to five shillings a head on every sheep. They could get no paying price for pigs. For five years their capital had been withering away by these continual losses, while their land fell in value to a quarter of what they paid for it.[43]

Many farmers simply gave up the struggle. At its lowest point, wheat stood at twenty shillings and ninepence a quarter, the lowest recorded figure since the English Civil War. A government report gave a dismal account of the consequences.

> Less arable land was to be seen in the landscape; the number of derelict fields, rank with coarse, matted grass, thistle, weeds and brambles, multiplied; ditches became choked and no longer served as effective drains; hedges became overgrown and straggled over the edges of other fields; gates and fences fell into disrepair; farm roads were left unmade.[44]

Up and down the country farmers demonstrated against government inactivity under the banner 'Wanted in 1914. Neglected in 1930.' The

farmers' lobby was becoming increasingly effective. By 1930 over two-thirds of them belonged to the National Farmers' Union. Political parties began to realise that something had to be done for agriculture, even before the National Government took over in the financial crisis of 1931 and made the change from free trade to a policy of protection.

Coming off the gold standard and abandoning free trade helped many British industries but also allowed them to continue their old ways unchanged behind the tariff barriers. But in the case of farming a partnership with government developed which was to be long-lasting and highly effective in the changes it brought about. Government, faced with the prospect of falling trade and greater difficulty paying for imports, now found an advantage in encouraging home agriculture. As well as the duties that were placed on foreign food imports, subsidies were available for both cereal and livestock farmers. Schemes to market farm products collectively were encouraged. A National Government propaganda film explained the proposition that was being put to the farmers very explicitly:

> The National Government said as it were to the British agriculturist, 'We are anxious to help you, and if you will organise your industry to provide an adequate supply of quality produce, we will help and encourage your schemes and protect you against foreign imports being dumped on the market.'

All this was done amidst considerable debate and internal division amongst the farmers themselves. Cheap wheat from abroad had ruined the wheat growers, but had been a blessing to the cattle farmers who could buy cheap feed. Farmers were frightened at the prospect of bureaucratic control from Whitehall. Not all milk producers welcomed the first and most successful of the marketing schemes, the Milk Marketing Board. Yet the fortunes of hundreds of small livestock farmers were transformed. In Devon, Michael Lee's family benefited immediately.

> The Milk Marketing Board started in 1933. My father kept bullocks, milked a few cows, and mother took butter to Exeter and sold it for about 1/10d a pound. We probably took £5 a week. It was a not a very good way of making a living. But through the formation of the Milk Board everybody was paid the same price for milk throughout the country. We were then getting the equivalent of double the price for liquid milk . . . and this stabilised Devon farming in particular because here was an ideal grass-growing area, and we could keep cows and it could be profitable.

Soon there were marketing boards for eggs, potatoes, bacon and hops. Farmers no longer needed to haggle with merchants, because the most individual of industries had acquired all the strength of a monopoly supplier. With greater security and better prospects, the modernisation of farming accelerated. On the dairy farms new milking

203

A tractor pulling a reaper-binder in 1936. Tractors spread fast in the late 1930s, as farm incomes rose again

machinery and portable milking sheds meant that more cows could be kept, and brought changes for cowmen like Arthur Amis.

> When machine milking came in for the cows it meant that you'd be milking four cows at a time, and two of you could easily look after that. So instead of having four or five men there was just two men left, or a man and a boy. The machinery did drive the men off the farms.

Farmers began to talk of 'mechanised agriculture', and though there were still horses on almost every farm, more tractors were bought to pull ploughs, reaper-binders, and the new balers. Combine harvesters were imported from America and demonstrated for the first time in the early 1930s, but only a few hundred were put into use. Farmworkers could see the progress of mechanisation, but were in no position to block it to protect jobs even if they'd wanted to. Productivity was improving. Labourers' wages were rising again, though the average was still only £1.15/- a week. They were granted paid holidays, but only seven days a year, not more than three days to be taken at once. Even with mechanisation the work could be as tough as ever. Len Sharman had looked after horses, but adapted to the tractor.

> The old Fordson Standards, they were really demons to start in the cold mornings. You'd have to swing for an hour before you'd get them going, and they wouldn't pull until they were hot. But on a very long day in hot summertime, they were boiling hot, the oil used to get hot and the gearbox would be so hot you couldn't put your feet on it. But in the wintertime that was a different story. You sat and froze with cold. You had no cab. I've had two overcoats on, two pairs of gloves, a pair of leggings, and then I've been frozen, I could howl with cold.

By 1939 British farming was recovering from its worst days. Up to £40 million a year was going in subsidies, but the benefits were not equally spread. Livestock and hill farmers were still suffering. Ken Jones ran his Welsh farm from 1937.

> When I took over this farm we had two teams of shire horses doing what ploughing was done here, and all the work; and it wasn't until 1942 that I bought my first tractor. Up until the wartime very few of my neighbours had a piped water supply. Very few of them had a road to the house, and housing conditions and general living standards were much lower.

Much remained to be done. Only one in ten farms had electricity. Grants were available to modernise farmworkers' cottages, but only a small proportion had the basic amenities by the war. Mechanisation had begun, but there were twice as many tractors in Germany as in Britain. Yields had almost stood still, and were in some cases lower than they had been before the First World War. Many of the improvements had only returned the industry to where it had been before the long depression.

With the Second World War, which began just as the harvest of 1939 was ending, the pressure was on the farmers again. Government used the full range of propaganda, financial inducement and emergency legal powers to get as much food grown at home as possible in the shortest time, which meant a concentration on wheat and potatoes. In the first plough-up campaign the target was two million acres. The farmer and writer A. G. Street recorded at the time:

> Just now British farmers can be divided into five classes. One, those who are ploughing up grassland; two, those who are cultivating and sowing ploughed-up grassland; three, those who are talking about their intention to plough up some grassland; four, those who are toiling and worrying on the local committees responsible for getting a certain acreage of grassland ploughed; and five, those who are objecting to any suggestions that they should plough up grassland.[45]

Farmers were directed as never before, by War Agricultural Committees set up in each county. The 'War Ags' were composed of both local farmers and officials and their job was to see that their area produced the amount set by the Ministry. They gave each farm a ploughing quota, and because their powers were so extensive, no farmer could afford to ignore them. Philip Woodward worked on his local committee.

> It wasn't an easy job, because a lot of them didn't want you at all. But you see, they couldn't get any feeding stuff, they couldn't get any petrol, they couldn't get any paraffin, unless it was allocated by the War Agricultural Committee, so they had to really toe the line a bit, and come down to it. Some people didn't want to be helped, some people were very pleased to have you.

To make the scheme more attractive farmers were given a subsidy of £2 for each acre ploughed, by the Ministry of Agriculture, and the Ministry of Food paid high prices for everything they grew.

The ploughing campaign also aggravated the old conflicts amongst the farmers themselves. Livestock farmers could no longer get cheap feed, and did not want to plough grazing land. Government pointed out, relentlessly, that an acre under crops fed far more people than an acre of pasture, and so production of beef, veal, mutton and lamb fell, and the number of animals dropped. But the newly-converted pasture land was fertile, and gave high yields. Public parks, golf courses and orchards were all ploughed up, as were Ken Jones's hillsides.

> With the shortage of labour, it was extremely difficult. I wouldn't like to say how many hours we worked in those days. During that time we took ploughs down everything that was ploughable, and on this farm I have got no flat land, and we turned it all up. If a farmer didn't carry out his ploughing quota he could be dispossessed.

In the end over 8000 were evicted for not co-operating, or farming badly. Derelict farms were revived and land that had not been properly drained since the nineteenth century was reclaimed. Farmworkers sometimes ploughed through the night by moonlight, or on occasions by searchlight. To provide the labour the Women's Land Army was formed once again. When there were not enough land girls, prisoners of war were sent to the farms. The achievement of all this exhortation and intervention, and sweat and toil, was that land under wheat rose by two-thirds, and an additional six million acres were ploughed by the war's end, when Britain was producing 80 per cent of its own food. Most important for the long run, the methods and practices of farming had changed more substantially in five years than in the previous twenty. What had been known in theory at the colleges or research centres before the war was increasingly put into practice. More fertiliser was used and new chemicals were introduced against weeds and pests. Mechanisation advanced rapidly. Though there were still over half a million horses in 1945, the number of tractors had quadrupled during the war. There were now 2000 combine harvesters.

As well as a technical change, there had been a financial improvement. In a situation of labour shortage, farmworkers' wages had begun to close the gap with town earnings, though they were still way behind. The Agricultural Wages Board now set a national minimum wage. Farmers themselves did better out of the war than almost any other group. Their incomes rose further and faster than the general level of wages or prices, and the efficient arable farmers prospered most. All this had been in a situation where they were told what to grow, and how to sell it, at a fixed price. The farmers' great drive had caught the imagination of the general public, who saw that they had ensured the nation's survival. Farmers also appreciated that doing their patriotic duty and

Tom Williams, Labour Minister of Agriculture, at the Smithfield Show. His 1947 Act gave farmers a stability no other industry enjoyed

working so closely with government had not been bad for their pockets.

In the early months of peace it was the turn of the National Farmers' Union to mount a propaganda campaign. Farmers were worried that they might be abandoned again as they had been in 1921. But things had changed and the new Labour government was on their side. The strategic need for self-sufficiency in food had twice been learnt, and with the dollar crisis home food production would save the foreign exchange cost of imports. The government brought in the 1947 Agriculture Act, to become known as 'the farmers' charter', which promised real long-term stability. The Minister of Agriculture, Tom Williams, was a former miner, and introduced the bill:

> During the war, the farmers and farmworkers of Britain stood between us and starvation. Today they are still fighting the battle for bread. When that battle has been won, they will be able to bring us more of the other foods we want: milk, meat, eggs, vegetables, fruit. But they must not be let down as they were after the 1914–18 war. The Agriculture Bill aims at giving farmers an assured market and guaranteed prices for their principal products, while at the same time ensuring a higher level of efficiency.[46]

The slogan was 'Full efficient production at home', and the 1947 Act was to be the basis of British agricultural policy under different governments for nearly thirty years. In that time farmers achieved much. Though the amount of land they farmed fell, they grew more food than ever. Though the population increased, they kept up a degree of self-sufficiency unknown before the war. But when their performance is contrasted with less successful industries it must be remembered that farmers had a degree of consistent government support and subsidy higher than that given to anyone else.

The 1947 Act was ingeniously designed to benefit the consumer, as well as the farmer, at the expense of the taxpayer. Though cheap food would still be imported and reach the shops, British farmers would not be subject to the vagaries of world prices. They would be paid a guaranteed price by the government, sufficient to give them a proper income and return on their investment. But the government also had powers to force them to farm to a certain standard. With guaranteed prices that they helped set themselves, they could hardly go wrong.

> Farmers were on a seller's market to some extent. If you are on a seller's market things are much easier. The truth was that we were very short of food, we were very short of foreign exchange, and therefore it was much easier to negotiate good prices than it later became.

At the heart of the new system was the annual price review, at which the farmworkers' trades unions, the Ministry, and the National Farmers' Union sat down together to review policy and set prices for the next year. The review was unique in industry, and to the NFU it was an ideal system.

The government and the NFU formed one team for this purpose. It was a marvellous exercise in that the industry and department of government, whether they had the time or the inclination or not, by law had to sit down once a year and go thoroughly into the whole thing. It was very wide-ranging, it wasn't just the interests of agriculture, it was how agriculture fitted with the general national picture.

The prospect of long-term security had an immediate impact. Regular profits could be made, and farmers could invest in buildings and improvements and plan ahead. Every kind of farming benefited, though the big farms felt the effects first. For the hill farmers prosperity came more slowly, but special provisions were made for them.

Tom Williams brought in his Hill Farming Act, and government recognised the importance of hill farming, and tried to increase the productivity and the status of the hill farmer. We had grants for roads, we had grants for buildings, we had grants for reclamation work, we had stock grants to compensate for living in this part of the world.

For the farmworkers there were fewer benefits, however. The union had increased its membership during the war, but was still weak. Farm pay was still far behind factory pay, and conditions were not much improved. Though Len Sharman was now earning £5 a week, he could see what his employers were getting.

They gave farmers subsidies on practically every commodity they had, on all the corn, on the milk, the cattle, on the fertilisers, the drainage, the ditching, practically everything. They had subsidies, well, they called them feather-bedded farmers and of course they were in those days. They had it jolly good.

The farmers were expected to keep their side of the explicit bargain and to become more productive. The National Advisory Service was established and officials toured the farms promoting better management, and cleaner and more scientific farming methods. New breeds and better crop varieties were put into general use, and more chemicals were used. Yields on Michael Lee's Devon dairy farm rose.

The government then were willing to plough a lot of money into research and so were the commercial firms. Fisons and ICI and people like that were quite prepared to spend a lot of money because they could see a good return on it, by increasing productivity on the farms. The farmers took it up and the amount of extra food and better feed that went into the stock altered very considerably over the following twenty years.

Carousel milking unit: the system of grants and subsidies encouraged farmers to improve farm buildings

One of the greatest changes resulted from the improvement of artificial insemination techniques for livestock, after 1947.

> If you imagine, then there were probably 200,000 farms each having their own bull. Now with the AI service that is available you are probably down to 40 or 50 bulls doing most of the work. And the breeding of these bulls is so good and so methodical that it must improve the productivity of the cattle. You've got bulls now that cost £80,000 which no ordinary farmer could afford. But you can afford the £3 to £5 AI fee, and for this fee you get the top bulls of the country.

In 1957, when farm production was 60 per cent above the pre-war level, a new Agriculture Act gave an even greater impetus to change. Sensitive to criticisms that farmers were doing too well from straight cash subsidies, paid as deficiency payments when market prices were too low, the government now shifted support towards grants which had to be spent for specific purposes. The cash incentives, for a broad range of improvements from drainage to new dairy buildings, encouraged even the smallest and most conservative farmers.

While the progress with yields was largely achieved in the laboratories, mechanisation did most to alter the look of the country and the nature of the work. The tractor, now much more powerful, became universal. In 1960 there were 470,000 of them. The combines took over the harvest completely, and men were no longer needed to run the reaper-binder, make the stooks, cart them in, stack them and run the threshing tackle. Ray Topham had started farming after the war.

> In those days to get a combine harvester you had to get an allocation from the Ministry, and they allocated us the small harvester, and I always remember I worked right through the harvest on it and I always used to take sandwiches with me and I'd go all day long, never stop until it was too dark or too wet. I

went contracting and I actually earned £500, its cost, in the first year. As I took on more land what I used to do was make my fields bigger, then in turn by making the fields bigger I could afford bigger machines to farm the bigger fields.

Farming was a business in which the most energetic and enterprising could get ahead, and raise the cash to put their ideas into practice more easily than for many commercial enterprises. But luck still played a part. One old farmer analysed the requirements as he observed them:

Some people were in here the other day, and they were highly academic people and they said, 'Now, Mr Muskett, what do you think it would take to make a farmer, and what ingredients would it take?' 'Well', I said, 'all it wants is 40 per cent muscle, 40 per cent brain, but he must have 20 per cent luck. Without good luck he couldn't exist,' and I am sure he couldn't.

Mechanisation was reducing the need for such a high percentage of muscle, but there was nothing that could be done about the luck factor. An outbreak of disease could kill a herd, and bad weather could lay low a crop just before harvest. Dairy farmers remember the foot and mouth outbreaks. Sheepfarmers recall the bad winters, when stock starved or froze to death.

1947 was certainly the worst winter I had, with the losses of stock, and the poor fodder that was in the barns to begin that winter. Sheep were coming across the wet ground here and through the pool and getting drowned under the snow. There were ponies frozen standing up, dead. Many people lost more than half their flocks, through no fault of their own.

In the early 1960s many farmers thought their long run of political good luck was about to break. The first bid to join the Common Market, in 1963, threatened their subsidy system, and would expose them to competition with sections of European farming that were more specialised. Though British agriculture was more efficient than it had ever been, some of its yields were well below those of Belgium, Holland and Germany. The NFU opposed entry, and the application was in any case unsuccessful. But ten years later, when Common Market entry finally came, the old certainties were removed. Agricultural policy was no longer controlled from Whitehall but from Brussels, and the priorities of the EEC were not the same. The 'intervention' price system worked quite differently, and though there was a transitional period, farming became a riskier business. Cereal growers, who had been in the ascendant since 1939, were helped more than dairy or meat producers. In 1974 the bottom fell out of the beef market, threatening financial disaster for thousands of British producers who had grown accustomed to long-term security. One of them was interviewed on television at the time:

The reason why the beef has collapsed is that the rug was pulled out. Our guarantee which we've enjoyed for 30 years was taken away from us. We feel let down to the extent that we responded to a national call, we have brought this about, we've produced efficiently the amount of beef that's on the market today, and it's reflecting on us.[47]

In practice the EEC proved less risky than many farmers feared. They had to be more flexible, and prepared to change what they were producing, but the intervention prices could be two or three times higher than prices on the world market. There were still bankruptcies but most farmers were able to make stable profits. The prosperity and stability promised in 1947 was maintained, but in a new context.

In the ten years that it took to join Europe British farming continued to change character. By the 1970s farming was big business. With general inflation, land values rocketed. Insurance companies and pension funds bought up land as a secure investment, and for some it became a way of avoiding heavy tax or death duties. At the same time, with existing tenant farmers getting security of tenure, and the high cost of land, it became almost impossible for newcomers to start farming. But the situation of those who had entered the industry in the thirties and forties was transformed. Many became paper millionaires, with huge assets of land and equipment. Farmers like to say that they 'farm poor and die rich', and are notoriously reluctant to reveal what they earn, but a prosperous East Anglian farmer admitted:

The profits to be made from cereal farming encouraged bigger machines, bigger fields, and higher inputs of fertiliser

As far as my actual worth on paper, I wouldn't really know. But certainly not less than five million, between five and seven million pounds . . . It's always been my philosophy that everything on the farm I can do myself, I'd never ask a man to do anything I could do myself. I am always on the farm before seven in the morning. When I am at home I am totally committed to the farm.

Not only have farms become major businesses, they have now become as modern and efficient as farms anywhere in the world. Productivity in farming grew faster in the 1960s and 1970s than in any other major British industry. On the livestock side, intensive farming methods have already altered poultry, pig and veal production in the 'food factory' direction, and beef and milk are moving that way. Yields have risen dramatically. In 1981 two-and-a-half times as much wheat was produced per acre than in 1939. Milk yields have doubled and so have the yields of potatoes and sugar-beet. By the mid-1970s Britain was self-sufficient in a dozen major foodstuffs for the first time. Some of these changes can be attributed to better farm management, and better supporting services.

We are much better at managing than we were thirty years ago. We are better trained. Nearly every farmer's son now goes to college and has got business training and he knows what is happening. In 1947 it was run from the seat of the pants, you just hoped you were going to be right. We've had to become more efficient.

Farming is not just farmers and farmworkers. You have got all the array of scientists and plant breeders, machinery designers and manufacturers, fertiliser manufacturers, veterinary science, all these things have been contributory to the progress.

The successful progress of farming has raised wider political questions. Since the 1930s farming has been subsidised by the taxpayer, with little of the fuss or outrage that attended other industries which became a charge on the public purse. Critics of the policy of subsidy have been an isolated minority. In 1950 a junior minister in the Labour Government was forced to resign because he rashly charged farmers with being feather-bedded. In the 1980s, Conservative MP Richard Body is a lonely voice who challenges the consensus. He questions the scale of the subsidies, and the effect that they have had on farming by encouraging the wheat-growers at the expense of livestock farmers.

We have been bringing into production poor-quality land to grow fabulous yields of wheat, and the triumph has been fantastic, there's no doubt about it. But it has been at tremendous cost. And it's time now to measure that cost. So far as the consumer is concerned it's £5 or £6 a week on top of the ordinary bills. That's a lot of money for the ordinary family. But then the taxpayer generally is paying something like five to six thousand million a year, as it will be very soon. This has all got to come out of profitable industries. Industries that don't have to go to the government and say let's have some more money.

Farmers challenge Richard Body's arithmetic. In 1980 agriculture received £358 million from the Exchequer, and £1570 million from the EEC's high food prices. Lord Woolley, a retired Chairman of the NFU who still farms in Cheshire, dismisses Richard Body's approach as a 'travesty of the facts'.

Our job is about filling the larders of the country and these esoteric arguments may be very interesting from an academic point of view but they don't fill people's bellies.

Michael Lee sees no difference between farming and other industries which have some degree of government help.

Every industry is subsidised to some extent. We are not feather-bedded. We have so many uncontrollable things, including government, stacked against us that if there were a few things stacked for us we hope the public won't begrudge us a few odd little bits. We don't want an easy life, we want a fair one, and we want to make a bit of money at the end of the day.

Every European country now protects its farmers, and if it were not for the Common Market contribution, the degree of subsidy to British farming would be less than in the late 1950s and 1960s. There is still a widespread belief that the benefits of home food production justify the cost. Nor have farmers sat back and lived off the subsidies they have been given. The money and support have allowed them to farm well.

The other price of success has been measured in farmworkers' jobs. While farming grew more efficient, a steady exodus was continuing. In 1946 there were 600,000 farmworkers, and by 1981 this had fallen to 159,000. It was a movement that took place with little publicity. As they bought machines, with government support, farmers needed fewer men, and laid them off or did not replace them. At the time, many farmworkers wanted to move their families from isolated cottages, and earn higher wages in the towns.

For those who stayed behind life has changed even more for the farmworker than for the farmer. Traditionally it had been a dedicated and often exploited workforce, in which sons followed fathers onto the land and accepted the conditions they found.

There was nothing else really to do. Agriculture was the main industry in the village. I wanted to be a carpenter but I just couldn't afford to be an apprentice and I went on to a farm, and gradually I grew to like the job.

213

There are some who regret the passing of what they regard as the good old days, and the radical changes in the country whereby the majority of people living in the villages no longer work in farming.

> In the old days we used to have communal shearing, and you used to go all round the neighbours and do it. And when labour was plentiful on the farms it was all done by hand. But now it's all machine-shearing, and you've lost those big days in the farming calendar. The farmer's wife had to feed perhaps thirty shearers. All the children of the parish would come in the evening. And we always killed a sheep on shearing day.

But for many old farmworkers there is a sense of relief, that so much of the drudgery is gone.

> We thought they were good days then but of course we didn't know any different. That's what we were brought up to, that was our way of life. But looking back on them today, I don't see anything good about them. I mean, it was slavery, slogging with very little money.

The long, backbreaking hours of muckspreading, beet lifting, hoeing, or shifting sacks and bales, came to be relieved by more mechanical horsepower. Old craft skills of hedgemaking and ditching and horse ploughing disappeared. Looking after animals came to involve veterinary knowledge, not just inherited wisdom. The new skills were technical and mechanical, and more training was needed. Many farms now have a range of complex machines that may only be used a few weeks of the year, but have to be used carefully and knowledgeably.

Farmwork became safer and more secure than it was between the wars. The 'tied cottages' finally disappeared, and housing standards improved. From 1971 farmworkers had three weeks paid holiday a year. Those who looked after animals could still work seven days a week, but there was proper overtime. By force of circumstances, farming had one of the most flexible and adaptable workforces anywhere. There were no demarcation disputes. New machines, which might put others out of a job, were worked willingly, and this helped farm productivity to rise by four or five per cent a year. But while in other industries employers tried to link pay rises to improvements in their workers' productivity, which they did not always get, farmworkers seldom saw the benefits of their own flexibility in substantially better pay. What some saw as most unfair about the system of rewards on the land was the application of a double standard. Because he worked in places where other employers were not competing for his labour, the farmworker's pay has been kept low by market forces. On the other hand, the farmer's income has been artificially maintained, from Whitehall or Brussels.

Yet farming is proud of its industrial relations, and the fact that people know each other well, and understand what is going on. A farmer describes the strengths.

Demonstration for higher wages for agricultural workers, 1969

I think one thing that has been a big help is the structure of our industry. We do work in small units and there is, shall we say, a team spirit between the farmer and his men. They work together, and nature is the master of us all, and we are all trying to serve the land, and you know we are all involved in the job. I know that it works in agriculture and agriculture has performed in this way, and I believe always will as long as we have the same sort of structure that we have now.

Farmworkers usually get on with their bosses, often call them by their Christian names, and work with a real commitment.

We all say this. If he is making money then we are in a job and that is as simple as that. We are making money if he is making money, and we like to see him get more land because we know we are that much safer in a job.

What complicates farming as a job and as an industry, when compared with others, is that so many of the attitudes to it are emotional. The public and the politicians like to see a prosperous and well-kept countryside, and place a value on its survival that they did not place on coalmining, for example. R. A. Butler expressed it in 1948.

In saving agriculture we are saving more than our own economy. We are saving a way of life in which the features are kindliness, freedom and, above all, wisdom. These are the qualities of the countryman and the countrywoman . . . they are vital to our existence.[48]

To match this, most farmers and farmworkers have an emotional involvement in the job themselves, and feel that the quality of working life in the country is better than in the city. Len Sharman was a farmworker for fifty years. He is highly critical of the conditions he put up with and the low pay, but passionate in asserting that he would not have done anything else.

I had two days in a factory at Leiston and I got so fed up that I packed it in. The noise was too much. I couldn't stand the noise, being shut up. I loved the life, I loved the horses, I loved the cattle and I loved the ploughing. I loved the job.

To be in the country, you know, in the summertime. All this lovely fresh air in the sun and all the country scenes. I could work in a field all day long alone and never be lonely. There's so much going on around you, all the animal life, the crops growing, the birds singing, you hear the cuckoo. Well, it's like being in heaven. That was my life. It was my father's life, my grandfather's life, that was born, that was bred in me, in my blood.

CHAPTER 10: CARS
THE TRACK

Mechanisation is now relieving the brain of the old tedium and giving it new stimulus. The slaves of metal labour, while the mind of man directs.

Sir Herbert Austin, BBC talk, 1934

The conveyor-belt is our master. If the management in the factory decide to increase speed by 10 per cent, a thousand hands work 10 per cent faster. I'm not exaggerating when I say that those of us who work on the conveyor-belt are bound to it as galley slaves were bound to the galley.

William Ferrie, untransmitted BBC talk, 1934

After lunch I would escort William Morris back to his car and I knew that I should be asked the same question. 'Are you putting up any new buildings, Smith?' To which I would reply, 'No Sir.' And he would then say, 'That's it, my boy, keep the walls bulging.'

Former company director

In 1919 the government handed back control of an old military academy at Cowley, near Oxford, to its owner, William Morris. Using stocks of spare parts left over from his small pre-war car business and the 150 workers he had employed during the war, Morris produced 367 cars in the course of that year. Six years later Morris Motors employed 14,000 people and produced 52,000 cars, nearly half the entire British output. This was a success story without parallel. Morris symbolised everything that was new and exciting about the motor industry. He was Britain's Henry Ford. From Oxford bicycle repairer to multi-millionaire in twenty years, Morris became an industrial hero in an age of economic doubt and uncertainty. When he was asked in 1924 to write about the secrets of his success he described his single-minded approach.

> My financial policies have been an important factor. They are so simple, that you may be inclined to smile at them. In the first place, I have insisted on financing the company from the inside. I have never gone to the public for capital. In consequence all the directors are 'still under one hat'. This not merely makes it easy for me to control finance. It gives rapidity of action which would appal many chairmen of limited companies. I can get things done while a board would be brooding over them. For instance, I rang up the principal of a certain firm and proposed buying their factory one Wednesday morning; the following Friday afternoon I had bought the concern and completed the financial arrangements. Six weeks afterwards, we were into production, when the average board would still have been weighing up the possibilities.[49]

Though Morris's own style owed as much to the Victorians as to Henry Ford, he helped create a new industry that was the prodigy of its time. The mass-manufacture of cars grew to employ hundreds of thousands, just as the old industries were in their steepest decline. By sheer energy William Morris and his rivals established giant new firms at the centre of British industrial life. Between the wars they expanded until they were producing half a million cars a year, far outgrowing the European competition. Their success continued for fifteen years after 1945.

But the entrepreneurial achievement is only one strand in the story of the car-makers. The new industry, with its American methods and moving assembly-line, also needed a new way of managing and working. For managers it required planning and organisation on a scale they had not known before. For the production workers it introduced pressure and monotony of a new order, as well as high wages. In these human terms the record of the car industry was poor from the start. There was little co-operation between the managers and those they employed, and no attempt to recognise the alienating effect that work in the noise and conditions of large car factories could have. Working practices did not change with the times, and the autocratic style of leadership became a liability.

Assembly line at Morris Motors, Cowley, 1933

The garage in Longwall Street, Oxford, where William Morris started his motor business in 1903

Ten years after William Morris died, foreign car imports were taking 40 per cent of sales at home, and cars had taken over as the British industry with the most days lost through disputes. Cars became one of the major industrial problem areas, like cotton and coal before, and those who searched for explanations began to look at the car-makers' history.

Before the emergence of the mass car industry, cars were handbuilt for wealthy customers. John Woods worked at the Vulcan car factory at Southport in Lancashire before the First World War.

> They were all fully-skilled tradesmen that were working at the Vulcan. You would have all sorts of machine operators, and turners, drillers, capstan-gear cutters, and then you would have smiths, strikers, moulders. There was no welding, everything had to be brass-brazed. When it came to Friday afternoon the customer would turn up and it was nice to see him drive away in it. It was a lovely finish, the paintwork. It wasn't even sprayed on.

At Vulcan they made up to six cars a week, and sold them for £350 each, and over a hundred small and scattered firms made cars on the same scale. Some had grown out of the old carriage-building trade, some out of cycle firms and engineering shops, but all were run by engineers and mechanics who concentrated on quality rather than quantity. One of the pre-1914 companies advertised, 'No car is finished or assembled before a definite order has been received, thus leaving the individual purchaser a certain limit to indulge his fancies.' Growing French and American imports showed the future lay in a different direction. In 1912 *The Times* castigated British car firms for concentrating on expensive cars for the rich, and neglecting the middle class.

> There is a huge and hitherto untapped public who would buy and are beginning already to buy from foreign sources – a really good cheap car. If a valuable market is not to a large extent to be lost at the outset, the British manufacturer will have to set himself seriously to work to produce small cars as good and as cheap as those now imported from abroad.[50]

The British makers realised they had to change their ways when the American competition arrived on their own doorstep. From the moment

Henry Ford's Manchester factory was organised with overhead conveyors and a moving line before World War I

that Henry Ford set up a new kind of car factory at Trafford Park in Manchester, in 1911, the days of the Vulcan car as John Woods remembers it, were numbered. Ford's breakdown of the assembly process into separately-timed jobs, and his emphasis on speed and delivery of standardised cheap parts, allowed him to sell the Model T in Britain for £135, when the nearest British models cost over £300. Just before the First World War a number of firms, including Rover, Singer, Wolseley, and Morris himself, were moving towards larger-scale production. Though they already employed around 90,000 and made 34,000 vehicles in 1914, there was still no cheap British car. In the United States production had by then reached over 500,000 a year.

For several of the old British industries the First World War was a trauma from which they never really recovered. Having seen a massive and hasty wartime expansion of capacity, steelmakers and shipbuilders returned to free-trade conditions to face strong new competitors and changed markets. The experience with cars was almost the reverse. For four years car-making as such almost stopped. Instead the pioneer car firms were diverted into making munitions on such a large scale that continuous mass-production methods had to be practised as never before. The experience gained, and the machine tools bought at government expense, stood them in good stead later. William Morris was able to perfect the sub-assembly techniques that made his fortune, putting together mine sinkers for the Admiralty. But the greatest benefit was a fiscal one. As far as the car industry was concerned the era of free trade ended in 1915 when Reginald McKenna, the Chancellor of the Exchequer, imposed a 33⅓ per cent tariff on imported cars. This duty continued after 1918 and became a major factor ensuring the growth of the infant industry in the post-war years. Even so the domestic manufacturers were not totally safe. American cars were being made so efficiently that, even after payment of the 33⅓ per cent duty, they could often be bought more cheaply than British vehicles produced in smaller numbers.

The American influence and example were paramount, and in the 1920s British manufacturers who learnt from them enjoyed the most spectacular success. Morris and others travelled to America to look at work methods and the flowering of mass-production techniques in Detroit. British firms then began to concentrate on lighter cars that could be made simply with as much standardisation as possible. Morris's best seller was the Cowley; Austin developed the baby Austin 7, and built the largest self-contained motor plant in the country at Longbridge. It was a period of hothouse growth, in which the smaller and less enterprising companies failed and the total number of firms was slashed by half. In 1926 Wolseley, one of the largest early companies, was taken over by Morris. But more cars were being made each year, and the price to the customer was falling. By 1930 output had reached 180,000 cars. At the end of the first decade of the modern British motor industry, Morris, whose company had gone public despite his earlier reservations, could tell his annual general meeting that whereas the Cowley had cost £390 in 1919, a much-improved equivalent now cost only £162. Most firms made a cheap family car for the fastest-growing part of the market.

The founding fathers of the industry in this period were powerful self-made men. But though they were dealing with the most advanced engineering techniques, their managerial style was old-fashioned. They drove themselves hard and expected the same commitment from the workforce. Hard-headed but paternalistic, they were twentieth-century survivors from the great age of industrial power into which they had been born. Tom Ward remembers seeing Herbert Austin at Longbridge.

Herbert Austin, first and foremost an engineer. He became Lord Austin in 1936

> Herbert Austin walked up the shop and these two chaps were leaning on the jig, and he came up and said, 'Where's your foreman?' They said, 'We don't know.' So he went and found the foreman and Herbert Austin said, 'Sack these two men, they're doing nothing.' He said, 'But they're waiting for parts.' Austin said, 'Sack these two men, they're doing nothing.' When Austin had gone and the parts had come through they were back on their jobs. He was a bit of a bully. It was everything had got to be done quicker and cheaper all the time. Quicker and cheaper.

The new entrepreneurs were opponents of the unions. During the First World War, with the shortage of labour and the importance of un-

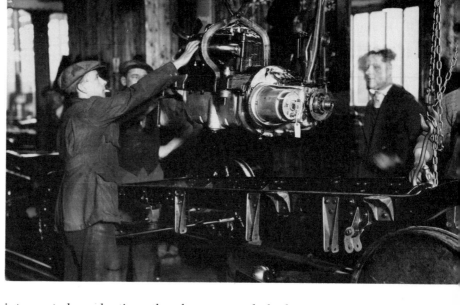

Above: *William Morris in 1934, the year he became Lord Nuffield. By the mid-thirties he had made a personal fortune of over £20 million*

Above right: *Fitting an engine to a chassis at Cowley. Gangs of men were paid on a piece-work system*

interrupted production, the shop stewards had risen to power in the engineering factories, able to confront management over wages and conditions for the first time. After 1922, and a major lock-out organised by the Engineering Employers' Federation, the power of the unions was broken, wages were cut, and the firms refused even to recognise them. In a time of rising unemployment the car firms could pick and choose between men who were glad of a job on any terms, and the proportion of skilled craftsmen with a union background was falling. Many of the assembly workers were former farm labourers, who cycled in from the villages and were quite prepared to put up with the discipline of the factories in return for the high wages they could earn. Morris understood this motivation and wrote:

> A low wage is the most expensive way of producing. A moderately high wage is the cheapest. The thirty-shilling-a-week labourer – and I have had ample opportunity of studying him in England – is bored to death when he leaves the works. And boredom in the evening breeds slackness during working hours. . . . A moderately high wage, particularly if it depends on effort, gives a man an interest in life.[49]

Making wages depend on effort meant piecework. In the Midlands payment by results was traditional to the engineering industry, and the car firms adapted it to suit their own methods of production. Individual craftsmen making a particular part by themselves in the machine shops could still be paid item by item, on a price list. But since much of the new car work was done by gangs of men working together making bodies, or fitting them on to the chassis, a bonus method was in use, with jobs measured in time. The faster the cars were produced, the higher the pay. Most car workers liked the system.

> When you are on piecework you watch your clock. You are either happy because you are in front, or you are a bit miserable because you are behind, but you are never bored.

At a time when there was so little union presence, managers could

ALL OUR WORKING LIVES

set prices and rates in an arbitrary fashion. Arrangements differed between factories. In Coventry, Rootes and Standard had a different pattern from Austin at Longbridge, or Morris at Cowley. In the complex business of making cars, payment by incentive was thought to be crucial to low prices and commercial success. Once the rates were set, the plant would almost run itself, with little need for management to chase or push because the car-workers set the speed themselves. But there were exceptions, most notably at Ford. The Ford philosophy was to pay a higher, fixed daily wage, and then use foremen to impose the pace of work by tight supervision, always backed by the threat of dismissal.

Apart from the character of the entrepreneurs at the top, the weak position of the unions, and the tradition of piecework, the new car industry had another characteristic which affected those who worked in it. A business which called out for steady and uninterrupted production was in fact erratic and interrupted. Partly because of the customer's habit of only buying cars in the spring and summer, and partly because of a policy of annual model changes announced at the Motor Show each autumn, car workers were used to fluctuations in their work and pay. There were months of frantic activity, and high wages.

> It was on the Standard 8, when no one really did bad, and we could work any hours we liked. So I worked all the hours I could. I had £7.17 10d wages and I was only a boy of 17. £2 was a week's wages for a bus driver.

A few months later the orders would be filled, and since the companies did not hold stocks of cars, skilled men who were not developing the new models would be put on short time.

> Work was seasonal. One firm had three busy months, three quiet months, three short-time months. There was no arguing then. It was just three days a week, short time.

Unskilled men would be kept on the records with a 'card' system and sent home and told to wait until they were 'called for'. A side effect of this was that trades unionists found it even harder to organise.

> What used to happen was this. If people didn't fit the bill during the period they were at work, they just didn't send for them back.

The world slump hit the car industry far less hard than most others. Production dropped only slightly, and soon recovered. The car business seemed to provide a splendid advertisement for the protection that other industries campaigned for. Not only had the car-makers prospered behind their 33⅓ per cent tariff, which had been in force since 1915 except for one brief interlude, but they had lowered prices to the customer, and had amalgamated and modernised as well. Six big firms now dominated, and came to have 90 per cent of the market. While the old export trades in coal and cotton and steel were collapsing, cars were

222

Preparing for the 1935 London Motor Show. The six big companies made over forty different models

developing a sizeable export business to the Empire. By 1933 car exports were double what they had been in 1930, and by 1937 three times as great. Britain moved into second place in the production and export league behind the United States. Only when the output per man of the British car industry was compared with the American could the real gap between the two be seen. With far longer production runs, and more mechanisation, each American car worker could already produce eight cars a year by 1930, the British only one and a half. Though they made different kinds of cars for different markets, this competition encouraged the spread of mechanisation in Britain, and productivity rose steadily. All steel bodies, instead of wood and fabric, or wood and steel, became standard.

The development which was to bring the greatest change in both the economics of car-making, and the lives of the car-makers, was the introduction of the continuously-moving assembly line, which reached its most advanced form at the new Ford works at Dagenham. On a marshland site in Essex, the American-owned company built a self-contained car factory designed to build vehicles for the whole of Europe, with a potential expansion to 200,000 vehicles a year, equivalent to almost the entire British output at the time. Fred Harrop was given the chance to go south from the old Ford works in Manchester, at short notice.

I went into work as usual on Monday morning, and in the early afternoon the foreman came down the line and told me, 'Oh, you will finish work here tonight and you'll report to Dagenham at eight o'clock Thursday morning.' So the Tuesday morning I went out with my mother and got all the things I needed, and on Wednesday we came down by train on a discounted ticket which had been arranged by Fords.

Ford dealers are shown construction in progress at Dagenham in 1931. The site would become the biggest integrated plant in Europe, with its own blast furnaces

At Dagenham the cars moved as they did at Ford's plants in the United States, slowly carried forward by a moving chain. Engines, gearboxes, wheels, and all the parts needed for the stations on the track, were fed in by overhead conveyors from other sections, or from the stores, in an intricate tributary system. Where before gangs of men had worked on each car together, they were spread out along the track, obliged to follow the speed of the line.

The new Ford works opened in 1931, and Morris followed quickly, transforming the main assembly plant at Cowley to four moving lines for different models. For almost all car-workers the coming of the track meant harder work. By shorter job cycles, monotony was increased while less skill was needed. If the line broke down at any point, or if one person could not keep pace, it disrupted the others further along so there was pressure on everyone to keep up, in all parts of the plant. The way in which the new methods were received also depended on the way in which people were paid. In the Midlands plants with a tradition of piece work and the gang system it was in everyone's interest for the conveyors and the track to be run as fast as possible because this increased earnings. At Standard, Tom Ward and the team he worked with used to try to beat the speed of the track itself.

> You had so much time for doing a job, and if you were on ordinary time you would get £2, and then you would have to go quicker and quicker to get more. So the track would start at perhaps time and a quarter. And it would go up to time and a half, £3 a week. Speed it up as you get used to it, double time. And when it got to double time they'd stop, no more, no faster. And what we used to do, we'd pick a body up and jump the pegs, and we could make about £5 a week. It was always good money in the motor trade if you could do the job. But if you were slow, you were in some trouble.

Stan Campbell was an inspector at Cowley.

> The pace of work was very high and the gangs would eliminate the weaker elements. Anyone who couldn't keep up with the job just disappeared, finished up by labouring.

A completely different atmosphere prevailed at Ford's. In a more controlled and less frenetic system the line ruled and Ford workers went at the speed the management decided on. As well as foremen, security men patrolled to see that company rules, no smoking, no eating, no running, were observed.

> They were great disciplinarians. You'd go down to where the job was, and hang your clothes up, and there'd be a man standing by this rack arrangement that the clothing was put on to. And as soon as the hooter went you would all start work immediately and out of the corner of your eye you could see this rack start to sail up into the roof with all your clothing. And there it stayed until 4.30 in the afternoon after you'd finished. If you didn't do your job properly and keep up with the line, you would obviously lose your job.

Conditions in the even larger, busier and noisier car plants increased the tension under which men worked. At Austin's at Longbridge there were 16,000 employees, and six miles of conveyors. Hayden Evans left the south Wales coalfield in the early 1930s to work at the Oxford factory of Pressed Steel, which made bodies for Morris.

> It was very frightening to start with. I had never been in a place where there was so much noise. The first thing that hit you when you went in a body factory was the terrific noise. The machine I was on was the equivalent of one of those hydraulic picks that they used to dig up the road.

The car-workers' main grievance was not the speed of the line, or the phenomenal din, but the continuing insecurity and the authoritarian style of management that went with it. Seasonal lay-offs continued right up to the Second World War. In any of the factories a failure on the track or a hold-up with parts could bring a stoppage, and a loss of earnings. Dismissal could still come at short notice. Marjorie Clarke had spent two years at Standards.

The rebuilt Cowley complex just before World War II, with the Pressed Steel body plant in the foreground

> On the Friday afternoon we saw the foreman coming down into the trimming shop with a long list of names. And she walked up and down between the rows of sewing machines, stopping at every third or fourth girl to tell them their name was on the list. She was coming down from the back of me and I couldn't turn to look, I daren't look. And then I felt a hand on my shoulder and someone said, 'Sorry love'. And that was it. I was out of work just six weeks before I was getting married. And there was nothing you could do about it.

So long as the unions were weak, management could carry on in this way. But in the process one of Britain's youngest industries was managing, in its most prosperous years, to create the same kind of distrust and hostility which characterised some of the oldest industries.

226

From the mid-1930s the unions won several recognition battles, with the first major victory coming at Pressed Steel. They began to recruit widely. The Amalgamated Engineering Union and the National Union of Vehicle Builders already had many of the skilled men. The AEU widened its scope to take in unskilled and semi-skilled as well. The greater number joined the Transport and General Workers Union.

In the years up to 1939 cars, like chemicals and electrical equipment, were one of the sunrise industries. Both Morris and Austin were rewarded with peerages, by a government which appreciated the benefits the car firms' prosperity was bringing to the economy as a whole. Morris himself had amassed a fortune of £20 million. But their success had been almost in spite of their natural inclinations. Morris said he was disinterested in money. 'I loathe figures and statistics, in a way, figures have always been out of my line.' Austin left the financial side to others. Alec Layborn served on the Austin board.

> Austin was a very dour, very quiet man, who spoke very little. He lived only for engineering, only for cars, and he wasn't the slightest bit interested in £.s.d. I remember he said, 'You know, Layborn, my cars are not run in till they have done 40,000 miles. So how can you expect to keep on having repeat orders? I make them to last, not just to go.'

The accountants at Austin sometimes despaired of him.

> Cost didn't worry him. I mean if he wanted to stop something half-way and start again he would do so. He wouldn't think what it meant for the costing thing at all, or whether the extra expenditure was justified. It ought to be done from an engineering point of view and therefore it was going to be done.

In terms of engineering the British firms had learnt much from America. Their factories used flow-production techniques to make reliable cars. But in a wider marketing and business sense the full logic of mass production had not been followed through. Despite the earlier amalgamations, too many companies produced too many types of cars in small runs. The 'Big Six', Morris, Austin, Ford, Vauxhall, Rootes and Standard, turned out forty different models between them. More than half sold fewer than 5000 and were quite uneconomic. In America the three giant companies produced fifteen basic models, and sold them in infinitely greater numbers. As a result, once protection was discounted, British cars were expensive. The export record looked impressive, but 80 per cent went to the Empire markets. In straight competition in the rest of the world, American exports exceeded the British by a ratio of twelve to one.

When serious rearmament began in the mid-1930s the government singled out the car firms for a special role. Herbert Austin helped to plan the 'Shadow factories' which were rushed up beside many car plants, to build tanks, aircraft and aero-engines when the need came. When war broke out civilian car-making stopped, and the entire industry was put on to war work. The large factory at Castle Bromwich set up by William Morris, who had now become Lord Nuffield, provided seven out of ten of the Spitfires made. As the wartime engineering industries merged together, the car-maker's knowledge of mass production helped build aircraft at a speed the aircraft firms themselves would never have been capable of. But their labour relations were less smooth running. The shop stewards' movement, and the unions, were in a much stronger position when every man was needed. Dick Etheridge started at Austin in 1940.

> What happened was that, as a consequence of the Emergency Power Act, the employer couldn't dismiss you, or at least you could appeal against it. That helped us to get consolidated and organised.

The shop stewards gained new power and recognition through the Joint Production Committees which reluctant managements were obliged by the government to introduce, to try to ease production. During the war the last bastion fell: Ford, and its body-supplier Briggs, finally recognised the unions and agreed to deal with the shop stewards over conditions, wages and hours. With the piecework system being used as a device to increase war output, and the government picking up the costs, wages in the west Midlands were the highest in the country.

When the car industry was demobilised, the aircraft jigs were moved out. At the Standard works at Canley they carefully unpacked the conveyor systems and special tools that had been dismantled in 1940, and started to produce the same models they had been making when the war began. In 1943 only 1650 cars had been made in Britain. By 1946 the figure was up to 200,000 again. Though the new Labour government had no plans to nationalise them, the car-makers had now lost their old freedom to do as they liked. They were to play a major role in the government's economic planning, and to be subject to guidance and intervention they had never known before. In the years of austerity, new cars for the home customer became a luxury, prohibitively taxed; there were waiting lists several years long. Almost all the cars that were produced were for export, to earn much-needed dollars and foreign exchange to repay the war debts. Steel rationing was the principal weapon the government used to bludgeon the car firms. Unless the cars were sold abroad, the manufacturer got no steel. So companies with only limited overseas experience began to export cars designed before the war for British roads, through dealers they had hardly met, and who certainly did not know how to service their cars. Alick Dick was assistant to the managing director at Standards.

> We only had, after the war, about three people in our Export Department. So there was no way in which we could export 80

per cent, and we appointed dealers without ever having been to the countries.

With both home and overseas markets desperately short, there was no difficulty in selling, and all efforts went into achieving the maximum rate of production. Almost two million cars were shipped abroad before the end of government controls. There was little time to test them for foreign conditions, and they proved to be too underpowered for the sustained long runs of North America, not tough enough for the dust and corrugated mud roads of Africa or South America, and to have the wrong springing for the paved surfaces of Europe. Nevertheless the Standard Vanguard was launched in 1947 as a 'world car'. Freddie Troop was his company's service manager in Scotland; he was also the only man in the service department with a foreign passport.

My boss said to me, 'We've got a few problems with the Vanguard in Belgium. You know how these continentals panic. We'd like you to go over there.' When I got there I found they really had problems, particularly with the chassis and suspension. The fractures in the chassis had to be seen to be believed. The shock absorbers were weak after a few thousand miles. The Belgians put a stiffer oil in, and that just made the shock absorbers go solid when they hit a bump. It used to fracture the bolts to the chassis, and it used to come up and over and straight through the wing. We got over that by fitting a sort of fireman's helmet.

Standard Vanguards and Ferguson tractors are paraded at the Coventry factory in 1948

Though Troop supervised repairs and modifications on a trail of Vanguards all over Europe, the damage had been done for Standard and
other manufacturers who encountered similar difficulties with their
cars. Through personal experiences with dealers who were unable to
make repairs or get parts after breakdowns, and through word of
mouth, British cars acquired a reputation for unreliability that would
take years to live down. In Europe the car industry was completing its
reconstruction with larger and more modern plants, particularly at
Volkswagen and Renault, and they quickly took over. In 1950 Britain
was the world's greatest car exporter, sending three times as many cars
abroad as the Americans, and was second to the United States in overall
production. By 1956 the Germans had overtaken in both exports and
output. Alick Dick, like most of the car managers, put much of the
blame for what happened on the government.

> It is little wonder the industry couldn't export in a proper or
> cohesive way. They required at least two or three years to
> design the cars, to research the market, and they were never
> given the chance. This is why the cars they were selling in the
> early 1950s were unsuitable for the car markets of the world,
> and why our continental rivals were able to come along at a
> later date with the experience of the British motor industry
> behind them, and design cars which were far more suitable.

Government influence was not confined to the export drive alone.
Successive post-war Chancellors of the Exchequer used the car industry
as a convenient 'regulator' of consumer spending. When the economy
was looking healthy, car sales were given a boost by easing purchase tax
or credit restrictions. When there were balance of payment problems, or
too rapid inflation, the same devices were used to slow car production
down. The level of purchase tax and hire purchase conditions were
altered no fewer than fourteen times in the 1950s. The industry complained that it was impossible to plan its future production with cer-
tainty, or to know how much to invest in new plant or in developing
new models, so long as government tinkering could sabotage their
calculations.

When they did put forward investment plans, they encountered
another government policy, aimed at directing jobs to the less prosperous regions of the country. Firms were not allowed to build the
factory extensions they needed, or new body or engine plants, in the
thriving south and Midlands. Industrial Development Certificates were
only granted if new plant was set down in places where politicians and
civil servants wanted to boost employment and the local economy.
George Turnbull, who also worked at Standard, could see the disadvantages at the time.

> We knew we were building inefficiency into the industry. But
> in those days to get an IDC, you just couldn't get one in the

Coventry area. If you were in the motor industry you had to go to Liverpool or to Wales or Scotland and that was very rigidly applied. It was a silly policy, because it may be all right if you are moving a whole industry up there and sufficient incentive is given to train the people, but if it is part of the conveyor belt, which runs from Coventry all the way up to Liverpool and back again, that's not a very efficient way of running a motor industry.

So the car plants moved northwards, to Speke and Halewood on Merseyside, to Linwood in Scotland. Instead of coming together to bring the economies of scale that were needed, the British industry was deliberately decentralised. A stream of lorries carried engines, axles, and body shells from north to south, and south to north. Body panels made in separate places were often damaged in transit, and did not always fit together. Alick Dick had difficulties with the Triumph Herald.

The Herald was made in pieces. Some in Liverpool. Some in Birmingham. Some in other places. It wasn't really a successful body construction at all.

The industry's own efforts at integration and amalgamation did little to compensate. In 1952 the two rival firms, Morris and Austin, finally merged, a proposal that Herbert Austin had first made in 1924, when he had been rebuffed by Morris. Austin had died during the war, and Lord Nuffield was withdrawing from the business. The merger was intended to offer a stronger resistance to Ford and the larger companies on the continent. But the new British Motor Corporation never fulfilled these hopes. BMC kept separate dealerships for Austin and Morris cars, and had sixty different plants, including the MG works at Abingdon where Alfred Smith was company secretary.

It was a merger that never was, because the Austin Motor Company and Morris Motors virtually traded on their own. There was some degree of rationalisation but it was absolutely minimal. The people in charge were desperately anxious to preserve good relations all round and not upset anybody by harsh closing down of factories and things like that.

So long as the car-makers could sell all the cars that came off the line, during the boom years of the 1950s that deceived and disarmed so many British industrialists, the problems of high costs were hidden. The level of spending on new capital equipment per worker was the lowest in Europe, yet output was expanding rapidly. Between 1954 and 1955 BMC's car production rose nearly 30 per cent, most of it going to the home market, which was now being allowed the new cars for which it had waited so long.

The men in charge of the motor industry were still the pre-war generation. Gloomy talk of growing foreign competition was hardly

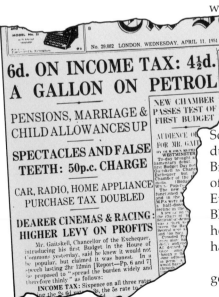

No. 29,882 LONDON, WEDNESDAY, APRIL 11, 1951

6d. ON INCOME TAX: 4½d. A GALLON ON PETROL

PENSIONS, MARRIAGE & CHILD ALLOWANCES UP

SPECTACLES AND FALSE TEETH: 50p.c. CHARGE

CAR, RADIO, HOME APPLIANCE PURCHASE TAX DOUBLED

DEARER CINEMAS & RACING: HIGHER LEVY ON PROFITS

NEW CHAMBER PASSES TEST OF FIRST BUDGET

Mr. Gaitskell, Chancellor of the Exchequer, introducing his first Budget in the House of Commons yesterday, said he knew it would not be popular, but claimed it was honest. In a speech lasting 2hr 12min [Report—Pp. 6 and 7] he proposed to "spread the burden widely and therefore thinly" as follows:

INCOME TAX: Sixpence on all three rates

credible to them, and an environment in which many firms produced a wide range of models, with frequent design changes, still seemed entirely natural. The autocrats at the top included the Rootes family, and Sir William Lyons at Jaguar, and the most dictatorial of them all, BMC's chairman Leonard Lord. But the old style of management faced a much more organised workforce, which had joined a variety of general and craft unions during and after the war. Labour relations and agreements were more complex, even though union membership was still not 100 per cent and the unions' true strength had not been tested. Wages were still among the highest in the country, and piecework still reigned. But with more mechanisation and higher speeds on the assembly lines, the job could be as oppressive as ever.

For the car-workers what had changed least since the 1930s was the basic insecurity. Despite the record-breaking production, the car managers seemed unable to organise production in a way that avoided periodic lay-offs and redundancies. Frequent changes of model still meant that lines were stopped while new cars were being introduced. Export orders were cancelled, or switched. The government's stop-go policy played an increasing role, with a tax or HP charge suddenly throttling demand altogether, or diverting it from large cars to small. Management continued to hire and fire to meet these fluctuations. When sackings were due, unions were seldom consulted; indeed, militant shop stewards were sometimes the first to be dismissed. Joe Dennis was working on the body for the Austin Metropolitan, specially intended for shipment to North America, and remembers the variety of explanations that were given when men were sent home.

> The best one was when they used to come down the line and say, 'We are laying you off because the Hudson's frozen up.' We just used to have to accept that.

For years car-workers had accepted the lay-offs and interruptions, and the foreman's arrival on the floor with the 'pink slips', as the penalties that went with high wages. In 1956 there was a turning point

Austin workers march against BMC's dismissal of 6000 at short notice in July 1956. Other firms also laid off men. High wages were accompanied by insecurity, just as in the 1930s

in labour relations when the unions were provoked into making a major stand for the first time. Following a government credit squeeze, the BMC Board ordered both Morris at Cowley and Austin at Longbridge to lay off 3000 men each, immediately. At Cowley the local management had been actively hiring more men for an expansion for the following year. Eric Lord was a manager at Cowley.

> We were in a ghastly position. People had already given up their present employment to come to us, and we were going round on Friday telling them not to come on the Monday, and there was no job after all. It was as much notice as that that we had. There was no doubt that this increased the strength of the unions. We seemed to be behaving very badly indeed.

Stan Campbell was an inspector at the Morris plant.

> People kept coming up to me and saying, 'What do you think's going to happen?' I said, 'This is so brutal it's bound to cause a strike.' And it did. There was a three weeks' strike and the unions realised they were in a strong position, and after three weeks they won. After that they were able to insist on closed shops, and the unions had power they'd never had before. It was a good strike in a good cause because the management had so little imagination they thought they could just go on hiring and firing as they had done for years, since the factory started.

The six thousand men did not get their jobs back, but management agreed to pay two weeks' wages to those leaving, and a formula for 'last in, first out' was agreed. The closed shop spread throughout the country. Management blamed the redundancy strikes on communist extremists, for many of the most active stewards were members of the party. But the cause seemed so just to so many car-workers that the activist leadership and union power were strengthened. After 1956 the number of disputes increased steadily. Some of the worst trouble came at Fords. The threat to 'stop the track' was used more frequently in everyday argument over piecework and conditions, made more anarchic by the divisions between the different unions themselves, and between the official leadership and the shop stewards. Official procedure laid down between management and unions was ignored and foremen and supervisors became more timid. Senior managers who were specialists in production, but not labour relations, found themselves devoting the major proportion of their time to them.

Not all plants were equally affected. There were far fewer stoppages in some of the new works built away from the Midlands, where piecework had never been introduced. But the prime evidence that a different approach by management could produce different results came at Vauxhall, owned by General Motors of the United States, which employed 20,000 car-workers at Luton. There a more enlightened managing director, Sir Charles Bartlett, had given the workforce greater security and a wide range of fringe benefits, and had introduced a formal system of consultation between management and labour, back in 1941. Vauxhall's Management Advisory Committee, with twenty-two elected representatives from different parts of the works, was closer to the new chemical industry in its spirit, and in the way it tried to identify the company's interests with that of the employees. Vauxhall had seen that a contented workforce was not to be bought, just through high pay, but had to be won, through more considerate treatment and good communications. Other companies studied Vauxhall and made belated attempts at consultation schemes, but they were too late to be convincing. Ford took more provocative action. After years of crippling unofficial stoppages at Dagenham they acted firmly, and contrived a way of firing seventeen men they identified as key troublemakers on the shopfloor.

In the 1960s a number of the industry's long-term problems came home to roost. Labour relations was only one of them though it became an alibi for others. Despite the full order books the profit levels of the many British companies in the 1950s had been low, with the exception of Ford. Not enough had been ploughed back into new plant if they were to compete with the more concentrated and often government-assisted industry in Europe. BMC had employed good engineers, including Alec Issigonis, one of the leading car designers of his generation. But the first small front-wheel-drive car, the Mini, was made in relatively small numbers and sold at too low a price, and the Austin 1100 was constructed in four different plants and was never sold aggressively.

BMC's Chief Engineer, Sir Alec Issigonis, with the Mini he designed. Despite the car's popularity, it made little money for the company

With low investment, models that should have been replaced were allowed to run on past their time. This made them less attractive abroad, and more expensive. Productivity in British car factories almost stood still, while abroad it climbed steadily. In 1955 Britain produced four cars per car-worker per year, Germany 3.9, the United States 19. In 1976 the figures were five cars in Britain, eight in Germany, and 28 in the United States. As exports stagnated, and overseas markets were taken by cheaper and often more reliable cars from France, Germany and Italy, smaller British firms ran into difficulty, and mergers seemed the only way of meeting the competition. Standard-Triumph was taken over by Leyland, a Lancashire truck-maker, in 1961, and Rover was absorbed in 1965. Jaguar acquired Daimler and was then taken over by BMC. Yet BMC itself, incorporating the two main streams of the country's motor industry, was living proof that mere financial amalgamation, the holding together of a loose collection of separate plants and activities, was not the same as the planned rationalisation that had been avoided in 1952.

At first it had just been the export markets that had gone. Now imports of European cars were rising, from three per cent of sales in 1960 to 15 per cent in 1970. When BMC's financial problems grew worse and the whole future of mass car-making in Britain seemed in doubt, government stepped in to try to force a true rationalisation, by creating an even bigger company. The successful but smaller Leyland firm, incorporating Standard, Triumph and Rover, was persuaded to merge with BMC, and effectively take it over, in 1967.

The new British Leyland Motor Corporation produced half the cars in Britain, and the other half was shared by the American-owned companies Ford and Vauxhall, and by Rootes, soon to be bought by Chrysler. Lord Stokes, who had made his reputation selling lorries and buses abroad for Leyland, became Chairman of BLMC.

> There were about fifty different sections in the group, all of which had grown up with their own custom and practices. You had people like Wolseley, you had Morris, you had Riley, you had Austin, you can go on and on. All these companies had grown up in the Midlands with their own particular traditions. We had to try and weld these together in one cohesive whole. The job should have been started not when we started it, but in 1914 if you like.
>
> We knew we were taking on a challenge. I don't think we knew, looking back with hindsight, how big the challenge was.

Stokes brought in managers from outside to help him, and his planners prepared radical schemes to integrate the eight old companies within the group, reduce the number of models, and raise productivity. They estimated that a loss of 30,000 jobs was necessary, with up to 20 factories closing. But a scheme of drastic redundancies on this scale would have been politically impossible, and would have caused long strikes that the

Start of the car recession: unsold Vauxhalls stored near the Luton factory in the 1960s

company, still privately owned, could not afford. Lord Stokes remembers how the schemes for the ideal rationalisation gave way to the realities of the time.

> It was not an age when you could shut factories. GEC had just had a tremendous industrial disturbance with the closing of their Woolwich factory. The unions were in a very strong negotiating position and they made it absolutely clear to us both publicly and privately that if ever we tried to shut down anything they would resist to the maximum.

Lacking either the finance, or the right political or labour relations climate to carry out the grand schemes the merger had been designed for, Leyland's central management had difficulty controlling such a vast organisation. Though they eliminated many models, Leyland still allowed its own cars to compete with one another, so that the Marina and the Allegro were introduced in opposition to each other while a replacement Mini was cancelled. They argued about whether to specialise in more expensive cars, or stay in volume production. But more significant than the short-term decisions that were taken was the human conflict as the attitudes of the old British motor industry, on both the management and the shop-floor sides, were seriously challenged for the first time. Bent on change, the new regime introduced managers to methods of control and planning that were common in most other parts of industry, but not in BMC. On the shopfloor the new men took on the cherished system of piecework and planned to dismantle it. In both areas the imbued traditions of the industry were being threatened.

John Barber had come from Ford to BLMC, where he saw different attitudes at the very top, in the way that decisions were taken. At Ford a decision to build a new car or make a new investment was taken after painstaking staff work and preparation.

> In BMC I got the impression that the chief executive tended to take almost off-the-cuff decisions by calling one person into the office, then another, and coming to a decision which wasn't well documented. We couldn't find out what the objectives were, so we didn't know why they were falling short of objectives.

The old autocrats would not have understood this language, of accountants and business schools, and nor did some of the plant managers who were confronted with tight new disciplines for financial control. Eric Lord was running the Morris works at Cowley.

> People were brought in from other companies and they came in complete with their manuals of procedure, and we were not used to working that way, but rather to using our initiative, and we were so tied down with rules and regulations that it completely stifled us.

With many of their own managers fighting a rearguard action against centralisation, and with the tensions that resulted from this, BL also took a major step to change relations with the shopfloor. The wave of strikes in the 1960s had many causes, but the central issue was the survival of piecework. A system which had once worked well to motivate traditional craftsmen to work as fast as they were able had become increasingly irrelevant to large automated factories where machinery dictated the speed at which parts could be produced or put together. Piecework produced constant conflict. In the past, because firms could not afford to waste time in negotiation, or by holding out, they had agreed to higher rates. This brought additional unrest over differentials from those still paid by the day, such as skilled toolmakers, or inspectors. George Turnbull was now running the Austin Morris division of Leyland.

> Once the price was settled that was fine, everyone worked very hard to maximise earnings, and it was an efficient method. When you wanted to make a small change in design, immediately a big bargaining point arose in the minds of the shop stewards. 'Let's get the maximum we can for this change, because most of the time is already settled and we have no way of increasing our wages. Let's ask for twice the time that this job should take, it's going to boost the earnings of the gang.' That was the general mentality.

Ford car-workers at Dagenham in the 1960s. They earned a fixed hourly rate, not the piece work which was standard in the British Leyland companies

The biggest delays came with new models, when management and shop stewards would spend thousands of hours in negotiation to agree rates for each different job that went into a new car's production.

> I've known a model take six months before a price was settled. Now if you are in a competitive business, and you have got to sell your cars in the market, and you have done a lot of advertising, there's an awful lot of pressure on the management to get something settled and get the thing going. This is what happened across the whole spectrum of British Leyland. There was no doubt in our minds that we had to go to day-work.

Every other major manufacturer in Europe and North America paid their men by the day, and could introduce changes quickly and make full use of new machinery. Starting with the men who were to build the new Marina at Cowley in 1971, BL 'bought out' piecework in plant after plant until three years later almost all their hourly workers were on day-work. They paid dearly, with generous new hourly rates of pay, and many new concessions. Under the new agreements shop stewards and management would jointly decide the number of men who were needed for a job. Just as with the equivalent change in the coal industry, the ending of piecework had the effect of making production smoother, with fewer disputes. But with cars it also made production slower, and encouraged overmanning. The old managers and foremen who had grown up with the system of piecework and saw its benefits as well as its disadvantages had expected this to happen. Hayden Evans had become a foreman at Cowley.

> We were doing over a hundred jobs by half-past-four. They introduced this new measured day work, they brought a third more men in, a ten-minute break in every hour, and the job went from 110, 120 an hour, down to 80 because the men were

on day-rate. When they were on day-rate the only way they could earn more money was by putting in more hours.

Whereas before you had to hold the men back, now you were shoving them, like taking the horse to water and he's not prepared to drink.

BL could see the consequences of the change, as they introduced it. A bold initiative to improve productivity had turned into a further obstacle to achieving it, at the time when price competitiveness mattered more than ever. John Barber thought the difficulty was a historical one.

In the Midlands people had lived all their lives with a bonus sytem, and the whole culture was different. The foreman didn't really have to be a manager. Men had the incentive to do a job, to get their pay. In the measured day-work system, on the other hand, the foreman is very much a first-line manager. In the early days I think we overestimated the calibre and experience of the BMC foreman, and we underestimated the time we should have allowed for this major change.

British Leyland's attempts to change the long-ingrained habits and attitudes of its managers and workers were accompanied by efforts to simplify collective bargaining. Each year there were 246 separate pay negotiations spread across their different plants. They worked to reduce the number of different agreements. As they tackled these internal issues, the problems they were meant to help solve grew worse. The entire British motor industry was now under heavy assault on its home ground. Between 1970 and 1975 the number of imported cars rose five-fold, to take 40 per cent of the market. Even when consumer spending boomed in 1972 and 1973 the British car-makers could not take advantage of it. The most popular British cars were made in such small numbers, or suffered from such interruptions, that buyers faced long waiting times. Loyalty to British cars evaporated in the face of better-made and often cheaper and more up-to-date European models. At a time when the greatest demand was for economical small cars after the oil price rise, the two British mini cars, the Imp and the Mini, had been on the market for 11 and 16 years respectively. Their imported rivals were two or three years old. The British car industry had almost stood still for ten years and was producing the same number of cars as in the early 1960s. In the same period the French and Italians trebled their output of cars and the Germans had almost doubled theirs.

In the league table of world manufacturers BL was now small, less than half the size of Renault, Fiat, Volkswagen or the major Japanese and American firms. But even with the size it was, potential economies were lost from having too many models, and too many different engines. Some of the differences in productivity came from the lack of capital investment, but it was reckoned that even with identical equipment, the labour required for assembling the same car in Britain, as against Europe, was nearly double. British production lines operated more slowly, with more interruptions. They had many more maintenance men, yet lost twice as many hours of production from breakdowns.

Three out of the four British car manufacturers had ceased to be financially viable, and only Ford was making enough money to finance its own capital spending from its own profits. When the government became increasingly involved in the motor industry's crisis in 1974, all the factors which had led it onto the rocks were studied, and devastating comparisons made with practice abroad. The government 'think tank', the Central Policy Review Staff, argued that the future depended on attitudes as much as investment.

> There is not the slightest prospect of the British car industry becoming viable at any level of production if the present constant interruptions to production, reluctance to accept new methods of working and capital equipment, and readiness to accept sub-standard quality continue. Fundamentally these problems reflect prevailing attitudes of management and labour towards each other, towards productivity and towards work.[51]

The diagnosis, that the central failing was a human one, was familiar to the older British industries. It had been made of the coal industry in 1919, and of shipbuilding from the 1920s. But plans for more industrial democracy, and increased participation, were secondary to the immediate need for hard cash. If British Leyland had been allowed to continue as it was, it would have gone into receivership. So government came to the rescue, and took the company into state ownership through the National Enterprise Board. Another attempt was made at reorganisation, as part of the rescue scheme devised by Lord Ryder, who gave new priority to volume car production. Yet even with additional funds the industry continued to nose-dive.

If proof were needed that the problem was human rather than concerned with capital investment and equipment, it came in the mid-seventies at Solihull, in a sequence of events that turned into a nightmare for those involved. Leyland had constructed a £25 million plant to make a new Rover model, the SD1, to compete with Mercedes and BMW and Volvo as a quality car. A combination of overmanning due to the end of piecework, demarcation disputes, and over-optimistic sales forecasts prevented the factory, full of the latest machinery, from ever fulfilling its promise. The plant became a battleground between Leyland headquarters and the old Rover management. Jean Rivers was shop steward on the final lines.

> The facilities were much better, because it was a much more modern plant than the old Rover. But facilities don't make a place happy to work in. The first thing the shopfloor always

notices is the times they change management. They were changing them every three months. It just wasn't running right.

After major difficulties getting the car and the line working properly before the launch, problems with the paintwork and the engineering of the car continued once it was under way. Peter Grant was production manager.

> I was at a dance at the Civic Hall in Solihull and a senior director of British Leyland came up to me and said, 'You Rover people are all the same. You worry about quality. We want quantity. We've got to get this SD1 turned out in quantity.'

As a consequence inspectors were overruled by managers, and substandard cars were produced in such numbers that they clogged the factory and were eventually sent on to distributors to be put right before they were sold. The car quickly gained a poor reputation with customers.

> Morale was very, very bad. We had sensible middle-aged people. They didn't want to be sworn at or screamed at and threatened with the sack if they didn't decide this that or the other. The plant director was despairing of the quality of the cars that were going into sales. It had to be seen to be believed.

Five years after the Solihull plant had been opened it was closed, and boarded up, and production of the Rover transferred to Cowley, where it could be made more cheaply. In the background to the SD1 story was the growing recession which hit the demand for all cars, particularly large ones. There was too much car-making capacity in the world, and British car firms suffered most.

The scale of the losses which all car companies faced at the end of the 1970s finally forced drastic changes, as a new generation of managers had to deal with the legacy of their predecessors. The man who epitomised the new approach was Michael Edwardes, Chief Executive of BL for five years from 1977. The man he brought in to sort out volume car production was Harold Musgrove.

> One of the things that appalled me when I came back was that we were establishing targets, we were establishing line rates, and only achieving 60%. Which meant the tracks stopped for 40% of the day. Now that was not the responsibility of the work-force. That had to be the responsibility of the management.

They did not get BL to make a profit. Losses totalled over £1300 million during Edwardes' time in office. But his style and message were direct and brutal. Taking advantage of a new political and economic climate he slashed the number of models, and accelerated the development of new ones, including the Metro and the Maestro. To increase productivity ten

Sir Michael Edwardes, British Leyland chairman, 1977–82

vehicle-assembly plants were closed and production concentrated at Longbridge and Cowley. Seventy thousand car workers lost their jobs. Management was slimmed with equal severity.

To his admirers, Edwardes' principal contribution was to seize power back from the shop stewards, and re-establish 'management's right to manage'. On many occasions he went over the heads of the unions and threatened to close down BL unless the workforce complied with what he wanted, but he also kept them informed about the company's true position. The number of disputes fell rapidly. Many work practices and customs were swept away, and with new conditions of service productivity rose fast. Output per car worker per year went up to 17. On some assembly lines, computer-controlled robots reduced manning to European and Japanese levels. The cars improved in quality and design.

Michael Edwardes proved that the car industry still responded to strong leadership from the top. But to many trade unionists it was a style of management reminiscent of the 1930s, against a background of high unemployment. Bill Roche is a Convenor at the body plant at Cowley.

> I wouldn't subscribe to the current method and style of management as being the only way. I would say that a different way has got to be found otherwise we would have a total disaster.

Whether or not there might have been another way, the British motor industry survived into the 1980s, something which was very much in

Computer-controlled robots making Metros at Longbridge increased productivity. Each robot line replaced 70 car-workers

the balance in the 1970s, and has much-improved prospects. It is likely to employ even fewer car-workers and more robots, and to produce a handful of models in larger numbers. But Britain now makes fewer cars than Spain.

The British excelled at making quality cars in small numbers. When they could make luxury and sports cars on an individual basis, they had no match. But the essence of the new twentieth-century industry was mass production and this they found difficult, even if years of protection and exceptional post-war demand delayed the discovery. One explanation has to do with temperament. At a time of rising aspirations, workers found less and less satisfaction on the production lines, with their particular tyranny. It was a form of work that was alienating wherever in the world it was done, but car-workers in other countries were more co-operative because so many were immigrants to the car cities, from the southern states in America, or from southern Europe, who could not afford to challenge the conditions.

But most car bosses now concede that, even though the nature of the job would always make labour relations difficult, the principal failure was on the management side. John Barber puts it in this way:

> Soon after the war management lost control of labour, because labour was in very short supply. There was competition, pay rates got out of hand, discipline weakened and from the 1940s to the 1960s a way of life developed which was very difficult to change. So management gave way in those difficult times. It was difficult because they had markets to meet, they had cars to get out. You could excuse them, on the other hand you can't avoid the conclusion that management was weak at the time.

The reasons for this weakness had much to do with the car industry's origins. Unlike electronics, it did not start with a clean sheet. The car firms grew from the Midlands engineering tradition, where the workers were on piecework, and where managers were used to taking quick decisions and backing hunches. Though the product was modern, the management of much of the car industry had remained stuck for nearly seventy years in the mould set for it by the tough Victorian engineers who began it. Michael Shanks worked at British Leyland at the time of the 1967 merger.

> We were still living in the afterglow of the great heroic figures of the industry, Leonard Lord, Lord Nuffield, and so on. It was the people who had been trained and brought up by them, who were their disciples, who were much influenced in their thinking by these great father figures, who had been operating in a much simpler age. I think there was this great legacy of the past, of the great heroic figures who created the industry, at a time when what was needed was something rather different, less heroic, more analytical, careful-thinking.

243

CHAPTER 11: ELECTRONICS
THE PACE OF THE NEW

It was very tedious, but we used to get a lot of fun out of it. We all had so many to do a day, and we've got to do this number, and there were ten of us, and we all tried to outdo the other one. We weren't allowed to eat sweets with wrappers on because it took too long to take the wrappers off.

Radio worker, 1930s

We felt that we were very much exploring new ground that had not been trodden in the past. We could find brand-new methods of manufacturing, brand-new devices, we could put them into the market place, and it was an exciting time for everybody involved. The rate of growth of the business was enormous. It was explosive.

Semi-conductor manager, 1960s

Just as the declining Lancashire cotton mills came to stand for Britain's industrial past, the growth of electronics has come to represent some of the greatest hopes for the future. Major industrial sea-changes often have to be deduced from statistics alone. But in Blackburn in the late 1930s the beginnings of this transition could be seen in direct and personal terms. Ethel Tillotson had started at 14 in one of the textile spinning mills that had survived the depression. She found textile work dusty, noisy and exhausting. When the Philips company built a new radio components factory in the town, and recruited with advertisements that said 'Come to the Friendly Factory' for a 'clean life and interesting work', Ethel Tillotson and many other mill-girls who had been on short time or unemployed applied for jobs, attracted by the prospect of better conditions and pay. The company was attracted by the girls' dexterity. Miss Tillotson started making condensers, and then went on to valves. In the mill she had to stand up all day. Making radio components she could sit.

> You had trays at either side of you, and you had to pick a grid up, and cathodes, heaters and all these and put them on top of each other. They were so fragile that it was really surprising how we didn't damage them, but it was a skill that came naturally to you, being in the mill. It's something that has come from generation to generation because of the fingers, the aptitude of your fingers.

The mass production of valves for the growing home radio market was the first real manifestation of an entirely new industry based on the applied science of electronics. The electron had been identified by the Cambridge scientist Sir Joseph Thomson in 1897. Hitherto electricity had been used just as a source of energy, to provide heat, light, or motor power. The discovery of electrons, and ways of controlling the flow of them, made it possible for an electric current to carry a coded message as well. This could be speech or radio sound, later a television signal, or computer data. It was the application of this principle that revolutionised communication, which changed the nature of warfare with radar and guided missiles, and which is now changing the nature of work itself through the computer and electronic automation. The electronics industry which developed with these changes was always hard to identify and define. Firms made parts for other industries as well as products in their own right. Many activities were involved, from laboratory research and top-secret defence projects, to the assembly of radios and televisions. Electronics firms made tiny components as well as whole computers. Later new companies emerged to produce computer 'software'. There was no workforce with the same sense of identity as there was in shipbuilding, or cars. But in the 1970s electronics had become one of the country's major employers.

Computers being assembled at ICL, Britain's largest manufacturers

Those who work in electronics have been part of a rapid expansion, but the risks have been high. The new industries that grew up earlier,

Girls making radio valves in a Lancashire factory in 1934. They worked for Ferranti, which, like Mullard, was expanding rapidly

chemicals and cars, were heavily protected by tariffs in their formative years. Electronics has been a cut-throat business, with fierce international competition between the most powerful companies in Europe, North America and Japan, aided in some cases by their governments. But the principal challenge for managers, scientists and production workers has been to keep up with the pace of scientific change. Of all the science-based industries, electronics has seen the shortest lead time between a laboratory discovery, and its commercial introduction. Whole technologies have been made rapidly redundant, to be replaced by new ones needing huge investment. The radio components that were made in Blackburn in the 1940s are as far from today's microchips as the penny farthing bicycle from the car, but the advance took less than thirty years.

The Blackburn workers were part of the radio boom between the wars. Electrical engineering companies had made military communications during the Great War. When a group of them started the British Broadcasting Company in 1922, to transmit entertainment from the Marconi headquarters and provide a reason for customers to buy their sets, a radio could cost £30. By 1939, with the BBC now well established as a public corporation, the manufacturers had the business they had hoped for. There were nine million licences in force, and much more reliable sets could be bought for £4 on hire purchase. Production, which had never flagged during the depression, was running at two million radios a year, and the number of radio jobs doubled within five years, to 43,000. Stanley Holden had also worked in the cotton mills.

> They had done every kind of different job before they came to Mullards. Joinery, sadlers, jewellers, tailors, you name it, they were there. And if you wanted jobs doing, kettles mending, watches mending, you could get it done at Mullards. I enjoyed every minute. It was like paradise to me.

Though the factories making valves and sets were clean and modern, and represented a major improvement on working conditions

ADVERTISERS' ANNOUNCEMENTS

SALESMANSHIP
1928 SALES
and
INITIATIVE
THE DRIVING
FORCE BEHIND
MULLARD
PROGRESS
1927
1926

Home and Overseas Trade

Modern manufacture—Modern marketing—
Modern methods of salesmanship, have made
Mullard the universal modern radio valve.

Mullard
THE·MASTER·VALVE

Testing radios at the Gramophone Company, Hayes, in the 1930s. Though there were jobs in the new radio factories, there could be seasonal lay-offs

in the traditional industries, much of the work was routine and monotonous, calling for assemblers rather than skilled craftsmen. Most companies paid piecework, and Ethel Tillotson found the pace hard at first.

> You had to build up and build up. They used to ask you, 'Can't you do a little more?' When I started work at first there were 20 to 30 starting the same morning as me. By the Friday there was only 10, because they weeded you out. They just wanted people who could do the work.

Many of the new workers were young girls, but as soon as they got married most companies insisted that they leave. Even in the Arcadian days of one of the growth industries of the thirties, when new designs were launched each year at the radio show, work was irregular, with seasonal lay-offs and other interruptions. Sid Todd began as an assembly worker for Pye in Cambridge, in 1929, putting radios in their cabinets.

> If we ran out of cabinets on Wednesday, and there was no supply of cabinets till Thursday or Friday, you were sent home and your money stopped. There was no payment. There was no paid holidays, or anything like that. They'd probably say when you got there Friday, 'Well we've got so many in, you had better work overtime and finish them off.' You were told to work overtime and that was the finish of it. If you didn't do it, you didn't bother to come on the Monday.

In another part of the same factory, Pye, like the other large manufacturers, was already conducting its own research into what was expected to provide the next major expansion, television. EMI and Marconi helped develop the electronic tube system in their own laboratories, and Pye had a 9″ set ready to go on sale when the BBC started television transmissions in the London area in 1936. But most firms concentrated on the simple broadcast radio receiver. The new industry's research effort was paltry compared with the millions of dollars that large American companies like RCA and Bell Telephone were already spending, and most research into other uses for electronics, apart from entertainment, was being done in British universities and the small government research departments.

Out of this basic scientific research came the second great breakthrough of the period. At Orfordness in 1935 Robert Watson-Watt demonstrated to the Air Ministry that it was possible to detect moving aircraft many miles away by the use of radio waves. Within a couple of years scientists had developed the first 'radar' defensive screen, able to locate attacking aircraft. By the outbreak of the war the east and southeast coasts were guarded by a chain of eighteen radar stations, stretching from the Orkneys to the Isle of Wight. Electronics and electronic theory were at a crucial stage in their development. The consumer-oriented manufacturers were already realising that government orders could be large and profitable.

During the Second World War the foundations were laid for the modern electronics industry. Military demands gave a new urgency to research, almost unlimited funds were available, and there was a massive recruitment of the best scientific brains to work on specific projects for which the forces saw a need, as well as more speculative ventures. F. E. Jones, who pioneered the Oboe blind-bombing technique for Bomber Command, was among the young scientists taken on.

> I was working on the electronics side of the British Empire Cancer Campaign as a young postgraduate studying for a Ph.D. And I had no qualms in stopping this and going into the radar business, although I didn't know it as such at the time. That applied to hundreds, maybe thousands of people.

There was no room for formality or professional jealousy. Even the most junior scientist could find himself called up before the Prime Minister to explain the importance of a new device. In the 'Boffins' war' scientists met face to face with the manufacturers in an exchange of ideas and information that was unprecedented. Sir Robert Telford, from Marconi, took part in the weekend meetings held at the Telecommunications Research Establishment at Malvern.

> They had quite frequently what they called 'Sunday Soviets'. They would get together people from the services operating in the particular field, people from industry, scientists and manufacturing people, scientists from government, to look at the problems, thrash out what could be done and then go away and quickly do it. Many of the wartime developments in the airborne radar field were done in a very short space of time in this way.

The major concentration was on radar, which made a greater contribution to victory than almost any other weapon. Increasingly powerful

Wrens working Colossus, the electronic decoding machine used to read German signals in World War II

radar was developed, in conjunction with the United States, and used to detect aircraft from other planes, as well as from the ground. Radar was used to track ships and submarines, and for navigation and weapons control. Radio communication was also vital for the war in the air, allowing pilots to talk to each other, and back to their base. Radio beams were used for the accurate bombing of targets in Germany, and radio technology was used to block the radar and bombing beams of the enemy. The need for portable and rugged equipment brought miniaturisation, with much smaller valves and components. Electronics took the leading role in the whole area of 'signals intelligence'. At a country house in Buckinghamshire, in conditions of utmost secrecy, Post Office research engineers helped build a machine to decode the intercepted German military radio messages. The largest electronic device that had ever been constructed, with 1500 valves, it was known as 'Colossus'. Dorothy Sands was one of the WRNS girls who operated it.

> I was sent to work on the Colossus computer in this huge room, these massive machines with wheels and valves and cogs, and it looked rather like a machine that a madman would invent. It hummed and clicked and ticked over, and it was very warm. I always thought of the machine as thinking. We used to climb up onto the ladders to load the tapes on, and then under the instruction of the Petty Officer, we would set it going.

Pat Pulford was another of the Wrens at Bletchley Park, working alongside the cryptanalysts and mathematicians.

> There was a mechanical typewriter which printed out jargon all the time, it didn't mean anything to us at all. Then if you were lucky and the actual code tape came up right, you'd get pure German through on the typewriter, which was always exciting.

Later the specialised Colossus would be regarded by some as having been the first electronic digital computer, though it had no storage memory. With Colossus, and the ballistic computers developed in the United States, the principle of the computer was now established. British scientists who had been involved went on to work on the computer projects at Manchester and Cambridge immediately after the war, though the Official Secrets Act forbad any mention of their experience with Colossus.

Just as electronic research and science was transformed by the wartime pressure, so was the manufacturing industry that was called on to make the new equipment and the valves and components that went into it. In 1939 the services spent £5 million on radio and radar. For 1944 the figure was £123 million. The number of jobs doubled again from the pre-war level, and new firms came into the field to fill the military contracts. Electronics was too new to be hampered by traditional attitudes, or ways of working. Unskilled workers learnt to do skilled jobs for the duration, with little of the trouble over 'dilution' that characterised the older war industries. Most of the managers were young, and came from a scientific or engineering background, and improvised quickly. At the age of 26 Robert Telford was organising the building of bomber radios at the Marconi factory at Chelmsford.

> There were lots of problems, but equally there was an enormous advantage that one had, because of the tremendous spirit and the will to overcome all difficulties. Despite the fact that components were short, everybody got stuck in and found alternative ways of doing things. You did it by cutting corners, and with the full backing of the Air Ministry, and of course the real co-operation of all the people prepared to work all the hours God made to get on with it.

The radio and radar factories suffered particularly badly from air-raids because many were in the south-east. The main Marconi factory was on 'Bomb Alley', the route that bombers took on their way into London. Plessey resorted to an underground factory in a completed but not yet opened section of the Central tube line. An instance of the industry's flexible thinking came in the way one firm handled the widespread labour shortage. At Pye, in Cambridge, the pre-war television section was making radar, and the radio factory was turning out two-way infantry and tank radios for the Army. When they got behind with a particular part they began to farm work outside. Queenie Culverhouse helped organise the scheme, which grew rapidly.

British television manufacture enjoyed a boom in the early 1950s, when over twenty companies were producing sets. Many had gone out of business within ten years

> My boss said, 'Why don't you get a hall in the village and see if you can get some women to come in and assemble them there?' So I saw the committee of the Women's Institute and I got permission to have the hall at £1 a week, and we went round and all the women of the village were very pleased to spend two or three hours there. I used to send car loads out, and fetch it back the next morning.

By 1945 Pye had 14,000 outworkers in the Cambridgeshire villages, as well as working three shifts in its main factories.

No major area of warfare was left untouched by the new science of electronics and no part of the industry was untouched by the wartime requirements placed on it. F. E. Jones saw it at first hand.

> Before the war the radio industry was really predominant in electronics, almost entirely linked to the consumer. The result of the war was that it in fact became engineering. Those that went into the business, the scientists and engineers who went into it, were given specific targets to do by the Air Force, the Navy, the Army, and we brought all the scientific men that we could onto solving those problems. At the end of the war you came out with electronic engineering, and you started the war really with radio.

As with the hugely-expanded aircraft industry with which they were closely connected, the electronics firms had to find a new role when peace came. Unlike the aircraft companies who had the foresight to start developing an ambitious programme for post-war civilian planes while the war was still in progress, the electronics firms were too scattered and preoccupied to think ahead. In the case of Marconi, company policy prohibited this.

> The managing director was an ex-Admiral of the Fleet who was put in to run us. And he would not allow anybody at all in the company to look to peacetime. Nobody at all. Everything had to be devoted to the war effort. So we were literally almost without a product after the war, or anything to do.

Firms had to choose between trying to remain in defence work, making use of their new contacts in Whitehall and staying in the vanguard of government-assisted scientific research, or finding commercial markets for the newly developed communications equipment by selling to airlines and shipping companies and police forces. Or they could return to the technically less exotic consumer market that they had known before the war. Sid Todd found his job changing overnight.

> The whole set-up as we had it before the tank sets, well it was absolutely useless for commercial production. So the whole set-up of the factory was more or less pulled out, and they had new lines laid down, and then we started making television. We had a very small one, about 10", I think.

For companies with much-increased capacity, making televisions had the greatest short-term promise. Work began at once in 1945, catching up with the United States where television technology had continued to develop throughout the war. Some of the firms had emerged during the war, others had been involved in traditional electrical engineering, like GEC and English Electric, and were now developing an electronics division side by side with their other work. For all of them television did in the early 1950s what radio had done in the 1930s. Six thousand sets were made in 1946 when the BBC service resumed, and by 1955 output was at 2,000,000 sets, and employment doubled again in the same period. Most of the work remained in the south, and the methods were little different from the way the radios had been assembled. A long line of men and women put components onto the chassis by hand, with soldering irons. It was still a labour-intensive business, with a largely un-unionised workforce. Audrey Swan made televisions at Pye.

> The sets came along on runners. We each did our own little bit of wiring, and soldering, and then it went on to the next person, and it was rushed. If you wanted to go to the toilet you had to call a float so that she could take your place, otherwise the sets piled up.

Though the product was modern, only a small investment was made in further television research, and the technology of production remained crude.

As many as twenty companies were making sets in 1950, and so long as demand was high, managers could almost ignore questions to do with costs and productivity, in favour of the engineering matters they understood better. But as the 'first-time buyer' market for televisions began to slow down, the competition between the British companies became more intense. When Arnold Weinstock became manager of Radio and Allied, which was bought up by GEC in 1958, he was appalled by the poor productivity and management he found there. Within weeks he had reduced the manufacturing costs by a third through better costing and production methods. The weaker firms with small production runs were gradually eliminated, or merged. Government financial policy, with the frequent changes in HP restrictions and purchase tax, made life more difficult for television makers just as they did for the car-makers. Doug Topping was at EMI.

> Every time the Budget came along some of the people on the production floor probably expected that it would affect them. They were on a week's notice, it was a way of life.

Only the largest companies, supplying the television rental firms, could weather these storms, and by 1963, after a round of failures and mergers, there were only ten television manufacturers left against 25 two years before. Unlike the Germans and the Dutch firm Philips, they produced only for the British market, not for the whole of Europe. The television workers did not necessarily lose their jobs. Other branches of the business making commercial products of higher value, or defence contracts, continued to prosper. One production worker remembers,

> Television gradually faded out, and we went into telephones and police wirelesses.

For many workers job satisfaction increased when the consumer production line stopped. Audrey Swan liked her new job.

> It was more interesting. Instead of doing just one part of a television set, one little bit, I built up a whole transmitter. The components came in, or the sub-assemblies, and then I built up the complete set, each one to a different coding.

Underlying the weakness on the consumer side of the British electronics industry, which showed itself in the lack of investment and research, was management's pronounced preference for specialised electronic engineering, and difficult one-off projects. This was a legacy of the war, when a generation of scientists and managers had cut their teeth on 'crash projects', in which money was no object, and the technical challenge much more exciting, than the more straightforward task of producing reliable consumer goods on an assembly line. The advanced work had not stopped at the end of the war. Money was available for electronic research connected with aviation, guided missiles, and signals. Sir Ieuan Maddock worked as a scientist in several government research establishments, and saw how the best brains were being directed.

> The main thing that happened after the war was that the impetus of all the techniques which had been developed during the war continued. Fewer people went back to straight communications and virtually everyone went into radar or into other forms of electronic or defence techniques. Contrary to the first expectations that people would leave the government laboratories and revert back to their universities or company laboratories, the size of the government laboratories actually increased. Most of the emphasis was on the defence ticket, and very much geared to government spending. And a particularly incestuous sort of relationship between government, and defence laboratories, and manufacturing industry developed.

The rearmament drive that came at the time of the Korean war, and the expensive aircraft projects of which new electronics were such a major part, meant that by the 1950s over a quarter of all electronic work was for defence. Foreign companies were unable to tender, so the work was protected, and much of it was on a 'cost plus' basis, so that it was impossible to make a loss.

Over half the research effort went on defence, and British universities and research establishments produced a stream of improvements and discoveries, on a par with work in the United States. But there was little feedback to the consumer field. Increasingly, there were two divided worlds, of specialised government electronics with lavish resources, and a limited range of consumer products with a much lower level of technology. No one imagined the explosion in the range of consumer products that would come later. The companies' policy seemed like commercial good sense. Ferranti expanded both sides of its business in the 1950s but closed down the television side later because of its poor performance. Other firms did the same thing. By the mid-1960s specialised electronics had become more important to the industry than consumer goods.

While this trend was developing, the technology was changing fast. The valve had been replaced by the transistor, developed at the Bell laboratories in the United States, and the whole emphasis of the massive American defence and space programme was to produce smaller and lighter and more reliable solid-state components which could be carried in rocket payloads and aircraft. But it was the Japanese, not the Americans or the British, who first saw the consumer implications of this. They bought the rights to the first transistor technology in America in 1948. Then they produced the first transistor radio and exported it back to the United States, as well as the rest of the world. In the United

States and Britain the defence application had seemed to be the only viable one, though exactly the same technology was available to British radio manufacturers had they been interested. Instead the British radio industry was to be devastated by cheap imports from Japan and Hong Kong ten years before British hi-fi equipment and television were struck down in the same way. Reg Edwards worked at EMI, at a factory engaged in both radio and defence work in the late 1950s.

> The radio side seemed to collapse. The whole factory was situated on one floor by then, that turned out tape recorders and radios, and gradually it seemed to disappear. Everything turned over, and the people that were made redundant at that time went over to the MOD side. I went over to the Ministry of Defence side and stayed with them. I've worked with them ever since.

There was one specialised field of electronics after the war which turned out to have the greatest potential of all, and which was also technically challenging and expensive to develop. The story of Britain's involvement with the computer provided the classic example of the gap between scientific innovation and successful exploitation of that research. The machines produced at Manchester and Cambridge in the post-war years were among the world's earliest. The team at Manchester University made the first storage computer anywhere. Professor Tom Kilburn remembers the day it first worked in 1948.

> We loaded in a programme which was a tiny programme to take the highest factor of a number, and at last it worked and there was great joy on the part of Geoff Toothill and myself. It was one of those marvellous days. Research is mostly a slog, but there are occasional days, and that was the greatest day of my professional life.

Unusually, this was a case in which the commercial possibilities of the research were recognised in Britain first. The Ferranti company helped finance the work at Manchester, and thought they might be able to sell several computers as number-crunching machines for universities and research establishments. In 1951 they made their first production model. The first working computer for business use anywhere in the world was commissioned, in an extraordinary act of faith, by the J. Lyons Catering Company of London. They were so enthusiastic with the machine that was delivered to them for tests in 1951 that they started a company to manufacture and sell the Leo computers in their own right. Dr John Pinkerton developed the first Leo, and saw what happened afterwards.

> We did have a visit from a vice-president of IBM, a Mr McPherson. The gossip that got around was that they thought, well, if a tea company in Britain can do it, well surely we ought

to be able to do it. The impression was that it was rather dis-
graceful for a company which was already the dominant company in office machinery at that time, not to be able to supply
what people were going to ask for.

A host of research computers were now being run in the United States,
and they moved quickly into the commercial field, led by Remington
Rand and IBM, who bought some of the Manchester patents. John
Pinkerton blames the slow development of British computers on the differences in scale between the two countries.

> The American companies were well aware of computing, but
> they had not recognised its potential impact in the office field
> as early as us. Not by a long way. But of course they had
> enormous industrial muscle behind them, they were trading on
> a very large scale, so once they recognised the potential they
> could afford to back it with very large resources.

In the 1950s British computer development, by Ferranti, EMI, Elliot,
Marconi and English Electric, who eventually bought out Leo Computers, saw much innovation. But the range of manufacturers was too
wide and the production runs too small to keep pace with the large
American companies. For a long time the British supplied most of their
own home market, but IBM had 60 per cent of the world market by the
1960s. IBM sold an increasing number of their computers in Europe and
became the technical standard with which other associated systems had
to be compatible.

The growth of the computer industry, and the space and defence
programmes in which computers were such an important element in the
United States, increased the demands that were made of the com-
ponent-making side still further. The transistor had been a major
advance, but in order to reduce the size of computers still further, and
cram even more complicated electronic systems into small spaces in
weapons, more research was going into new semi-conductor materials,
and further miniaturisation. The British research establishments were in
the forefront of this work, that led to the silicon chip and the age of
micro-electronics. At what had become the Royal Radar Establishment
at Malvern, a government scientist, Geoffrey Dummer, suggested a way
in which an electronic circuit with a number of devices could be integrated onto one piece of silicon.

> In 1957 we made a model showing our ideas on how this would
> work. It wasn't possible to make one yet because the techni-
> ques were not available at that time, but the idea was reason-
> ably sound. But we could not place contracts because we had to
> have equipment into which to fit it, before the Ministry would
> place a contract, and the firms were dubious about putting
> money on something which hadn't yet been developed.

Once again the basic concept was grasped in Britain at an early stage, but it was exploited faster and more effectively in the United States. In Britain the Ministry would not underwrite the further research necessary to put these ideas into practice, and Whitehall rules prevented joint exploitation of the idea with a British manufacturer. But the American Air Force paid Texas Instruments $2 million dollars to do the development work, and two years later they produced the first commercial integrated circuits. One British company was doing independent work. Derek Roberts, then doing semi-conductor research at the Plessey laboratory, had his own ideas about how silicon integrated circuits might be achieved.

> Having got the ideas we obviously turned to the Ministry of Defence for some initial support, and this led to the award of a contract for the grand sum in the first year of £10,000.

It was not simply a lack of government finance that held back British semi-conductor development. Most of the other British manufacturers were extremely cautious about the new ideas, and did not believe that the enormous technical difficulties of getting reliable circuits onto the silicon would be overcome.

By the mid-1960s the large American firms had achieved the same dominant position in components for micro-electronics as IBM had with computers. Against the background of this phenomenal growth, and with the space and defence programmes forging ahead, American companies needed as many trained scientists and engineers as they could lay hands on, and many British graduates were attracted by the prospects of more demanding work and a better salary. George Wells, now in California, had done postgraduate work at Glasgow University.

> After two years I went to work for GEC in Wembley on microwave research. A few months into this I began to wonder if I'd made the right decision, because the pace of the work seemed somewhat slower than what I had expected. Around about that time an American semi-conductor company were advertising in a London newspaper so I followed that through.

What began as a trickle developed into a flood. After a government minister had spoken out about 'brain snatching', the movement that was christened the 'brain drain' became a highly organised traffic. American recruiter William Douglass came to London in 1963 and set up a consultancy to find skilled scientists and engineers for clients in the United States. His first advertisement had 2000 replies, and soon up to 4000 were responding. Every year for five years he brought over representatives from twenty American firms to take their pick of his selection.

> I think American recruiters made friends very quickly because they were so much more disarming, easy to work with. There was no question of letters back and forth. Everything was

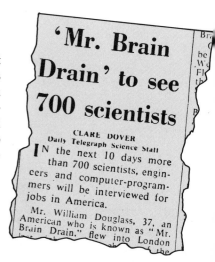

'Mr. Brain Drain' to see 700 scientists

CLARE DOVER
Daily Telegraph Science Staff

IN the next 10 days more than 700 scientists, engineers and computer-programmers will be interviewed for jobs in America.

Mr. William Douglass, 37, an American who is known as "Mr. Brain Drain," flew into London

handled on the spot. We were just different from what they'd run into before. They would tell us stories about having to requisition a slide rule. They just felt they were wanted, and that we were going to do everything possible to make it easier for them.

At the height of the brain drain a government committee found that 42 per cent of the output of the most relevant university departments was migrating. At least 1000 graduates a year were going through William Douglass's agency alone. At a time when the average wage for a young scientist in Britain was £1500, they could expect £4500 in the United States. As well as the pay and the work, many of those who left liked the ambience of the American firms, which was very different from what they had known in Britain. John Page, who now has his own company in California, worked on computers in London until the Leo factory was closed down following a merger.

When I left Leo's I wound up with an American computer company, Hewlett-Packard. The feeling of the company was entirely different, just from the physical environment. You could tell it was an open company, there weren't any office walls or partitions, and the company was run very much that way. The communication lines were open, there was no real élitism. The people who ran the place didn't have any special offices or trappings of power.

The company knew what its objectives were, where it was going, what its goals were. I knew what my part was, and what was most exciting for me was the feeling that my ideas, and extra things that I could contribute, were actually welcomed, and sort of integrated into the whole. Which is a kind of heady feeling, especially when you are young and just starting out.

The effect of the brain drain was much debated. Many of those who left were on the research side, and yet few complained that Britain was not doing enough research. The real gap lay in the ability to exploit the pure research and put ideas into production. What was needed was investment so that the brains could be used to better effect in the United Kingdom. The traffic worked in both directions, and many came back to the home country bringing valuable experience from the United States. Some, including David Jackson, found the British approach constricting.

I decided to spend a year in England working for ICL. So I did and for the first week I was there, I really tried to help them, I tried to work within their format. But I only found committees, nothing but committees. Every time I sat down to try and do something it would be resolved partially in committee. I couldn't get anything done and after a couple of weeks I really stopped.

Late in the day, British companies did start to make integrated circuits commercially, but it was an uphill task for those involved. Mullards, the largest of the old valve manufacturers and owned by Philips of Holland, started a factory at Southampton. They could not get the amount of government assistance they hoped for, and encountered technical difficulties at first achieving a high enough yield of working chips. Dr David Heard became production manager of the new unit.

> We knew that we were taking the world head on, particularly the Americans. The Americans had not at that stage had much competition from us. In 1966 it was very clear that the Americans had a start on us, and we were going to have to struggle very hard to catch up and keep up with them.

Most of the major British manufacturers, who were using large numbers of imported solid-state devices in their defence and commercial work, took a decision to continue to buy abroad. They felt it was now too late to start their own production. Lord Nelson, Chairman of English Electric and subsequently General Electric, thought it was the scale of production that counted for most once more.

> By the time it came to the question of manufacturing these, they were already making them on such a scale in the States that it wasn't easy to catch up. You could buy the same plant as they developed for doing it, but if they were making at five or ten times the volume, it was difficult to remain competitive and you could not afford not to be competitive.

British firms concentrated on the more specialised sections of the chips market, designing complex circuits for special purposes rather than what became known as all-purpose 'catalogue' chips.

By the end of the 1960s the British electronics industry was still narrowly based, on a range of large-scale government-sponsored projects in defence and communications in which it had proved very successful. Though the work was protected from competition, British defence exports to other governments were also rising, and in the era of electronic warfare specialist companies like Ferranti, Plessey, Racal and Marconi could offer a dazzling array of radar and electronically-guided weapons systems. But on the civilian side, whether with computers for businesses to buy, or products for home use, there were great weaknesses. The computer companies were small and increasingly vulnerable. It was reckoned that IBM, with their long runs, had production costs on each computer that were half those of its European competitors. Consumer electronics had shrunk still further.

The Labour government which came to power in 1964 pledged to industrial regeneration spent much energy and money trying to revive the flagging fortunes of the old industries. But the new Ministry of Technology was also determined to strengthen electronics, and thought the best way to do this was through amalgamation to produce bigger

Putting together computers at an ICL factory at Letchworth. The difficulty lay in competing with America's IBM

companies with stronger resources. The big three electrical companies were encouraged to merge together. In 1968 GEC took over the ailing AEI, and a few months later English Electric, which had earlier absorbed Marconi. The highest priority was given to the two remaining computer makers, ICT and English Electric computers, who had themselves absorbed a succession of companies but were still a financial embarrassment to the groups of which they were a part. At the Ministry of Technology Tony Benn was the Minister, and Sir Ieuan Maddock his chief scientist.

> It was obvious in the mid-sixties that the booming technology was computers, and everything to do with computers. We were already dropping behind in the whole technology which affected computers, and there was a multiplicity of little companies striving to succeed in the face of some very heavy-powered competition from overseas. The government itself took a hand in merging some of the effort which produced ICL, to allow some chance of competing in a fiercely difficult field.

The newly-created International Computers Ltd was still small in relation to its principal competitors, but it was the biggest firm in the world outside the United States. The new managing director, Arthur Humphries, said confidently at the time:

> We can't expect to be able to out-produce a large American company, but there is no reason why we can't out-think them. They haven't got any more people that are involved in the art of thinking than we have, and, with all their skills and experience, I believe ours are better.

The creation of ICL, combining almost all the British-owned computer effort in the country, and with a 10 per cent government stake, ensured that Britain kept a computer presence through the 1970s, though it needed a further government intervention to keep it there. ICL did little to shift IBM's share of world computer sales, which had now risen to over 70 per cent, but managed to keep over a third of the British home market for themselves.

The concentration on financial reorganisation, in order to compete in the area of the large and expensive main-frame computer, obscured what was really happening technically and in the market. Integrated circuits and the reduction in size of components had been proceeding so fast that applications for electronics were widening all the time, beyond computers, across all of manufacturing industry and into new consumer products. On the west coast of the United States the physical proximity of equipment-makers to chip-producers, and to university research, was producing a new synergy. In the dense concentration of electronic companies that were settling south of San Francisco, in Silicon Valley, an astounding rate of economic growth was directly linked to month-by-month advances in the technology and the state of the art. Yet the big firms which dominated in Britain were not geared to the riskier, innovative, but potentially hugely profitable new business. Their directors did not always understand what was happening.

In Britain many of the new and most successful electronic firms had younger managements and were American owned. Honeywell, Hewlett Packard, Burroughs and IBM all set up profitable subsidiaries. Having brain-drained, and spent a distinguished career in semi-conductors in the United States, Dr Ian Mackintosh came back from America in the mid-1960s to start the first chip-making company in Scotland at Glenrothes, for Elliott Automation. When he left shortly after a merger, he tried to establish his own micro-electronics company in Britain. The difficulties he faced showed the financial problems which stood in the way of any new venture in Britain at that time, as well as the general unawareness of the changes that were taking place.

> I can remember about 1969, going around trying to raise the reasonably humble sum of half a million pounds going on two million pounds, to start a British independent semi-conductor company. I went to quite a number of senior civil servants and financiers but the result was completely disastrous, nobody wanted to know, nobody really seemed to care.
>
> There was during the sixties an extraordinary lack of awareness on the part of the men in power in Britain, the ministers, people in the city, members of the academic research establishment, managers of electronic companies, that we were at an industrial watershed, that we were at the beginning of a major new industrial revolution of enormous economic significance.

Ian Mackintosh failed to start his own manufacturing company, but four years later his old firm at Glenrothes, which had been closed down by GEC because it duplicated work being done in other plants, had been revived under new American ownership, and had successfully invented the circuits at the heart of many video games.

Through the 1970s, at an increasing pace, the nature of the watershed became clear to civil servants and politicians, and impinged on the general public. The results of the new technology could be seen everywhere. In the high street, calculators and wristwatches based on chips became both cheaper and more sophisticated at the same time. Television incorporated microprocessors to provide teletext, and a plethora of hi-fi components came into the shops, followed by video recorders and video games. Small computers were installed in primary schools, and bought for the home. In industry microprocessors gave new controls to tools, and allowed greater automation, even before the arrival of robots on production lines. Time-consuming design processes could be done with the aid of computers. Office work began to change with word processors, and terminals, telecommunications and computers were linked in what has become known as information technology.

The British electronics-makers took part in this growth, and it would have been hard not to have done so. The market for all electronic products was growing at about 17 per cent a year at the end of the 1970s. But the level of imports was rising to nearly 50 per cent of the British market, and many of the most advanced products were coming from Japan and the United States, or were being made in the United Kingdom by foreign-owned companies. The remaining part of the old-style consumer industry, hi-fi and television makers, were hit first. Doug Topping was a senior manager on the television side of EMI, which felt the full force of the Japanese onslaught at the same time as the car-makers, in 1971.

> It was the time that the first receivers from Japan arrived in volume, and demonstrated something that was quite new to the British consumer and the British market. That was that the receivers worked when they came out of the box first time, and they kept on going.
>
> Our chairman called all the senior executives together about ten years ago and told us quite frankly that unless we did something about the quality performance that we were putting up at that time, our company as we then knew it would absolutely cease to exist.

Though defence and specialist work continued to prosper, the financial mergers of the late 1960s did little to help Britain recover the ground lost in micro-electronics. A more radical change was needed not only in the way that managers approached quality and productivity, and the market, but also in the funding that was available. It became increasingly clear that, although electronics was a prosperous new industry which might have been expected to be able to stand on its own two feet, its development costs were extremely high. Other governments, grasping the future benefits of micro-electronics sooner than Whitehall, had been far more helpful to their own manufacturers. Whether through their procurement policy for government and defence orders, or through closely co-ordinating government research activities with industry's own, or by providing cash grants to nurse promising schemes, the American, Japanese, German and French industries all received far more government backing. By 1978 the British government had recognised this and began to provide more substantial sums, with grants totalling £70 million. In a late attempt to take Britain into the production of the next generation of micro-chips, the NEB funded Inmos. Britain had its first Minister of Information Technology from 1982, and there was a major propaganda campaign to make industry more aware of the potential uses of electronics.

Young as it is, the electronics industry has already been the subject of critical reviews. In 1982 a report by the industry's own Economic Development Committee pointed out that though Britain had many strengths in specialised fields, there was a growing trade deficit in electronics.

> UK manufacturers have not concentrated on leading-edge businesses, and in consequence the UK industry continues to lose its share of the world market . . . The UK electronics industry is, in short, in relative decline. A continuation of present trends would imply a further decline in the UK share of the world market and an equivalent loss of trade, profit and job opportunities.[52]

Sir Clive Sinclair with his innovation for 1983, a 2" flat-screen television

In Britain's particular situation, of large and rather unwieldy firms that found it hard to move quickly into the new areas of electronics because they lacked the cash, or were otherwise engaged, it has been the small companies, offering very specialised products or services, that have done best. By focusing on a particular part of the market, they have been able to do what ICL hoped to do with IBM, out-think the opposition. Sir Clive Sinclair started his firm in the 1960s. Like others, he found it difficult to raise capital. But in 1972 he devised a technically ingenious method of reducing the power needed by a factor of ten, and produced the world's first pocket calculator. When the Japanese manufacturers caught up with him, which they quickly did, he turned to a programmable calculator, then to a digital watch, then to a pocket television, then to a cheap and simple computer. Each product was new, and though his company collapsed at one point, he made a fortune.

> When I came into the business at the beginning of the sixties the industry was run by giants. There was Jules Thorn at Ferguson, C. S. Stanley at Pye, businesses that had started before the war and had become very large indeed. But they sold principally to the British and to a lesser extent a European

market. When the Japanese came into the consumer electronics field they tended to sell on a world scale. They had an economy of scale that made them very tough competition. They were also putting in new technology. They were able to recruit into their consumer industry the very brightest engineers, whereas the brightest engineers in Britain were going into the aircraft industry or atomic power. So there was very little innovation in British companies. We set out to be innovative, that was our strength. And we learned through the years that in order to be any use at all in the business we had to be on a world scale of production. The firms that are succeeding now are those that perceived the need to sell worldwide.

The small British firms avoided the huge research cost of developing their own components, while exploiting the inventiveness of their engineers and designers. The fastest growth was in computer servicing and programming, with firms that produced no tangible product at all, and which therefore had even lower overheads. New companies grew up to provide 'software' for computer users and computer manufacturers, instructions that tailored a general-purpose machine to do a specific job, whether to handle airline reservations or deal with driving licence records. New software firms developed into worldwide businesses. Philip Hughes is chairman of Logica, one of the earliest companies.

Up until very recently the City had a total lack of interest in the software industry. It didn't meet requirements. They felt it wasn't big enough, it wasn't solid enough, it didn't have assets, didn't have desks, didn't have machines, didn't have factories, just had people.

We have come to realise that instead of being a disadvantage it's an advantage to have a people business. If you've got a pool of 1400 highly skilled people gathered together over a 10- to 15-year period, this is in fact far more stable than a company that's got all its future in one of two products that could suddenly become obsolete. Each year we recruit about 10–12 per cent of our current size from universities. This is our investment. It is really our sole critical investment for the future, investing in people.

The requirements of the software industry represent electronics work at its most cerebral. David Blease, working on a contract for British Telecom at Logica's office in London, described the appeal that he finds in programming.

I design my programmes, I write my programmes, test my programmes. At the end of the day I've got a working product. There's not many jobs where you can do all that.

In the second half of the twentieth century the progress of electronics has provided a crucial test of British scientists for their ability to innovate, and of entrepreneurs and managers for the speed of their reactions and their production ability, and of politicians for their attitudes to new industries. F. E. Jones, one of the scientists who started on radar during the war, went on to become managing director of Mullard, and campaigned for more government help in the 1960s.

> One can't say that we have had disasters in electronics, but we have been slow, and we have been held back on investment, which is really the key to success. Techniques change so rapidly that what you make now in large numbers are out of date in two years time, needing more investment, new skills and training.

Lord Nelson, of GEC, acknowledges that opportunities were lost.

> We were slow to see the opportunities of developing this electronic technology towards a consumer market. I think we ought to have moved a bit quicker in hindsight. The Japanese spotted that, they developed their own home market, then they got into the American market, they got into our market. By that time the size and scale on which they were doing it became increasingly difficult to match.

With all the developments in software and micro-computers, as well as the continuing telecommunications and defence work, electronics still has a divided workforce, many of them working in small units, doing many different types of job. Most of the new brain workers are in the cluster of companies that have grown up around Slough and Maidenhead in the Thames Valley, as well as the science parks that have been opened in university cities. The greatest number of jobs for the unskilled and semi-skilled remain in assembly work, putting together components to make micro-computers or defence electronics. In the central belt of Scotland there are now 40,000 electronics workers, many of them working for American- and Japanese-owned companies. They make 50 per cent of Britain's semi-conductors. The greatest transformation has come over the television factories. Five out of the six that survive are now in Japanese hands, and are run with a management style and a level of productivity that British ownership never achieved. But though the value of the goods that the electronics industry produces has doubled over the past ten years, the total number of jobs has fallen. Higher productivity and automation have meant that, even in the new industry with the most promise, the total number of jobs has dropped from 575,000 ten years ago, to 500,000 in 1980.

Barbara Abrahams was one of the first workers in the 'clean room' where integrated circuits are made at Mullard. She works through a microscope, with tweezers. But machines will soon be available to do the work she does.

Examining components at the Japanese Mitsubishi television factory which employs 200 people near Edinburgh

It frightens me that we could be making silicon or micro-processors which are going to put us out of work. We have got higher-technology machines coming in which can do what we can do, with less operators. When I first came here there were 1700 operators. There's 700 now, producing the same amount of work.

Iain Barron of Inmos, the microchip company set up in Newport in south Wales with heavy government funding, sees the future in the employment created indirectly by the new wealth of the microchip age.

Inside the clean room where advanced microchips are made, at Inmos in south Wales

I think it is wrong to think of an industry like semi-conductors as creating jobs. It will undoubtedly create jobs in small numbers. We are planning to employ about a thousand people in this building. But really with an industry like semi-conductors, it's creating wealth for the country. It's generating money, and it is the use of that money which is more likely to create jobs.

CHAPTER 12
HINDSIGHT

Britain had a good reservoir of technical skills. That was not always translated into effective and competitively manufactured products.
Graham Day

The problem has been that the manager hasn't perceived the need to keep his labour force, his workers of any sort, properly informed of what was happening. The lack of knowledge bred fear, and the fear bred bad labour relations.

Sir Clive Sinclair

In this country, uniquely, industry is looked upon as a means of providing jobs, and that actually isn't the job of industry. The job of industry is to create wealth.

John Harvey-Jones

In the nineteenth century Britain, as the first industrial power, had been able to do things her own way at her own speed, untroubled by self-doubt or competition. The hard-headed Victorian businessmen ran the workshop of the world, and later became the world's bankers as well. The consequence of this early start was that in the twentieth century Britain had to make a series of fundamental readjustments. At home, employers who had grown accustomed to treating their workers in a certain way found that they were better organised, more politically educated, and had greater expectations for themselves. They could try to repress these expectations for a while, but they had to alter their assumptions about markets and customers more rapidly. Abroad, new competitors developed who were able to take traditional export markets, and then send cheap imports to Britain itself. This process of coming to terms with a changed situation has provided the principal theme for all the old industries whose stories have been told here. The new industries had to measure themselves against international criteria from the very start.

Despite these changes the British economy has grown steadily since the First World War. British industry produced 60 per cent more in 1939 than in 1914, 100 per cent more by 1950, 250 per cent more by 1970. These increases brought a better standard of living and higher real earnings, more government services and improved working conditions. But when set against the progress of other countries, the record has not been impressive. In the 1920s Britain failed to match growth in Europe and North America. In the 1930s she performed better, with the help of tariffs. During the 1950s and 1960s the gap widened. Britain's economy was growing at two per cent a year, that of West Germany at six per cent, France at five per cent, Japan at seven per cent. Productivity was certainly rising, but far more slowly than in other countries. As a result many British goods became less competitive, and there was less to spend on re-equipment, which in turn left productivity further behind. When Britain still dominated international trade in 1900, her share of world exports in manufactured goods was a third. But though Germany's export share stayed about the same over eighty years, Britain's had fallen to 15 per cent in 1960, and to only eight per cent in 1982. The level of manufactured imports to Britain has trebled in the last twenty years. Britain now imports almost as many manufactured goods as she exports.

In the 1970s and 1980s there was not only low growth, but an absolute decline in manufacturing output. The relative decline of manufacturing as an employer of labour, and as a contributor to the economy, seemed to suggest that British managers and workers, and British governments, had over the years got things wrong. Explaining Britain's industrial record has become a full-time occupation in itself for many economists and historians. One diagnosis puts great stress on social attitudes, and on the way in which the tensions of the class system worsened industrial relations and held back change. Other explanations

Car-workers leaving British Leyland at Cowley in 1983

267

emphasise the role of government, and the extent of public spending and taxation; or the way industry is structured; or the inadequacies of scientific training and education. It was not just the pundits who took part in these debates. Those who work in British industry have had their own ideas about where things went wrong, and their own particular perspective.

Some of the sharpest observations have been made by foreign managers who came to work in Britain. To many of them it was the social divide in British industrial life that was most striking. In 1971 a Canadian businessman, Graham Day, was put in charge of the Cammell Laird shipyard on Merseyside.

> I was there before half-past seven, which caused everybody great consternation because I guess they did not expect the gaffers until a little later on, and I used to perambulate through the yard most mornings because I was learning and I wanted to talk to people, or wanted them to talk to me so I could listen and start to appreciate what the issues from the shopfloor were. I remember going aboard the accommodation section of a ship we were fitting out, going into a cabin, and there was one of the workmen fitting in a window, and so I said, 'Good morning', and there was no real response and I thought, well, he's not a steelworker so he can't really have a hearing problem, so I raised my voice and said, 'Good morning'. And he turned round and said, 'Are you speaking to me?' And I said yes, and I said, we haven't met, and I am Graham Day, and so on. And he said, 'Oh yes, I knew you were here, but I wasn't sure you were speaking to me because I've been here 27 years and that's the first director who's ever spoken to me'.

> When I used to walk around the shipyard people used to avoid me. If I was walking, for example, straight in that direction and they were coming towards me, they would sidle off to the left or right.

The gulf between managers and workforce varied very much from company to company, and was often a factor of size as much as anything else. But evidence for it, summed up by the phrase 'Them and Us', could be seen everywhere, even in the newest industries. Paul Murphy was a supervisor in a Manchester aircraft factory.

> The tradition in the industry is of separate canteens, even separate toilets. It still exists today where on the toilet door you can see 'Ladies' and 'Gentlemen' on the staff side, and 'Male' and 'Female' on the shopfloor. There are four canteens still today at British Aerospace, Manchester. There's a special mess for the directors, there's a mess for middle management. Below them there's another mess for supervision, and ultimately the larger canteen on the shopfloor. And yet when things go

wrong the directors tell us we're all working for the same company. I can't square that circle.

Pension rights, holiday provisions, the way people were paid all emphasised the differences between management and workforce, white collar and blue collar, skilled and unskilled. Charles Lisgo worked for a company which applied two standards.

> It was one of the goals for you to get on to the staff, because a) it was more money and b) in those days it was more security of employment. If you were on the staff, you were on at least a month's notice, and if you got onto the senior staff you were on three months' contract. If you were on the clock it was a week's notice.

The hierarchies even among those on the clock were just as pronounced. In the mills, spinners thought they were superior to weavers. The stratifications and internal divisions were at their most complete in the shipyards. A joiner recalls:

> Each trade seemed to have its own particular pride, and seemed to be very clannish. Electrical engineers thought they were better than boilermakers, they were more highly skilled. Boilermakers used to think they were the salt of the earth, because they literally built the ship, and if they didn't build the ship, the engineers couldn't finish it. There was a sort of class warfare.

One worker described the yards as 'like the Indian caste system'. The same distinctions were transferred to the much newer car and aircraft factories.

> All through my working life the toolrooms have always considered they were just a little better than the everyday common or garden fitter. They used to say that without us, you can't build aeroplanes. We make the jigs, we make the tools, therefore we are better.

Some have found the hierarchies of the shopfloor and the divisions between 'Them and Us' a sufficient explanation for Britain's problem in itself. For others it was just one obstacle among many to meeting common difficulties in a co-operative way.

The heritage of the nineteenth century must play a major part in explaining these difficulties, which dictated so much about British industrial life. Social divisions were only part of this tradition. The Victorian entrepreneurs and their fathers and grandfathers had determined where British industry was located, close to the coal and near enough to the sea for export; and how it was organised, in small and individualistic family firms that held back the growth of trusts or combines. They also set a tough, hire and fire style of management which in turn forged the attitudes and organisation of those who worked for them.

Most of the worst labour-relations problems, as well as the strict demarcation among skilled men, could be traced back to the ruthlessness of Victorian employers. In the fifty years before 1914 a whole series of small, separate craft unions grew up, whose purpose was to defend the interests of their members against tough employers, as well as against other workers skilled or unskilled. Because of widespread insecurity workers were anxious to safeguard their craft, but the outcome was widespread restrictive practice and inter-union rivalry that lasted well into the present century. Managers in many industries were compelled to deal not only with one national union, or one union for each factory, as in the United States or Germany, but with ten or twenty small unions.

In the days when labour was cheap, and foreign competition had not yet struck, arguments about demarcation and restrictive practices were not so critical. But after the First World War, when managers realised they could only survive by cutting costs and improving efficiency, they found themselves faced with an organised and sometimes highly political workforce. It had learnt to resist efforts to eliminate old skills, to alter pay or piece rates, or to bring in new equipment. Attempts to increase productivity from the 1920s onwards provoked regular conflict, partly because of the growing feeling of insecurity which mass unemployment encouraged; partly because of the authoritarian character of much of British management.

As Britain's industrial structure changed, away from the old industries of cotton, coal and ships, to the new industries of cars, chemicals and electronics, many were forced to seek new jobs or move from one part of the country to another. They took with them the conservatism and distrust of management that was part of their past. These inherited attitudes were in turn fed by the way some of the new industries behaved. Hayden Evans came from south Wales to an Oxford car-body plant.

> I had been brought up in Merthyr Tydfil, in a strong trade union, as an ex-miner, and when I went to Pressed Steel I found there was no trade union and you didn't have any representation. They could pull any punches they liked and threaten you with the sack. I thought this wasn't quite right.

Many British managers still continued to use insecurity as a tool of control, and kept to the tradition of hiring and firing at short notice, with welfare facilities kept to a statutory minimum, and little consultation. Even before 1914 there were notable exceptions, in the companies which took a more enlightened line. Brunner Mond was the leader in its treatment of its workers, and fifty years later its successor company, ICI, was still well in advance of much of British industry. It was easier to be a model employer in a new field than in the old export-based industries whose contraction was so rapid between the wars. But there were great variations in the way in which management dealt with labour relations even there. The most progressive coal companies, or steel companies, who treated people better, usually benefited from this even during the recessions.

In the period of full employment after the Second World War, when changes might have been towards ending restrictive, or protective, practices, the memory of the recession was still strong. Workers were suspicious of the post-war productivity drive, though it had the full support of the TUC leaders between 1945 and 1951. In hindsight many managers feel that it was in the fifteen years after the war that most chances were lost. Sandy Stephen was a director of a Scottish shipyard.

> I think one has to blame the management at that time for not taking more vigorous action to get the problems sorted out. It's easy to blame the unions now. With hindsight we should really have tackled all these demarcations vigorously, and they were capable of solution when times were good.

Sir Campbell Adamson remembers the lack of imagination he saw in the meetings of the Iron and Steel Employers' Association he attended in the 1950s.

> There was a sort of tradition that you never gave any increase in money unless the men's side could prove what was called change of practice, that something different was happening. We spent hours on this. I never remember one single occasion in that body when we constructively said to ourselves, 'Well now, if we paid twopence, threepence, fourpence, sixpence more per hour, and actually got something back from it, in increased productivity, more efficient working, then it would be worth our while to do that'. We never seemed to talk about it in anything except the negative sense, trying to hold down the amount we could give.

As a result, management became defensive too, resenting the apparent unwillingness of the unions to 'co-operate' with them, and irritated at having to devote so much time to labour relations. As shipbuilder Sir John Hunter saw it:

> More and more, management had to spend their time on sorting out labour difficulties and demarcation, to an extent where they really hadn't got time to do their proper jobs at organising and getting production efficiently arranged.

The definition of the 'proper job' of management was central to industry's difficulties. In the most successful firms, management had long since grasped that looking after their employees, with welfare provisions and better conditions, was not just a matter of generosity, but of self-interest. A more secure and comfortable workforce was usually more co-operative when it came to improving productivity and profits.

If labour was inflexible, and found it hard to change its ways, it was partly because management was so slow to change, too. The stereotype of the British manager or owner as the paternalistic, shrewd, practical businessman, despising formal training and taking markets for granted, endured into the 1950s and 1960s. Learning by experience, by being 'put through the mill', they distrusted paper qualifications. Part of the appeal of William Morris as a great business success story in the inter-war years was the fact that he started with no formal technical training and had grown rich entirely on his own efforts. The anti-educational prejudice sometimes reached absurd lengths even in major companies. Sir Leonard Redshaw joined Vickers in the 1930s.

> I remember when I decided I would go to university, I made enquiries and I found that only two people employed in the whole of Vickers' at Barrow had degrees, but the bossmen did not know. They dared not tell because we had one particular boss who would have sacked them as being the wrong type.

British managers put much more emphasis on practical production questions, and engineering, than on personnel matters, or on selling what they made, or the new skill that became known as marketing. There had always been a complacency about markets. Before the First World War the Germans used trained export salesmen who spoke the languages of their customers, backed up by a commercially-minded consular service, and were already taking orders away from British companies as a result. In the 1920s Japan's seizure of the textile markets was based not only on price, but also on an energetic sales effort in India and Africa. British companies became used to being chided for their poor salesmanship. In 1930 the then Prince of Wales spoke in the Guildhall, where his father had told England to 'wake up' thirty years before.

> We have all got to realise that the world markets of today are not those of the times of Queen Victoria . . . What we need is to realise that our best men must not be concerned with production only, or even mainly with production. A goodly share of the best brains to be had must be concentrated on the difficult, complex but most interesting job of fighting competition in the world's markets.[53]

The measures taken to help British industry in the 1930s took a form which made competitive selling less necessary. Tariffs protected the home trade. Within the Empire, preferential agreements provided British companies with captive markets. Joining international cartels, with fixed prices, protected the chemical industry and the steelmakers. After 1945 a generation of managers who had learnt to concentrate on all-out production during the war found there was still no need to worry about selling, because major rivals were temporarily out of action and there were extreme shortages. Shipbuilders made ships at 'cost plus'.

Car-makers had long waiting lists. Goods sold themselves and managers grew used to this.

In the 1960s and 1970s every major British industry, with the exception of retailing which is by definition committed to selling, could point to a failure of the sales side. The shipbuilders did not see the changing demand for new types of ship. The car firms, with the exception of Ford, did little market research into what sort of cars customers really wanted, and were still run largely by engineers. The aircraft industry made planes that were among the most advanced in the world, but could not sell them to the international airlines in sufficient numbers. The penalty had to be paid, as one after another Britain's major industries were attacked by aggressive marketing from abroad. Sir Monty Finniston remembers the attitude to selling he found in the renationalised steel industry, in 1967.

> I went to see a sales director whom I shall not mention by name, but from one of the leading steel companies, and I said to him, 'How do you sell your steel?' He said, 'I don't sell it at all. I haven't sold any steel since the end of the Second World War.' I said, 'What does that mean?' He said, 'I ration it. People come to me to ask for steel because they are short of it, and I give it out.'

Having been heavily protected in the 1930s, and enjoying an apparently irrepressible demand after the war, the chemical industry had the same bias towards production and away from selling. Sir Michael Clapham was a Deputy Chairman of ICI:

> I'm afraid that salesmanship was always rather despised in ICI. There was a time when there wasn't a single commercially trained man on the Board, partly because we'd always taken our best brains in on the technical side. We'd got brilliant research people coming in, and we'd never recruited people of the same quality on the commercial side. I think that arose from the old monopolies in soda ash and fertilisers, and from the protection that kept our competitors out.

The same trait was present in the new electrical and electronics firms, which preferred specialised defence electronics, where sales were to governments only. Lord Nelson is a director of GEC.

> I don't think we recognised early enough the importance of the commercial base as distinct from the technological base. A terrific effort was put in to create a good technological base, and pretty successfully, but what people hadn't realised was that in the end it wasn't the technical thing that mattered, it was the marketing side. We were slower at picking that up.

What was missing from many British companies was a systematic, planned approach to their labour relations, to selling, and to production.

Many senior managers still prided themselves on intuition, and were shy of the careful planning and research which characterised the modern style of management, particularly in North America. Graham Day describes the situation he found when he became Managing Director of the Cammel Laird shipyard.

> It wasn't focused on basic business principles. The concentration was on technical items. I remember eventually establishing what we called a corporate plan, which said, 'This is the business we are in, this is the time horizon we are shooting for, these are the capital implications, the people implications, the market implications, these are our selling targets, these are the markets we are going for, here's our projected cash flow'. There wasn't anything like that.

The new team who moved into the collection of companies that comprised BMC, after the Leyland merger in 1967, made similar comments about the management they found. Michael Shanks was planning director for the new group.

> They were extremely energetic, dynamic, but they didn't think, most of them. There was a tendency to operate by the seat of your pants, to operate by instinct. Now that's fine when you are operating a small business and you can control everything, but it's much less successful when you are running a huge mammoth enterprise. Those are not the decisions you can take on a Saturday afternoon. You really need to think and work out a great deal.

Many British managers doubted the need for large corporations, in any case. The nineteenth-century structure, with its small companies, ran on for a long time. In the inter-war years all the calls for amalgamations to form stronger units, with more money for re-equipment, were resisted by the cotton firms, the shipyards, and the private coal-owners, often until it was too late. When large firms did become widespread there was resistance to centralisation, and a new sort of divide between those who produced and those who ran the new corporate bureaucracies. The arrival of the multinationals was also greeted with suspicion by many managers, as well as by the unions. Like the workforce, management had retained the prejudices and values of an earlier age.

Yet in the end it is too simple to explain the performance of British industry in terms of management and labour alone. Neither the defensiveness of labour nor the conservative traditions of management grew up in a vacuum. They were shaped by historical circumstances and the wider social environment of which industry was just one part. A crucial factor was the anti-industrial bias of British education, particularly of the public schools to which those who had made money in industry sent their children. There they were taught the classics in preference to science, and practical education was eschewed in favour of academic learning for its own sake. An ethos of gentility and service was implanted, that was hostile to industrialism and economic growth. Fred Cartwright joined the steel industry in 1929.

> You've got to remember that in England people were either Indian Civil Service, Sudan Civil Service, Army, Navy. That was the sort of thing the ambitious young man went for. He certainly didn't say, 'I want to go and work in a steelworks in Dowlais'. He certainly didn't.

John Harvey-Jones, Chairman of ICI since 1982, believes that some of these social values still continue.

> Industrialists in this country are not looked upon as a particularly desirable thing to be. The gentleman farmer is viewed as being a far more desirable thing, or a lawyer, or a member of parliament. You don't get much social standing in this country through being an industrialist.

John Barber was Finance Director of the Ford Motor Company in the 1960s.

> I think the blame is probably on the education system, in that industry wasn't regarded as a place where the best people went. If you look at the more able people over the years, I think you will find that merchant banks and others probably get a higher share of good people than industry. Industry was almost a dirty word in universities and schools at one stage.

The prejudice against industry sent the best brains into the civil service, the professions, or the city, but it could also be seen at every level in the low status given to vocational training. In West Germany over 65 per cent of school leavers have gained some sort of vocational qualification, usually in a technical field. In Britain the figure of those leaving with any qualification is 35 per cent, and those with a vocational training a mere 15 per cent.

Another disadvantage for industry, not unrelated to the bias in education, has been the strained relationship that manufacturing has had with government and the civil service. It was unsettling that the two main parties held sharply different views about how industry should be owned and run. In Germany governments were informed about, and helpful towards, industry from before the turn of the century. In the United States there was a continuing belief in the virtues of the free market. In Britain governments were critical. They intervened, then withdrew. They had different standards for different industries, changed their priorities, and spent far more time and money on propping up old industries than on encouraging new ones.

The first real intervention came in the First World War, when the Ministry of Munitions took an unprecedented control over the war industries, pumped in funds, built state factories, and proved how effective central planning and direction could be in an emergency. The modern chemical and aircraft industries were created in this period. But in the 1920s government withdrew to the sidelines again, from where it criticised employers and trade unions in lengthy enquiries which made sound recommendations that were usually ignored. To meet the depression in the 1930s government introduced tariff protection, and backed reorganisation schemes that gave more direct aid to cotton, coal, and shipbuilding. But though the industrialists desperately needed the help that was offered, they were often resentful, and disliked taking advice from Whitehall. Laissez-faire attitudes disappeared very slowly.

After 1945 government moved from advice and regulation to direct intervention and control. Labour believed in state ownership, and running the main industries of the country in the public interest by public authorities, as a matter of principle. But the limited degree of nationalisation that was carried through, of the railways, coal and steel, was not based on political dogma alone, as Herbert Morrison pointed out in 1945.

> The Labour Party offers a short-term programme of socialisation of a limited number of industries, and in each of these industries it rests its case on the practical facts and necessities of the situation – facts which cannot be argued away, neccessities which cannot be escaped. Its argument for socialisation is based on the practical business merits of each case.[54]

The hope was that the new Boards could put up a better performance than the private owners had done between the wars, and that planning and public funds would bring efficiency and competitiveness which the old regimes had failed to achieve. At the same time the private sector was to be disciplined and organised with new controls and directives.

After 1951, when central planning was out of favour again, industry was expected to modernise and invest in new plant of its own accord. Yet this was made difficult. Successive Chancellors, who were more concerned with financial stability and the balance of payments, switched demand on and off through squeezes and changes in purchase tax, which in turn affected sales and investment rates and made it hard to plan ahead. Governments continually preached the need for rationalisation and increasing productivity, but were reluctant to cope with the political and social consequences of job losses and job mobility. When industrialists wanted to create new jobs they ran into regional policies they found onerous. Alick Dick was Managing Director of Standard Triumph in the 1950s when the Conservatives were in power.

> I don't think any minister really understood the industry. They wanted to solve social problems in development areas. We wanted to establish markets on a long-term basis. And they never came to grips with this question. They put an enormous

burden of taxation on the industry. It was quite fantastic. Sixty per cent purchase tax. Only 20 per cent production for the home market. There is no way you can run an industry like that. If you look at any motor industry in the world today you will find that they have to have a strong home base, in order to export.

The car firms wanted to build new body and engine plants alongside their works in the Midlands. Instead they were dispersed to Scotland or Merseyside, thus increasing costs. The steel industry saw a need for one new strip mill, but the politicians insisted that the jobs be shared out between Scotland and Wales, and so two mills were built instead of one. Governments tried to maintain employment in industries that faced inevitable job losses. The effect was to neutralise gains in efficiency, and to hold up the transition to faster-growing areas of the economy. When the cost finally became insupportable, and governments shifted their tack, the social impact was all the more damaging.

Within Whitehall there were conflicts between one ministry and another that added further confusion. Nationalised industries, like the Coal Board, were instructed to keep their prices down as a service to the rest of the industry. Later they were criticised for not being able to finance their own investment. The electricity industry was urged to convert to nuclear power, or to oil, while millions had been spent to re-equip the coal mines to supply them. When the Board of Trade was trying to help the Lancashire textile industry, the Colonial Office was representing the interests of Hong Kong. The state airlines were urged to buy the cheapest planes, after the government had poured public funds into the British aircraft industry. In other countries there was more consistency. The French took a firm decision to build up their aerospace industry, and did so over a period of thirty years. The Japanese co-ordinated research and export efforts, and targeted their support to specific areas. But in Britain the relationship between government and industry was one of mutual distrust and criticism, regardless of which party was in power. Sir Michael Edwardes described how many businessmen saw it, in 1977:

> Industry has been like an overloaded donkey, being driven uphill by someone who apparently dislikes the donkey intensely – and I speak of successive governments.[55]

One of the additional complaints was that politicians and civil servants could not understand the issues they were dealing with, particularly with the science-based industries, electronics and aircraft. Sir George Edwards was Chairman of BAC for twelve years from 1963.

> The central civil service in this country, their integrity is second to none. They're highly intelligent chaps, but they've been reared in a classical tradition and therefore find it very difficult to understand the big technological problems with which they were confronted. They're suspicious of the scientific chaps in

the civil service who give them their briefs, largely because they don't understand what the briefs are about.

It was not only scientific and engineering matters that the civil service found difficult. Graham Day dealt with Whitehall when he was Chairman designate during the Labour Party's first attempt to nationalise the shipyards in 1976. He found that though the Department of Industry had come to understand the shipbuilders' problems, the civil servants with whom he had to discuss the detailed financial structure were generalists.

> One would discuss a commercial issue, for example the question of debt equity ratios which I thought were important to the future success of the company. The people with whom one had to deal neither had an insight into the industry, nor did they have what I would have considered an appropriate educational background. Of three chaps, one had done the history tripos at Cambridge, one was a classics scholar and one had done religion, and I had great difficulty relating that to a financial structure. I still can't get my mind over that kind of situation.

Even the farmers, who had little cause for complaint, sometimes grew a little impatient with Whitehall. Lord Woolley tells how the Treasury could behave at the annual Price Review at which the National Farmers' Union and the government agreed levels of price support.

> The Treasury always were very sticky. They don't open their money bags with very great enthusiasm. I remember one chap who had come from the Treasury, at the Review, and Sir James Turner was being pretty forceful and said, 'Well, I want to know whether the answer is yes or no'. This official had a great habit of clearing his throat in order to gain time and so he cleared his throat for some time and he said, 'Well now, if you press me, the answer to your question, Sir James, is – yes and no. But I say that with reservations.'

Farming was lucky. It was the one industry which was treated in the same way by both Labour and Conservative governments, and which could plan ahead safely.

Despite the difficulties which British industry has faced when it comes to organising itself, and producing and selling effectively, there has been one respect in which it has been second to none. The major strength has been a continuing ability to innovate. British brains produced a long series of breakthroughs, from the steam-turbine engine to the jet engine, from radar and the first computers to the pocket calculator, from polythene and penicillin to the Harrier jump jet. But it became a truism that the financial investment, and the sales or marketing ability that were needed to make the most of them, were often missing. Sir Ieuan Maddock, who was Chief Scientific Adviser to the Ministry of Technology, believes the pride in innovation was itself a snare.

> One of the chronic problems we have with this nation is this intense national ego in things that have a scientific base. This kind of feeling that by some divine ordinance we have all the talent in the world focused into this little island, and therefore we've been cheated by the fact that we have produced so many brilliant ideas and inventions and wicked people overseas exploit them. I prefer to invert the argument and say we are too preoccupied with being first and we have too much conceit about being originators and we have a chronic reluctance to be willing to learn from other people.

Throughout the twentieth century, it has been the firms and sectors that were prepared to learn from others, and put into practice management methods and production techniques acquired abroad, that prospered most. Very often foreign-owned firms in Britain did better than locally-owned companies because they were more professionally managed. This was true of the American consumer-goods plants that sprang up between the wars, and of the new electronics factories opened by Americans and Japanese in the 1970s. Many foreign-managed companies also find it easier to bridge the 'Them and Us' divide of British industry, and to deal with their workforce in a straightforward way. They could also be tougher. It was no coincidence that government ministers eventually chose a South African, Michael Edwardes, a Scottish American, Ian Macgregor, and a Canadian, Graham Day, to try to turn round the most troubled nationalised industries, cars, steel, coal and shipbuilding.

When Japanese firms came to Britain and introduced their own management style, they were sometimes able to create profit-making businesses out of plants where home managements had failed. At Lowestoft, in Suffolk, the Sanyo company now produces televisions in a factory once owned by Pye. In the Japanese manner, management and shopfloor all wear the same uniform, and have a daily meeting to discuss production. Noel Salmon is Personnel Manager.

> We have common conditions of service for everybody. We try to get rid of the traditional irritants, whereby office staff have different conditions, hours of work, holidays and procedures from shopfloor workers. So we all clock in and out, and we all have the same holidays.

By transferring Japanese methods to Lowestoft the company has reached productivity levels up to 75 per cent of those obtained in Japan. Faced with this competition on their own doorstep, the surviving British television company, owned by EMI, has tried to learn from Japanese methods. Douglas Topping is a senior manager.

We had to put a lot of effort into learning from them technically, we put a lot of effort into learning from them on the production lines. We thought that the time had come at which we
ought to try and learn from them about the relationship between the companies and their staff. The real thing which one
sees when one goes to Japan is the enormous degree of co-
operation which takes place between the workforce and the
managers. The way in which they recognise common objectives and seek common solutions and put them into practice.

In the mid-1980s British industry, and British working life, are once
more in flux. The fierce world recession has forced both sides of industry to make long-overdue changes. The overhaul has been made
more urgent by the policies of a Conservative government which un-
ambiguously set a higher priority on the long-term need for industrial
efficiency and restructuring than on full employment, and put its faith
in monetarism and market forces to achieve this. With a policy of 'survival of the fittest' the process of de-industrialisation, under way for
twenty years, has moved faster. The manufacturing workforce stood at
nine million in 1960 and has dropped to under six million. In 1981 the
haemorrhage of jobs from manufacturing reached 1000 a day. This was
not due to falling demand and the recession alone. The human impact,
measured in the millions of men and women thrown on the dole and
children who leave school seeing no prospect of work, has been made
more severe by the increasing speed of technological change, led by
electronics. As yet little is being done to find ways of sharing work more
equitably, through a shorter working week and less overtime.

Though there is a belief that all these changes are forcing a new
realism, and that a fundamental turning point has been reached, few of
Britain's industrial problems are new, and there have been false dawns
before. People believed that the mould had been broken in 1919, during
the recovery of the late 1930s, and after 1945. The same claim was made
in the boom years of the 1950s, the period when so much was left
undone that might have been done. In 1956 the *Manchester Guardian*
could report in a survey of industry:

> The spirit of industry is progressive, expansionist, and free . . .
> The crust that has been lying on this country for thirty or forty
> years is cracking and breaking up . . . We found almost com-
> plete unanimity that this country is embarked on a venture in
> economic expansion which has gone beyond the point of no
> return.

The crust was not broken then, nor in the 1960s, when a Labour government announced a commitment to industrial regeneration through
technology, but found itself pouring hundreds of millions into run-
down heavy industries.

Britain's industrial problems have been of two kinds: the technical and structural, and the political and human. Many of the technical and organisational weaknesses are being cured. The overcapacity of the old export-based industries, and the legacy of out-of-date nineteenth-century plant in old locations, are no longer the overriding handicap that they once were. The under-investment of the 1950s and 1960s is also being remedied, often at great public cost. The steel and motor industries are now as well equipped as any in Europe, if far smaller. Industrialists have been given the tax changes that they have long campaigned for, and find it easier to raise venture capital from banks and the City.

But even with the latest plant, better-designed products, better-educated managers and better marketing, political uncertainty remains, while industrial relations vary from the excellent to the sour. For industrialists, the political uncertainty affects investment and morale. The see-saw of government policy, whether right or left, has continued since 1945. John Harvey-Jones is Chairman of one of Britain's largest companies, ICI.

> I think British industry has been operating under an almost uniquely hostile environment. We operate in 46 countries in the world and I don't think I know of one which is more difficult to operate in than the United Kingdom. There are all sorts of reasons for that. I think the sort of people who came into industry have not always been the best natural leaders, but there are so many other things. I don't know of any other country where apparently it's impossible to have a bipartisan industrial policy. In this country, every five years I'm either about to be nationalised, or being glorified that I'm not being nationalised. We're either heading towards protectionism or we are glorying in free trade. There seems no common ground over the valuation that is placed upon industry. In this country, uniquely, industry is looked upon as a means of providing jobs, and that actually isn't the job of industry. The job of industry is to create wealth.

The political disagreements about the value and purpose of industry have been repeated within industry itself, and on the shopfloor. Through their treatment of the workforce, many industrialists have failed to convince their own employees that the creation of wealth was a worthwhile objective. Employees have remained suspicious of attempts to improve efficiency or productivity, because they, or their fathers, so often suffered from them. Certainly in the recession of the 1970s and 1980s many changes in manning and working practices have at last been pushed through. But the fact that people went along with them has not necessarily implied a greater identification with the company than before. Often there was no alternative, except going out of business. One Cowley car-worker described the new realism from his point of view:

> You are just a number. We have all got clock numbers and that
> is the be all and end all of it. As long as that clock number gets
> out x amount of bodies and makes x amount of pounds, that is
> all they are worried about. They would walk right over you just
> to get the cars on the road. That is all they worry about.

Though British Leyland devote great efforts to improving communication, another bodyworker, producing the Maestro, complained:

> They are not telling us enough about what is going to be going
> on over the next ten years. They keep saying, 'The computers
> are there', but how does it affect us? Is it going to do us all out
> of a job? They say no, because of the high volume, and you will
> need service industries. But we just don't know that. They are
> not telling us anything, and really that is industrial relations, to
> be kept informed.

The arrival of the robot era will produce more spectacular changes
in working life than any of the new tools and machines that have been
brought in, often painfully, over the past 80 years. As in the past, the
way in which they are introduced, and the degree of co-operation with
which they are being received, differs widely. In many companies, particularly small ones involved with electronic technology itself, there are
new forms of consultation, new types of agreement with the trades
unions, profit-sharing schemes, and a degree of involvement that can
outlast the recession. In other cases, larger and older firms where a more
traditional management ethos survives, there has been little sign of a
real improvement in co-operation, only a sullen acknowledgement of
where power lies in a time of high unemployment. Many managers have
reasserted their 'right to manage' in an aggressive way reminiscent of
the 1930s, rather than attempting to find a new relationship between
capital and labour that can run into the 1990s. Most British firms remain
as cautious as ever about the degree of consultation, or direct industrial
democracy, which has been a feature of some of the most successful
economies in western Europe. Yet it remains demonstrably true that
many of the greatest commercial achievements have come from those
firms, large and small, which have gone out of their way to produce a
spirit of collaboration, and to break down the barriers between manager,
engineer, and shopfloor. Unless these gulfs are bridged, all the arguments about monetarism, or an alternative economic strategy, may
prove to have been irrelevant.

REFERENCES

Chapter 1
1 *The Times*, 20 March 1902.
2 *Daily Mail*, 'Our German Cousins', 1912.

Chapter 2
3 Watney, C., and Little, J. A., *Industrial Warfare: the Aims and Claims of Capital and Labour* (London: Murray, 1912).
4 Armitage, G., *The Lancashire Cotton Trade: Great Inventions to Great Disasters* (Manchester Literary and Philosophical Society, 1950–1).
5 Whittam, W., *Report on England's Cotton Industry* (US Bureau of Manufacturers, 1907).
6 Bowker, B., *Lancashire under the Hammer* (London: Hogarth Press, 1928).
7 Macara, C., *Why We must have Control* (1924).
8 *Report of the Committee of the Economic Advisory Council on the Cotton Industry* (Cmd 3615, 1930).
9 *Report of the Cotton Textiles Mission to the United States* (Ministry of Production, 1944).

Chapter 3
10 *War in the Air*, Vol. 6.
11 *Report of Civil Aerial Transport Committee* (Cmnd 9218, 1918).
12 Lt Col. Moore Brabazon (*Hansard*, House of Commons, 17 November 1938, Col. 1162).
13 F. J. Erroll, Parliamentary Secretary to Minister of Supply (*Hansard*, House of Commons, 8 December 1955, Col. 688).

Chapter 4
14 Atha, Charles, Evidence to Board of Trade Committee on Iron, Steel, and Engineering Trades after the War (PRO BT 55/40 (040517)).
15 Evidence to Board of Trade Committee on the Iron and Steel Industry, 1916.
16 Mcgeown, Patrick, *Heat the Furnace Seven Times More* (London: Hutchinson, 1967).
17 *The Times*, 17 March 1934.
18 *Hansard*, House of Commons Debates, 16 November 1948.

Chapter 5
19 Hoffman, P. C., *They Also Serve: the Story of the Shop Worker* (London: Porcupine Press, 1949).
20 *The Listener*, 14 February 1934.
21 *Co-operative Independent Commission Report* (Manchester: Co-operative Union Ltd, 1958).

Chapter 6
22 Webb, S. and B., *Industrial Democracy*, 2 vols (London: Longmans, 1897).
23 Pollock, D., *The Shipbuilding Industry* (London: Methuen, 1905).
24 *Board of Trade Committee on Shipping and Shipbuilding after the War* (Cd 9092, 1918).
25 *Joint Enquiry into Foreign Competition and Conditions in the Shipbuilding Industry*, June 1926.
26 Reid, J. M., *James Lithgow: Master of Work* (London: Hutchinson, 1964).
27 Pyman, F. C., *Shipbuilding Rationalisation* (Liverpool: C. Birchall, 1933).
28 Bullock, Alan, *The Life and Times of Ernest Bevin*, Vol. 2 (London: Heinemann, 1967).
29 Transactions of the NECIES, October 1946.
30 *The Times*, 23 March 1960.
31 *Commission on Industrial Relations*, 1971.

Chapter 7
32 *Chemical Trade Journal*, 9 March 1901.
33 *Commission of Enquiry into Industrial Unrest, North West Area* (Cd 8663, 1917).

Chapter 8
34 Coombes, B. L., *Those Clouded Hills* (London: Cobbett, 1944).
35 *Royal Commission on the Coal Industry*, 1919.
36 Wilson, H., 'New Deal for Coal' (*Contact*, 1945).
37 *Coal Mining. Report of the Technical Advisory Committee* (Cmd 6610, 1945).
38 *Mining Review*, June 1947 (PRO INF 6/388).

Chapter 9
39 *Recent Development of German Agriculture* (Board of Agriculture, Cd 8305, 1916).
40 Astor, Viscount, and Seebohm, R., *British Agriculture: the Principles of Future Policy* (London: Longmans, 1938).
41 Liberal Land Committee, *The Land and the Nation: Rural Report of the Liberal Land Committee, 1923–5* (London: Hodder and Stoughton, 1925).
42 David Lloyd-George, 'Whither Britain', radio talk, March 1934.
43 Gibbs, Philip, *England Speaks* (London: Heinemann, 1935).
44 *Report of the Committee on Land Utilisation in Rural Areas* (Chairman, Lord Scott) (Cmd 6378, 1942).
45 Street, A. G., *Hitler's Whistle* (London: Eyre and Spottiswoode, 1943).
46 Tom Williams, to Pathe News, 20 October 1947.
47 Beef farmer on BBC TV *Money Programme*, October 1974.
48 R. A. Butler, Speech to Conservative Party Conference, October 1948.

Chapter 10
49 Morris, William, 'Policies that built the Morris Motor Business', *System*, 1924.
50 *The Times*, 20 August 1912.
51 *Future of the Car Industry* (Report by the Central Policy Review Staff, 1975).

Chapter 11
52 *Policy for the United Kingdom Electronics Industry* (National Economic Development Office, 1982).

Chapter 12
53 At Sales Managers Association, *The Times*, 17 December 1930.
54 *The Times*, 30 April 1945.
55 Lecture to the Royal Society of Arts, 1977.

PRODUCTION CREDITS

Aircraft: Film Editor, Hugh Tasman; Production Assistant, Cecilia Coleshaw; Assistant Producer, Charles Furneaux; Producer, Jonathan Lewis. *Cars:* Film Editors, Max Wheeler, Philip Elliott; Production Assistant, Beverley Harkus; Assistant Producers, Holly Aylett, Peter Grimsdale; Producer, Peter Ceresole. *Chemicals:* Film Editor, John Nash; Production Assistants, Sue MacGregor, Sheila Johns; Assistant Producer, Roger Parry; Producer, Angela Holdsworth. *Coal:* Film Editor, Peter Delfou; Production Assistant, Lareine Bathe; Assistant Producer, Nikki Rendle; Producer, Ruth Jackson. *Cotton:* Film Editor, Dave Lee; Production Assistant, Sue MacGregor; Assistant Producer, Charles Furneaux; Producer Angela Holdsworth. *Electronics:* Film Editor, Stuart Davidson; Production Assistant, Beverley Harkus; Assistant Producer, Colleen Toomey; Producer, Michael Waldman. *Farming:* Film Editor, John Nash; Production Assistant, Cecilia Coleshaw; Assistant Producer, Maggie Brooks; Producer, Jonathan Lewis. *Retailing:* Film Editor, Dave Lee; Production Assistant, Lareine Bathe; Assistant Producer, Joanna Davies; Producer, Averil Ward. *Shipbuilding:* Film Editor, Dave Lee; Production Assistant, Sue MacGregor; Assistant Producer; Maggie Brooks; Producer, Angela Holdsworth. *Steel:* Film Editors, Roy Deverell, David Head; Production Assistants, Deirdre Devane, Christina Hamilton; Assistant Producer, Averil Ward; Producer, Glynn Jones. Graphics, Alan Jeapes; Series Videotape Editor, Chris Booth. Series secretaries: Marian Dawson, Liz Green, Carmen Poole, Cassie Phillips. Narrator, John Woodvine. Music composed by Carl Davis and arranged by Ray Farr for the Grimethorpe Colliery Band. Series Adviser, Professor Leslie Hannah. Stills Researcher, June Leech. Film Researcher, Christine Whittaker. Executive Producer, Peter Pagnamenta.

INDEX